WWW

WEBSITE NEWS UPDATED WEEKLY
WWW.INDEXONCENSORSHIP.ORG • CONTACT@INDEXONCENSORSHIP.ORG
TEL: 020 7278 2313 • FAX: 020 7278 1878

CONTENTS

A MATTER OF WORDS
URSULA OWEN

Judicial reviews are rarely comfortable for governments, but few people would have predicted how rapidly the Hutton Inquiry into the death of the weapons expert Dr David Kelly exposed the deepest internal processes of key British institutions.

And certain things will never be quite the same again: there will surely be lasting consequences for foreign policy, security, the operation of government. Significant, too, is the fact that dispensing with the 30-year-rule and disclosing dozens of contemporary emails and documents from the heart of government has, with no observable harm to the country, blown a hole in the case against greater freedom of information (p11).

The inquiry has been uncomfortable for the media, too, revealing much about editors' relationships to their journalists, about journalists' commitment to protect their sources (p26), about the practice of journalism itself and the power of the media – something that John Lloyd (p84) and Julian Petley (p75) address from different perspectives but with critical concern.

Secrecy, hidden agendas, freedom of information – all aspects of *Index*'s business – have been crucial to this inquiry. But it has also exposed the clash between those who deal with words as a means to presentation, spin, exaggeration and half-truths, and those who believe that words matter, must be chosen with care, mean what they say. In short: it has told us a great deal about the world we're living in.

Thrown up more starkly than ever has been the question of trust in authority, or rather the lack of it – something that does not bode well for democracy. This issue of *Index* looks at the law and its authority at a seminal moment, examining in particular its relationship with free expression nationally and internationally. While Marcel Berlins reports on how the courts have been treating freedom of expression since the 1998 Human Rights Act (p36), Anthony Scrivener is disturbed by the recent erosion of civil liberties in the UK (p54), Bob Woffindon by the role of the tabloid press in preventing fair trials (p67) and Philippe Sands by the dangers globally of the US abandoning international law (p116). Imran Khan discusses how impact cases break taboos (p62), Irena Maryniak analyses the curious relationship of countries of accession in Eastern Europe to the 'rule of law' and Anthony Hudson looks at the law's complex relationship with hate speech (p45).

Sara Roy's own title for her piece in the last issue of *Index* was 'Living with the Holocaust: the journey of a child of Holocaust survivors'. This is the title by which she prefers her personal reflections to be known.

IRANIAN REVOLUTION

KAVEH GOLESTAN
8 JULY 1950 –
2 APRIL 2003

Kaveh Golestan, self-portrait

Many fine words have been written about the BBC cameraman and photographer Kaveh Golestan who died when he stepped on a landmine in Iraqi Kurdistan in April this year. I, who lost a personal friend of 20 years' standing, want only to do one thing: remember Kaveh through his pictures, chosen here by his wife Hengameh and his son Mehrak.

In 1979, the year of the Iranian Revolution, Kaveh was awarded photography's highest honour, the Robert Capa Prize (not the Pulitzer as claimed in most obituaries), for his dramatic shots of the uprisings in Tehran and other cities that led to the flight of the Shah, the return of Ayatollah Khomeini and events that followed. They were reproduced in *Time* magazine and sped round the world, anonymously at the time to protect the photographer's identity back in Iran. They continue to inform our image of those heady days. ❏

JVH

- Kaveh's family and friends in Iran have set up a foundation in his name to encourage the development of young photographers, something Kaveh did much to foster through his courses in Tehran university and elsewhere. The foundation will present three awards annually.

For further information ➪ hengameh_g@yahoo.co.uk or www.kavehgolestan.com

Opposite, top: Isfahan 1979: the first night of curfew under martial law

Opposite: Tehran 1979: the first student uprising, outside the university

Above: Tehran 1979: members of the public lead away the brother of a man who has been injured during a demonstration

Right: Tehran 1979: a student grieves for a classmate

NAPSTER AND THE DOGS OF WAR

JIM D'ENTREMONT

MANY MUSIC FANS CONSIDER TRAFFICKING
IN MUSIC DOWNLOADS FAIR REVENGE ON THE
INDUSTRY FOR EXORBITANTLY PRICED CDS AND
CONCERT TICKETS, CONTENT RESTRICTIONS,
DISRESPECT FOR CONSUMERS AND CORPORATE
BULLYING OF ARTISTS. NOW IT'S ILLEGAL

Napster, a service enabling internet users to obtain recorded music without paying for it, was disabled through litigation in 2001. But traffic in downloaded music has persisted through newer software options furnished by KaZaA, iMesh, WinMX, Morpheus, Grokster and other entities. The practice of peer-to-peer (P2P) sharing of music files free of charge raises issues of ownership, intellectual property rights and free expression. The Recording Industry Association of America (RIAA), the trade group that represents US producers and distributors of recorded music, regards the sharing of copyrighted music files among private individuals as theft. But some music fans interpret the response of the RIAA as extortion.

On 8 September 2003, the organisation filed lawsuits against 261 internet users allegedly engaged in free exchange of music harvested online. The RIAA had already obtained US$3,000 settlements from ten internet subscribers who came forward after discovering that their Internet Service Providers (ISPs) had received copyright subpoenas. Pursuing evidence of illegal activity, the RIAA had been granted more than 1,500 subpoenas opening ISPs' customer records to industry lawyers.

The defendant named in each case was a person paying a monthly internet charge – in many instances, the parent or guardian of a putative cyber-bandit as young as 12. At each billing address, someone with access to a home computer had collected more than a thousand songs in MP3 format and was making them available to others without compensation. Each defendant may be liable for US$750 to US$150,000 per song. The RIAA threatens an avalanche of additional lawsuits that will be funded, in part, by cash settlements received from the present wave of defendants. Only internet users in the USA have been targeted thus far, though online music circulates worldwide.

The September lawsuits were timed to coincide with the start of the academic year at US colleges and universities, where file-sharing has become widespread. Several months ago, the RIAA reached a settlement with students who had operated song-trading networks on school computers; now it is beginning to target informal P2P activity. A growing number of US educational institutions, such as the University of Florida, have installed filtering software to block music swapping altogether.

As a public relations gesture, the RIAA has unveiled a programme offering amnesty to people who admit to sharing copyrighted music and swear to delete all illegal music tracks. Writing in the *Los Angeles Times*, attorney Fred von Lohmann of the Electronic Frontier Foundation notes that 'the RIAA promises not to assist copyright owners in suing you. But its major-label members reserve the right to go after you, as do thousands of music publishers and artists like Metallica. In other words, once you have come forward, you are more vulnerable to a lawsuit, not less.'

Meanwhile, the RIAA persists in its efforts to stamp out file-sharing services themselves. On 19 August, the RIAA joined music publishers in appealing against a district court ruling that Grokster and Morpheus could not be held liable for the copyright infringements of their customers. Two days later, the US Department of Justice obtained a guilty plea from Mark Shumaker, head of Apocalypse Crew, described as 'an internet music piracy group'. The RIAA has been working with law enforcement officials to expedite such prosecutions.

An estimated 60 million Americans download MP3 files and share them. Many young music fans are just beginning to understand that what they have been doing is illegal. The habit of music-sharing among peers is culturally embedded, and predates the technology that now facilitates its expansion. In the 1950s, American teenagers with reel-to-reel tape recorders distributed home-made tapes of singles and albums among their friends. Many fans have a strong sense of entitlement to their music, resent its tightening link to corporate greed, and find the RIAA's tactics heavy-handed. 'If industry honchos think they're going to terrorise people into buying more CDs, they're crazy,' says one occasional file-sharer in New England.

Among recording artists, the issue is divisive. The heavy-metal phenomenon Metallica, which owns the copyright on all its music, found it expedient to help bring down Napster. But most artists in the mainstream music business signed away significant rights to their own creations when they signed coveted contracts with major labels. Many singers and songwriters believe that music downloads serve to promote their work and increase sales. 'Who gets hurt by free downloads?' asks singer Janis Ian in the May 2002 issue of *Performing Songwriter*. 'Save a handful of super-successes like Celine Dion, none of us. We only get helped.'

Despite the pieties about starving artists voiced by the RIAA and representatives of the National Association of Recording Arts and Sciences (NARAS), the industry is chiefly focused on the fiscal health of retailers such as Wal-Mart and media conglomerates such as AOL Time Warner and Vivendi Universal. Some fans feel that the music industry is itself stealing money, and consider trafficking in music downloads fair revenge for exorbitantly priced CDs and concert tickets, content restrictions, disrespect for consumers and corporate bullying of artists.

According to a recent study by the consumer research firm Soundscan, CD sales have dropped by 8.7 per cent in the past year – less than industry sources claim. The extent to which falling sales can be attributed to online music theft is debatable. Many US consumers are spending their dwindling disposable income on other items, such as DVDs. Some music labels may soon reduce CD prices to lure back customers; some are experimenting with commercial MP3 download services that may charge about 79 cents per song or up to US$8 for a complete album (CDs now cost roughly twice that). Legal online music services may represent a significant part of the industry's business within five years. Meanwhile, the RIAA's law and order campaign can be expected to alienate thousands of consumers.

Copyright protection is mandated by the US constitution in order 'to promote the Progress of Science and useful Arts' by giving 'Authors and Inventors' exclusive rights to their creations for a limited time. But thanks to corporate intervention, copyright laws intended to protect creators now protect capitalism. ❏

Jim d'Entremont is an arts journalist and playwright, and is head of the Boston Coalition for Freedom of Expression

HALF OPEN, HALF SHUT

DAVID GOLDBERG

WHILE THE PRINCIPLE OF FREEDOM OF
INFORMATION IS NOW SAFELY ENSHRINED
IN UK LAW, THERE'S A LOT TO DO TO GET
THE SHOW ON THE ROAD BY JANUARY 2005

Recent articles in *Index* have noted the tentative steps being taken towards freedom of information in the UK (*Index* 3/2000). However, there are actually two laws in the UK: the Freedom of Information Act (2000) and the Freedom of Information (Scotland) Act 2002.

Nor does it end there: the States of Jersey has published a consultation paper on enacting a separate law; the Isle of Man government operates under its own 1996 Code of Practice on Access to Government Information (a select committee, however, decided against enacting a law). There is also the Welsh Executive Code of Practice on Public Access to Information and the Welsh Cabinet publishes its minutes – whatever one thinks of the slur that it does so because it has so little of interest to conceal, it is setting the standard for the rest of the country.

Future elected English Regional Assemblies will be subject to the FOI Act, as are the important, but neglected, inter-administration concordats – date-sharing agreements between public authorities. The position with regard to UK/Ireland bodies is less clear. Which, if any, freedom of information regime covers the North–South Ministerial Council, given that the Irish FOI rules do not apply at present – the British–Irish Council or the British–Irish Intergovernmental Conference?

So freedom of information is now a legally rooted plant in the UK: another symbol of New Labour's constitutional modernisation programme as far as Westminster is concerned; and the delivery of a 20-year-old promise by old-style Liberal Jim Wallace as far as Holyrood is concerned.

The BBC recently opened a website dubbed 'Secret Britain'. But, only a few weeks later, the Hutton Inquiry website was deluged with most of the documentation presented in evidence – foreshortening the normal delay by some 29 years and 11 months. The release prompted a *Guardian* correspondent to write that it was 'a moment beyond our wildest expectations'. Perhaps it's time to review the old adage that Britain is the most secretive state in the world. With due apologies to Harold Evans, Britain may be best described as a 'half-open, half-shut' society.

These days, the task of implementing an effective FOI regime is the main game in town. The heady campaigning days of the 1980s and 90s are now but a memory. The focus is on information commissioners – from their country seats in Wilmslow and St Andrews – receiving and deliberating on draft publication schemes; consultations on codes of practice on how authorities should deal with requests for information and how they should manage their records ('the key to FOI'); and reviewing official annual reports on progress made in bringing the legislation into effect.

FOI is also a growing economic activity: employment opportunities at the two commissions; training contracts and conferences; newsletters; a blog; and consultancies are mushrooming as authorities try to gear up for January 2005, the still-too-far-off date when the individual right to request information comes into force.

Meanwhile, for the training and education businesses the future is bright. The Stationery Office, for example, found that 'the Civil Service is unlikely to meet obligations set out under the 2005 FOI Act'. The Henley Management Centre found that 'only a minority of public sector organisations will be ready to cope with the demands of the Freedom of Information Act when it takes effect at the beginning of 2005'.

There are differences between the Westminster and Holyrood laws. In itself, that's nothing new: since the Treaty of Union in 1707, two distinct legal standards operate within the UK. The UK Act is often misconstrued as the 'English' Act as opposed to the 'other' law covering Scotland. The real difference, however, is that the Westminster law applies to (mainly) UK bodies that hold information; Welsh and Northern Irish bodies come under the UK Act, too. The principle is that each public authority is subject to only one FOI regime; which particular one depends on whether the authority holding the information is a UK body or a cross-border, Welsh, NI or Scottish public authority. 'Public' authorities may include private sector companies operating under publicly funded contracts.

A crucial issue is coverage: which bodies are covered? Compared with the Human Rights Act, coverage is not defined in a formulaic manner; public authorities are defined by virtue of their inclusion on a schedule appended to the act and listed separately. While it is possible to know who is covered, some glaring omissions are evident – Scottish Housing Associations, deliberately excluded at Stage 3 of the bill, for instance. The laws provide for a system whereby bodies not currently in the schedule can be designated by Ministerial Order laid before the parliaments on a case-by-case basis.

Environmental information will be the subject of separate, subject-specific regulations, to conform with new EU rules that will make operational the Aarhus Convention – the UN Convention on access to information, public participation in decision-making and justice in environmental matters. But decisions on access will be subject to review by the Information Commissioners.

Other salient differences include:

- under the UK Act, information can be withheld if it would (or would be likely to) cause 'harm'; under the Scottish Act, the higher standard of 'substantial prejudice' applies;
- since there is no reference to the Information Tribunal, the appeal process under the Scottish Act is more streamlined;
- in Scotland, unlike England, data protection is a reserved matter and the Scottish Commissioner deals primarily with freedom of information;
- the SIC is nominated by the Scottish parliament and not appointed by the government in Westminster; and can order the disclosure of information, rather than merely requesting it;
- where an authority is considering whether the public interest test should apply, the authority is under a tighter deadline under the Scottish law;
- factors to take into account when considering whether the public interest test should apply are spelled out in the Scottish Code of Practice;
- and there are differences regarding the substance and exercise of the ministerial veto.

Both laws are weak on permitting the facts underlying governmental policy decisions to be released.

Protecting and promoting freedom of information is akin to keeping the Forth Road Bridge well painted – a never-ending task – and the UK Act is often criticised as being a pale shadow of the original White Paper 'Your Right to Know' of 1997. But recent events in Ireland are a salutary reminder that a good situation can be compromised at a later stage. At issue are the new charges being levied on those who request information. The fee for a request is €15 (cUS$15); €75 for an internal review and €150 for an application to the Information Commissioner. This prompted the Irish Information Commissioner to comment recently: 'The government's proposed [sic] Freedom of Information (Amendment) Act, 2003, which was enacted in April 2003, curtails access to non-personal or "official" information.'

In the meantime, freedom of information radicalism lives on. The site has shifted from the national terrain to the access policies of intergovernmental organisations, such as the EU, international financial institutions and multinational corporations. Interesting civil society initiatives on this front include Article 19's Global FOI Campaign (financial institutions); Statewatch's efforts to access EU documents; the International Right to Know Campaign (US corporations have no legally binding obligations whatsoever to disclose comparable information for their operations abroad); Publish What You Pay (international oil, gas and mining companies), which aims to help citizens hold their governments accountable for how these resource-related funds are managed and distributed; and the Access Initiative, a global coalition of public interest groups collaborating to promote national-level implementation of commitments to access information, participation and justice in environmental decision-making. In addition, a global freedom of information portal has been set up at www.freedominfo.org.

Not all the initiatives are from civil society. Following the Johannesburg sustainable development conference, the UK coordinates the Extractive Industries Transparency Initiative (EITI). A recent meeting in London agreed a Statement of Principles and Agreed Actions to increase transparency over payments and revenues in the extractives sector.

Finally, there is one deficit crying out for attention: the protection of the right to access information at the European level. The new EU Charter of Rights applies only to EU institution documents. Article 10 of the European Convention on Human Rights does not guarantee a general right of access to information. The Council of Europe's Committee of Ministers did adopt a political recommendation on access to official documents in 2002, and a follow-up seminar, in November 2002, concluded that there should be a binding treaty on access to information. While that might be useful, far better an additional Protocol to the Convention that would make the centuries-old Swedish *offentlighets-principen*, the principle of publicity, the legally enforceable, foundational principle of contemporary European governance. ❏

David Goldberg *is a co-convener of the Campaign for Freedom of Information in Scotland*

LIFE IN BLINKERS

ADONIS

FRENCH PROPOSALS TO RE-EXAMINE
THE SECULAR HEART OF THEIR
CONSTITUTION HAVE AGAIN RAISED
THE ISSUE OF THE WEARING OF THE
VEIL IN PUBLIC INSTITUTIONS SUCH
AS SCHOOLS AND UNIVERSITIES

Despite what the fundamentalists would have us believe, nowhere in the Quran or *hadith* is there a single, unequivocal passage that imposes the veil on Muslim women. Their view is based on a different reading of the text. Is it acceptable then, on a religious level, that a mere 'interpretation' can have the force of dogma and law? The veil remains a bone of contention. By what right or authority can a select few impose their interpretation on everyone else? Would these few go so far as to use violence against women; against all those whose opinions differ from their own; against the world?

The issue of the veil has a long history in Muslim societies and remains a live one in that largely traditional world. But when fundamentalist Muslims import this and other internal issues into Western societies, all they succeed in doing is to create problems for their own communities and to do irreparable damage to Islam's vision of man and the world.

Émigré Muslims, particularly those who have become citizens of the country in which they live, should acknowledge and establish a sharp distinction between their lives in public and in private. Those Muslims who insist on the veil must realise that their very insistence demonstrates that they do not respect the feelings of people with whom they share a homeland; that they do not respect their values and are questioning the fundamental tenets of that society; that they are making a mockery of the laws and liberties for which these people have fought over time; and that they are denying the principles of republican democracy in the countries that have welcomed them with work and freedom.

Some people claim that Muslim women in the West who wear the veil have chosen to do so of their own free will. There may well be something to be said for this view. However, when one sees girls as young as four years old wearing the veil in the streets of Paris, for example, can anyone seriously claim they are doing this voluntarily? More serious still: why do fundamentalist Muslims who have emigrated to the West see in the openness of their new home nothing more than an opportunity to proclaim their own narrow-mindedness and isolation? Why do they choose to 'emigrate' once more from their point of arrival? Their presence in these countries is made possible only by the openness of their host societies. When they express their beliefs by parading in the veil or a beard, they undermine Islam by reducing it to superficial questions of form: holding up mere slogans and rituals to the world's eye.

Those who call for the imposition of the veil represent only a minority of the Muslims living in the West; indeed, in the Arab world itself. If wearing the veil were made the subject of a democratic decision, it would be dropped immediately. But, instead of respecting democracy and its principles, this active minority is trying to overthrow these principles and impose its convictions by force. I cannot see how such a position might be defensible, how it might help the cause of Islam or how it might be a legitimate response. Anyone who looks carefully at the fundamentalist position cannot regard its supporters as men of religion, as simple pious souls. They are politicians embarked on a political mission. Muslims and Westerners ought to deal with them on this basis: they represent not religion but a party.

The mosque is the only place where a Muslim should demonstrate his 'difference'. While in the West, this is the place where he can freely express his religious 'identity' – as should be the case in the Arab world generally. All social and public practices outside the mosque are a challenge to the values of the host community. Public institutions belong to all citizens: schools and universities, in particular, are open to all. They are places from which all external marks of denomination and distinctive 'signs' should be excluded.

And to this category of 'public institutions' we can add streets, cafés, meeting places, cinemas, conference halls, and so on. The wearing of religious signs and symbols in these places is a violation of their very meaning and function. It is, in fact, the symbol of a desire for separation: it means we refuse integration.

This insistence on visibly demonstrating difference has a theatrical and exhibitionist element, which has nothing to do with religion. There is an intimacy, secrecy almost, at the heart of religious experience. It is suffused with simplicity, modesty, silence and contemplation – a long way from this cult of appearances.

France 2000: veiled Muslim,
Disneyland.
Credit: Abbas / Magnum

When certain Abbasid Caliphs ordered non-Muslims to wear distin-
guishing symbols, it provoked unrest throughout the kingdom. It was a sign
of anxiety, of retreat. And it is the progress of society that will reverse such
measures.

It is strange and incomprehensible that certain Muslims in the West insist
on wearing such distinctive symbols. By insisting thus, they insult their
history, and condemn their culture and their presence in the world. If we
look closely at this business of the veil, we realise that it is not a simple
violation of the law and culture of another; it is, above all, an insult to
oneself. It is a different relationship with life, one more akin to flirting with
death.

In conclusion, let me say that the religious interpretations that compel
Muslim women to wear the veil in secular countries where church and state
have long been separated and where equality of the sexes is firmly established, reveals a mentality that is not content merely with veiling woman,
but seeks to shroud man, society, life in general – to pull the veil over the
eyes of reason itself. ❏

Adonis *is the leading poet in the Arab world*
First published in Hayat, *London. Translated by Will Bland*

CHILDREN OF ISRAEL

HAIM TAL

THEY GREW UP IN THE SETTLEMENTS
AND WERE EDUCATED AS RELIGIOUS
ZIONISTS BUT NOW THEY ARE CALLING
FOR A WITHDRAWAL FROM THE
OCCUPIED TERRITORIES

For more than 20 years, Jewish settler Shlomo Wegman managed to look right through Palestinians crouched down beside the road waiting for permission to pass through Israeli military checkpoints.

'It was as if they were transparent,' says Wegman, 28, a financial adviser and former member of the youth wing of the extreme right-wing party Moledet (Homeland). 'I simply never identified with them at all.'

Then, one day last year, as he passed through the checkpoint at the entrance to the Alon Shvut settlement in the Gush Etzion region, he noticed an old man and a young girl waiting to pass. 'The soldiers were not ill-treating them. They were just stopping them from going through. Suddenly it dawned on me. I understood then that all these measures were not really there for security reasons. It came to me that this gigantic military apparatus was there to allow me to live, with those I love, in a plush villa in spectacular countryside: that is to say, at Alon Shvut.'

It was at that moment that Wegman decided on his own personal with-drawal from the occupied territories.

'I knew how much I would miss the place because I loved it so much,' he says. 'Now I live in an ugly urban area inside the green line (inside inter-nationally recognised borders).'

Wegman cannot explain his former membership of Moledet, his earlier blindness or the continuing blindness of his friends and family, who still live in the settlement. 'We no longer see reality in the same way,' he says.

Wegman is among the signatories of a petition started by a movement calling itself Realistic Religious Zionism. The petition vehemently criticises the leadership of the religious Zionist community that it sees as sacrificing 'efforts to live an observant religious life on the altar of the struggle for Judo-Samaria [the West Bank] and the Gaza Strip'.

The signatories of the petition are convinced that there can be no public debate about the future of religious Zionism while the millstone of the occupied territories remains around their necks. Anyone familiar with the extremely close-knit world of the religious nationalists knows that the many signatories of the petition will pay a high price for taking this stance. It is virtually impossible to be an observant Jew without belonging to and taking part in a *minyan* (a prayer group made up of six adult males).

'This petition could well be suicidal,' says Shay Binyamini, one of the several hundred religious young men and women who have signed it. 'We are trying to draw up a list of young people that is not just an extension of Netivot Shalom [Paths of Peace, a religious peace movement] or Meymad [a religious peace party] because these organisations are no longer effectively making themselves heard.'

Many of the signatories to the petition say they feel themselves to be victims of the dogmatism of traditional religious education. 'A short while ago I took part in a debate,' says Sheetreet. 'At the end of it they told me I did not belong in the Jewish seminary. That wounded me, both personally and ideologically. For me the Jewish faith is steeped in the idea of debate but they told me, "No. No, we don't want any controversy. You have no place here." I understood at that moment how deep is the crisis facing Judaism today.'

Next week, when Sheetreet wants to go to Bet Midrash (religious study seminar) in the Golan Heights, the chances are he will find himself locked out. Given the monolithic Jewish education to which religious nationalists are subjected and the belief that 'the land of Israel, the people of Israel, the law [Torah] of Israel are one,' the petition that Sheetreet signed will unquestionably be viewed as heresy.

This controversy is yet another symptom of the serious crisis into which religious Zionism has been plunged. For the past several years it has become more religious, more nationalist and more extremist. At the same time, many in the younger generation are looking for new and more personal ways to express themselves.

On the right this produces young people who throw themselves into creating 'unauthorised' settlements; on the left are those who signed the petition. The old guard among the settlers find it difficult to come to terms with; all of a sudden, their children have embarked on a quest for a more complex identity.

The best of the young men do their military service in elite combat units then leave immediately for India from where they return with mystical ideas that push them towards Hassidism (a popular spiritual movement founded in the eighteenth century and characterised by religious zeal and joy). Or they drop out and take to drugs. Sometimes they turn their backs on their faith.

'Inside the settlements, those in the realistic camp believe that we have to occupy the territories to ensure the defence of Israel,' says Noam Huppert, who began to lose his faith at the age of nine. 'Then there are the unrealistic ones who believe that settling the territories is a metaphysical act. They no longer talk much about the recovery of Israeli land because it has no impact on the public. They mostly stress the need for security and a kind of pride at seeing the Jewish state occupying these territories.'

Noa Malikovsky, who studies art at the Hebrew University, says, 'Of course I don't believe there will be peace as of next year. But my dream is that one day I will eat hummus in Damascus. When I was a little girl my favourite song was 'Ani noladeti la-shalom' ('I was born for peace'). If we don't keep this goal in sight there is no point to any of it. God does not whisper in my ear to tell me what it suits him to do today, and the path [to peace] is paved with questions.'

For several years, prominent rabbis have used the traditional weekly leaflets containing extracts of the Bible that are distributed in the synagogues to foster a subtle campaign against secular life and Western culture. Realistic Religious Zionism also has its eye on the use of this method of publication to get its ideas more widely known, even if they are unsure of its chances of success.

One of its members explains: 'As far as we are concerned it isn't a case of talking about peace but about the end of occupation and as soon as possible from now on. Our goal is realistic. First you have to learn to see things as they really are. It is not being pessimistic, but you have to put your illusions behind you. We don't need any more extreme ideologies, just reality.' ❏

Haim Tal *writes for* Yediot Aharonot, *Tel Aviv*
Translated by Veronica Forwood

FREEDOM OF EXPRESSION: FOR WHAT?

ANDREI KOLESNIKOV

IT'S INSCRIBED IN THE CONSTITUTION,
BUT IN THIS PERIOD OF 'PUTINESQUE
STAGNATION' NEITHER POLITICIANS,
JOURNALISTS NOR READERS HAVE ANY
REAL USE FOR IT

Here's the conundrum: news is a commodity and the media is a business. The state, however, has a right to keep its citizens informed about its doings and therefore needs its own media.

To some extent these two assertions – banal as they are – ring true. But the opposite is also true: news has a value in itself as a vital piece of the jigsaw in a democratic society, which is why the media should not necessarily operate as a business. Moreover, for democracy to mature, the state should most definitely not force its own ideas on society, which is why the media should remain independent.

Over the past ten years, the post-Soviet media have been through every possible stage, following the successive twists and turns of the economy, politics, the very existence of dailies, periodicals, TV channels, radio stations and the internet.

While most state publications (in the broadest sense) have gradually modernised themselves and have become virtually autonomous, private publications, financed by capital that is dependent on the state, have become more Catholic than the Pope when it comes to defending the interests of government.

The vast range of the Russian news industry, in which the media remain relatively small cogs, is shot through not with censorship but with self-censorship. No press magnate would ever allow his group to criticise the government. An editor-in-chief will always make sure that his heads of department do not deviate one jot from the official line, while they, in turn, have no desire to lose their jobs over a political mistake and comb their journalists' pieces obsessively. Journalists – also wanting to hang on to their employment – weigh every word, every thought, every expression. As a result, the media has become a public information agency without the state having to pay a penny for the service.

This internal control system is highly effective. Even those publications financed by disgraced oligarchs such as Boris Berezovskii, now in exile in London, behave themselves because they want to stay in the news business and avoid problems. Complete freedom of expression is not in the interests of proprietors, founders, publishers or editors-in-chief.

Apart from a few sticklers for democracy and liberalism, readers themselves feel the need for news less and less. The consumer of news is depoliticised, his curiosity about government at a low ebb, and he no longer wants to engage with politics even via the press. The current stability or Putinesque 'stagnation' [the term used to describe the end of the Brezhnev era in the 1970s when the Soviet Union, which was apparently stable and relatively prosperous, was in fact heading for decline and fall *Ed*] encourages this approach.

Every professional knows the unspoken limits of freedom of expression, and every politician knows that if his party goes too far out on a limb it will be squeezed out of the political scene and from the TV studios – tantamount to the same thing. 'Freedom of expression' is now as empty an expression as 'multi-party system'. The former can only operate where there is no longer self-censorship; the latter can only work when there is a real opposition within the country and not one that is marginalised or imaginary.

Russian media have no economic independence. As long as the quality press cannot survive independently, it is dishonest to talk about success in the media business. There are, indeed, a few examples of serious and prosperous mass publications – in the field of financial journalism, for instance – but they are the exceptions.

The media are in fact unable to flourish economically without advertising revenue. It is only through advertising that a good newspaper with a serious reputation can survive, as is the case in developed countries. There, advertising is carried in newspapers whose circulation is proportionately higher than in Russia. People are used to reading newspapers, they can afford to do so and they know how to tell advertising from advertorial – a regular feature in the Russian press.

In Russia, the big-circulation tabloid press has grown out of the ruthless editorial policy that only knows how to attract readers by descending to the lowest possible level. The Italian daily *Corriere della Sera* (circulation 715,000) sells as many as *Komsomolskaia Pravda* and remains a serious, non-specialist newspaper. *Izvestia* (circulation 235,000), a newspaper of reference that its competitors consider has a 'mega-circulation', can scarcely match that of *Giorno,* a virtual outsider in the Italian press scene. And that takes no account of the vastly different size of the population in the two countries.

To quote another example, this time from the old socialist bloc: Russia is still far from being able to produce a publishing phenomenon such as the Polish group Agora that produces *Gazeta Wyborcza.* The group is quoted on the stock exchange and its flagship publication, a quality political newspaper, is economically and politically successful.

The sole area of freedom, the one that more or less evades all control, is the internet. But even there the most trenchant criticism is gagged. The satirical site in the style of Daniil Kharms (a famous satirist of the 1920s and 30s), vladimirvladimirovich.ru, has been shut down.

Freedom of expression exists. It is inscribed in the Constitution. One can make use of it. But almost nobody takes the risk, nor has any wish to. ❑

Andrei Kolesnikov *writes for* Novoié Vremia, *Moscow*
Translated by VF

Amina Lawal and her 20-month-old child Wasila enter the Katsina State Judiciary Sharia Court of Appeal, Nigeria, on 27 August 2003. Lawal was found guilty of adultery – evidenced by the existence of her child – and sentenced to death by stoning in 2002 (Index Index 4/02). As we go to press, she is appealing against the sentence.
Credit: Jacob Silberberg / Panos

SPEECH IMPEDIMENT

KAREN K LANE

When Singapore's Speakers' Corner opened, many hailed it as a victory for free speech in this tightly controlled city state – but on its third anniversary, the voices are growing fainter. The number of people airing their views at the government-approved free-speech venue fell to 177 last year from 365 two years ago, police spokeswoman Rachel Yeo said on 1 September.

Speakers' Corner, marked by a sign in part of a small downtown park, is loosely based on its historic, freewheeling namesake at London's Hyde Park, where virtually anything goes. But in Singapore – where some call their local version 'Hide Park' – it's a different story. Race, religion and other topics that authorities deem sensitive are banned at Singapore's corner. Loudspeakers are also outlawed, and speakers must register their names with police before holding forth. Traffic sometimes makes it hard to hear, and the corner is only open in the daytime, when relentless equatorial sun or monsoon rains beat down on Singapore. Activists have been urging opposition politicians and civic groups to show up and speak out to mark the anniversary. But Yeo said just four people registered to speak on the anniversary day.

Many opposition politicians dismiss Singapore's Speakers' Corner as a cosmetic attempt to create the appearance of freedom in a country where political activities and the media are strictly regulated and where top leaders have often successfully sued their critics for defamation.

'Why commemorate such a sham and a fraud?' said local opposition leader Chee Soon Juan. 'I don't think there will be a lot of people there. It wouldn't be productive or meaningful.' In 2002, Chee was fined 3,000 Singapore dollars (US$1,709) for speaking about banned topics – race and religion – at Speakers' Corner. He has not returned since. ❑

Karen K Lane is an *Associated Press editor*

Prince Claus Fund to withhold support from the 2003 Havana Biennial because of increased suppression of cultural expression in Cuba

Prince Claus Fund *for* Culture and Development

75 Cuban cultural and social activists have been arrested in recent months and sentenced to prison terms of up to 28 years. Because of this, the Prince Claus Fund has decided not to provide financial support to the 8th Havana Biennial in November 2003. All those sentenced were engaged in the Cuban cultural and social arenas; their convictions signal a significant deterioration in the situation for intellectuals and artists. The body responsible for organising the 8th Havana Biennial, an internationally acclaimed platform for non-Western art, is associated with the government and has not distanced itself from the policy of prosecution. Therefore the Prince Claus Fund is forced to withdraw its collaboration.

The Fund was a key financier of the 7th Havana Biennial in 2000. It contributed €90,000 because of the high quality of the exhibition and its emphasis on intercultural exchange with artists in Latin America, the Caribbean, Asia and Africa. The Biennial also gives Cubans access to international cultural developments in a country where independent provision of information is scarce. The Fund considers, however, that it would be inappropriate to collaborate directly or indirectly with a government that pursues a policy of severe repression.

The Prince Claus Fund sees its task as drawing attention to the difficult situation of artists and intellectuals in Cuba at the present time. It is particularly important to stand up for those who struggle peacefully for freedom of speech and for free cultural expression.

The Prince Claus Fund for Culture and Development
A platform for intercultural exchange, the Fund realises contemporary activities and publications in the fields of culture and development. The Prince Claus Awards are part of this policy. Special attention is paid to what are called 'zones of silence' – areas where people are deprived of the opportunity for free cultural expression. In 1999 the Fund gave an Award to the Cuban cultural periodical *Vitral*, which operates as a volunteer organisation, albeit on the fringe, supported by the Roman Catholic Church in Cuba.

For more information please contact Prince Claus Fund for Culture and Development
Hoge Nieuwstraat 30, 2514 EL Den Haag, The Netherlands. www.princeclausfund.nl
Tel.: 00 31 70 427 4303. Fax: 00 31 70 427 4277. E: m.tummers@princeclausfund.nl

A DUTY TO WHOM?

MICHAEL FOLEY

DOES A JOURNALIST'S COMMITMENT TO PROTECT THE IDENTITY OF ANONYMOUS SOURCES OVERRIDE THE DUTY TO READERS AND VIEWERS?

Few relationships are more fraught than that between journalist and source. Journalists wine and dine their sources, spend long hours on the phone to them, get let down by them and are even willing to go to prison to defend their anonymity. In Britain, a senior judge, Lord Hutton, is currently investigating, among other things, the relationship between a senior government scientist, the late Dr David Kelly, who acted as a source for a number of BBC journalists, and the BBC reporters Andrew Gilligan and Susan Watts. Meanwhile, the National Union of Journalists has deemed another journalist, Nick Martin-Clark, 'not a fit and proper person' to be a member of the union. Mr Martin-Clark's offence was to give evidence against a source, a convicted member of a loyalist terrorist organisation, who told him he had murdered a Catholic taxi driver.

The centrality of the source to journalism is considered so evident that most journalists see little point in going further than stating this and saying no more. Journalists are defined by their contacts books, that collection of names and phone numbers without which most could not function. At the centre of this journalist/source relationship is the anonymous source.

So crucial is this relationship that there is hardly a code of ethics anywhere in the world that does not call in the strongest terms for journalists to maintain the anonymity of sources. Refusing to give the name of a source and abiding by a willingness to honour the contract of confidentiality, even by going to prison, is something many journalists maintain is a fundamental tenet of their craft. In a number of jurisdictions, journalists have some legal rights in protecting their anonymous sources; these are often known as Shield Laws. The European Court of Human Rights has even ruled, in the case of British journalist Bill Goodwin, that protection of confidential sources is an essential means of enabling the press to perform its function of public watchdog and should not be interfered with except in exceptional circumstances where vital public or individual interests are at stake.

However, while journalists in Britain and Ireland welcomed the ruling of the European Court of Human Rights, few looked at that all-important qualifier. Instead of pondering on the issues of public and individual interests, journalists are taking an increasingly absolutist view of protection of sources. Commenting on the Nick Martin-Clark case in the *Journalist*, the magazine of the National Union of Journalists in Britain and Ireland, NUJ official John Toner wrote:

> Some have argued that Nick Martin-Clark was acting in the public interest by informing on a notorious killer. We must take a broader view of the public interest than this. Sources must believe that a promise of confidentiality is as binding on a journalist as it is on a doctor, a lawyer or a priest. Any weakening in that belief will result in sources drying up and countless issues of public interest may never see the light of day. (*Journalist*, July 2003)

There are problems with the position taken by Toner. If we ignore priests, whose justification for upholding confidentiality are theologically based, then we are left with lawyers and doctors. Both professions are highly regulated and licensed. The professional bodies that run both professions have the powers to grant and take away the right to practice. Such a scheme would be anathema to most journalists.

Doctors, lawyers and priests offer anonymity in order to ensure privacy, so that what is said can remain private. Nothing said to either the doctor or the lawyer will be put into the public domain without agreement from the patient or the client. For the journalist the opposite is true. Not only will the journalist report all that is said, but will try, with all the skills at his or her disposal, to get the source to talk more and get more information, which again will be made public.

One of the problems for the absolutist case is that the use of anonymous sources is increasing. Day after day the media, especially newspapers, are full of quotes from sources close to the prime minister, or from industry sources and so-called 'friends' who tell all. No names are given; often only one source is quoted. Is the public to believe that the journalist is to risk imprisonment in order to keep the anonymity of the ubiquitous friend in celebrity news? And if they do, are they to be admired as doing something central to democracy and journalism?

How can the public, those who are to be informed by journalism so that they can make the decisions necessary in a democracy, trust journalists who offer so much information without any meaningful indication of where it came from? In many cases, the anonymous source is not a fearless whistle-blower, but a manipulative spin doctor, working for the rich and powerful and hiding behind a journalist's promise of anonymity.

The absolutist position also places the journalist above the ordinary citizen. With a demand for the legal right to withhold the identify of sources of information, journalists are seeking, and in some cases getting, a right denied to others. In that case, the journalist has ceased to be a citizen using the right to free expression granted to all in a professional way, but a special sort of citizen, one with rights granted by Parliament or the courts, who might, of course, one day, have a view as to who can operate that right.

Sources with genuinely important information concerning the public interest are more likely to go to a journalist they believe is trustworthy rather than simply rely on a principle that cannot be policed. The doctor or lawyer can be struck off, the journalist cannot. A source, I would maintain, is more likely to take the word of a journalist who appears committed to the same things he or she is, the betterment of the society they live in or the end

Credit: John Donegan, Punch

"Did Esme Draycott really go to her lover that night? Is Selwyn Plunkett dead, or alive and well in Peru? Was Melanie Frayle asleep or drugged? Who was the man in the green Lagonda? Stay with us for Part Two after the break?"

of the corruption the source wants exposed. It is more likely to be the word of an individual journalist rather than a principle enunciated by a group of people who cannot decide if they operate as a profession, with all that implies, or a trade, with a few rules as to how to do the job.

With anonymity, the source holds all the cards. A decision as to anonymity has to be agreed before the information is given: even before the journalist has heard what the source has to say, he has given a binding undertaking never to reveal the name, whatever the outcome. If that outcome leads to a miscarriage of justice, for instance, is that going to instil confidence in another person whose information is of great public interest, but who now fears giving it to a person who would rather see a guilty person go free than give a name to a court?

This is not an argument for abandoning the principle of defending the right of anonymity. It is right and proper that codes of conduct state clearly and unequivocally, as the NUJ's does, that 'a journalist shall protect confidential sources of information'. The International Federation of Journalists' code, which is often used as a model for journalists' codes in emerging democracies, states: 'The journalist shall observe professional secrecy regarding the source of information obtained in confidence.' Codes lay down guiding imperatives and all journalists must have a strong duty to follow such codes. Such a duty ensures continuity and also helps the public to know what journalists themselves believe are the principles of the profession.

However, the problem for journalists is that for the most part they are condemned to live without hard and fast rules, and all they have to guide them are ethical principles. They can adopt a legalistic Kantian allegiance to rules that tell them to follow the codes out of duty to the rules and for no other reason; or they can adopt a more reasonable approach, one that insists they consider the consequences of their actions. As John Merrill says in *The Dialectic in Journalism* (Louisiana State University Press, 1989):

> Journalists must be flexible, or willing to moderate a basic ethical tenet in order to reach a higher ethical objective dictated by a reasoned analysis of the situation. A significant point, and it should be emphasized, is that the journalist should never capriciously or unthinkingly break an ethical rule or maxim. An exception to a principle because of a specific situation must be made only after serious thought.

Throughout this article the word trust has been used and maybe it is now time for journalists to adopt a new imperative to judge and guide their actions: trustworthiness. Are my actions or decisions likely to increase the trust between me and my readers? Such an approach would have journalists seriously question the use of anonymous sources and ensure that they are used rarely and, when they are used, a full explanation is given as to why. With trust placed central to journalist practice, fewer anonymous sources would be used and the problem of protecting anonymity would arise less often.

Trust also brings us neatly back to an issue mentioned in the first paragraph, the events surrounding the establishment of the Hutton Inquiry. Hutton, established to investigate the death of Dr David Kelly, also gave us an insight into the relationship between the government, journalists and the BBC and also a rare look at how journalists work.

The events that have occurred since Andrew Gilligan first broadcast his story based on information given, at least in part, by Kelly, has been a battle between the New Labour government and the BBC for the hearts and minds of the viewers, electors and listeners. In other words, it was about who you trust: the journalism of the BBC or the government?

One interesting discussion centred on sources and the number of sources a journalist should rely on. The BBC's Andrew Gilligan, who, it appears, will be the second victim of the whole saga, was accused of relying on only one source. The implication was that this broke some sort of journalistic rule. The so-called two-source rule that is often invoked is a rule formulated by some US journalism schools; it comes back to the 'rule' about anonymous sources. Journalism schools have often felt insecure within the academic world and attempt to overcome this by creating a body of knowledge, or a list of rules, to satisfy traditional academics.

In the real world of journalism, reporters use single sources all the time. The question is not the number of sources but whether the sources are in a position to have the information and have integrity. The other issue is whether the story is in the public interest. By that standard Kelly was an ideal source. Other questions might profitably be raised that relate to how information is found, the relationship between the source and the reporter, the motivation of the source and whether money changed hands. The narrow range of sources regularly used by journalists might also be investigated, in order to satisfy the notion of the 'authoritative source'; the somewhat slavish pursuit of this 'rule' means many people not considered authoritative are excluded from the media whether as named or anonymous sources.

The outcome of Hutton will have far-reaching consequences for the BBC, journalism and possibly for government public relations or spin. It will also call into question the relationship of journalists to their editors and of that between journalists. If the protection of sources is such a central tenet in a journalist's craft, why were Gilligan's colleagues and editors not only so willing to reveal his source, but to throw him to the wolves when the tide of opinion appeared to be moving against him? If this inquiry has told us anything about that central relationship in journalism, the relationship between the reporter and the source, then it will have done something worthwhile. ❑

Michael Foley *is a lecturer in journalism at the Dublin Institute of Technology. He is vice-chair of the NUJ's Ethics Council and has worked on formulating codes of conduct and other ethical issues with journalists in Eastern and Central Europe*

HAVE YOU HEARD THE ONE ABOUT?

SANDI TOKSVIG

Q: Why should blondes not be given coffee breaks?
A: Because it takes too long to retrain them.

Sorry, have I started by offending you? Do you want to sue? Well, move to Bosnia. Did you know that 'blonde jokes' have been made illegal there? Savima Terzic, director of the International Group for Human Rights, announced that a new law on gender equality would 'enable blonde women to sue anyone who tells jokes that offend them, even if those jokes were based on the colour of their hair'.

I like the sound of a gender equality law but do you not think the International Group for Human Rights might have better things to do? Actually, I'm blonde myself. I would have sued but I didn't understand the joke.

I move from the blonde to the dark world of Section 315 of the Federal Communications Act in the US. Are you gripped yet? Basically it's a rule that says that anyone broadcasting pictures of a politician running for office has to give equal airtime to his opponents. At its heart it is a good rule but it didn't reckon on one Arnie Schwarzenegger standing for governor of California. According to legal experts, no Californian television station could show, say, *Terminator 2* without giving all the other 134 candidates a chance to spend two hours dressed up as benevolent cyborgs as well. At that rate there would have been nothing on television but robots taking over the world. Mind you, I've watched TV in the Golden State and I don't think it would have been a big change.

So no blonde jokes and no showing of *Kindergarten Cop*. Both good ideas taken to slightly silly extremes but there is a tricky question lurking in the midst. How do you draw the line between not letting people broadcast defamatory or inciting remarks and maintaining the critical right to free speech? It's not something I've had to deal with much. I've only been directly censored twice in my life. Once in my youth when I wrote an article for the school paper about anorexia that was deemed too racy for the fourth form who, as it was, wouldn't eat their pudding, and once when an ad I made with the actress Imelda Staunton for Atora Beef Suet was judged to be anti-Russian. (Come to think of it, I've never seen a commercial for beef suet at all and I wonder if the incident put them off the whole idea.) So just those two incidents in a life awash with opening my mouth and never using an edit button. Recently, however, I have been cheek by jowl with the whole subject of watching what you say.

Every weekday I do a two-hour talk show for LBC, a London radio station. In it I run the gamut of topics from heavy political discussion to reading excerpts from *The Warne Pleasure Book for Girls* published in 1929 (do read 'A Muff at Games' – it's a cracker). A little while ago the presenter of the phone-in that airs before me was censored by the Broadcasting Standards Commission for encouraging racist attitudes towards immigrants and asylum seekers. Now it is fair to say that this particular gentlemen has a political standpoint that is about as far as you can get from me without actually taking a plane. He is of the very fox-hunting right and I am of the very bunny-hugging left. During the last 'conflict' he was given to playing stirring tunes from an album of military hits that I then countered with pacifist pan-pipe music. Despite our differences we get on very well because at his core he is a supremely professional broadcaster.

I think the BSC is right to keep an eye on who says what but the fact is that these two polar opposite radio shows follow each other directly. Here is a radio station broadcasting a complete spectrum of opinions and I think that is important. We hide our head in the soft sand if we think there aren't people in this country with unpalatable views about immigration. On the whole I think I'd rather hear and refute them than try to pretend they don't exist. What is that quote about hating what you say but defending to the death your right to say it?

The LBC management refused to censure my colleague and I was delighted because they don't tell me off either. I say some appallingly critical things about the conduct of foreign and domestic policy in this country and I am free to say it. I am free to be as liberal and leftie as I like. We do have to be careful that we don't just want to censor the things with which we don't agree. Talk radio is an invaluable asset in the UK and we should leave it alone even if there is the odd blonde joke. ❑

Sandi Toksvig *is a writer and broadcaster*

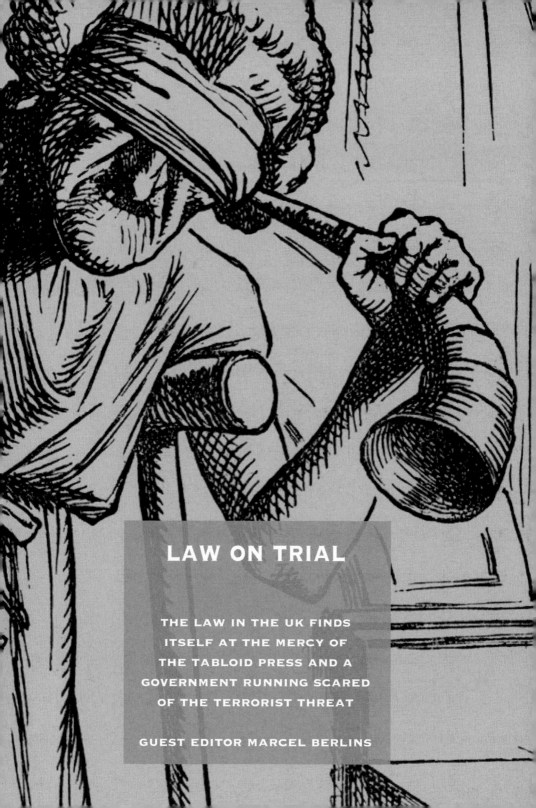

LAW ON TRIAL

THE LAW IN THE UK FINDS
ITSELF AT THE MERCY OF
THE TABLOID PRESS AND A
GOVERNMENT RUNNING SCARED
OF THE TERRORIST THREAT

GUEST EDITOR MARCEL BERLINS

MORE EQUAL THAN OTHERS
MARCEL BERLINS

FEW RIGHTS SUCCESSFULLY CHALLENGE
THE SUPREMACY OF THE RIGHT TO
FREE EXPRESSION. IN LAW THAT IS;
GOVERNMENTS ARE ANOTHER MATTER

It goes without saying that the ultimate human right is the right to live. The unjustified taking of a human life by the state or one of its satellite institutions stands alone as an act of ultimate international banditry. It acts as a sure measurement of a nation's wickedness. But if that human right stands alone in terms of its possible brutal finality, the right to freedom of expression stands with it as a mark of a state's civilised behaviour. Or, to put it more crudely, as a gauge that distinguishes democracies from dictatorships and totalitarian regimes. No other in the growing family of human rights possesses such influence and importance.

'Give me liberty to know, to utter, and to argue freely according to conscience, above all liberties,' the poet John Milton wrote in 1664, in his *Areopagicita*. Voltaire is believed to have offered to defend to the death a person's right to say something with which he disagreed; there's no evidence he did speak those words, but the sentiment gives freedom of expression its due significance. Over the course of history, many have, indeed, died defending their own, or others', right to speak out.

The writer Junius put the pre-eminence of freedom of expression thus in 1772: 'The liberty of the press is the Palladium of all the civil, political and religious rights of an Englishman.' Not long afterwards that view was confirmed by a great dictator: 'If I were to give liberty to the press, my power would not last three days,' Napoleon remarked.

Freedom of expression is a rambling sort of right, imprecise and impossible to define neatly. It includes, most importantly, freedom of the press, but its ambit encompasses also the individual's right to free speech. We tend to think of freedom of expression mainly in terms of the right to criticise authority or reveal iniquity and malpractice, but it includes too – though not unlimitedly – the creation of works of art or literature without censorship, a system of open justice 'seen to be done' and the protection of

London: statue of John Wilkes, 'father of press freedom' in the UK. Credit: Tony Callaghan

journalists' sources. In Britain, it affects profoundly the laws on defamation, contempt of court, copyright, breach of confidence and privacy.

It's not easy to draw up a balance sheet that tells us, simply, whether this government is sound on freedom of expression or these judges have clearly upheld the right or diminished it. But the passing of the watershed Human Rights Act 1998 allows us to assess whether the judges' approach to freedom of expression has changed, whether there is a new judicial spirit abroad making Britain a country in which free speech and freedom of the press flourish with an added enthusiasm.

The problem with the Human Rights Act is that it has been hugely oversold. In one sense, by incorporating the European Convention on Human Rights (ECHR) into our national law, it did little more than change the setting in which Britain's adhesion to a human rights regime operated. British citizens, instead of having to take the elaborate, expensive and lengthy (six years was commonplace) path to the ECHR in Strasbourg to have the wrongs done to them righted, can now approach the national courts directly and quickly. But the content of the human rights package remains broadly the same.

The UK was not just a signatory of the ECHR in 1952, but one of its principal drafters. Article 10, the freedom of expression provision, has not changed in the half-century since it first appeared. For all that time, and not just since the Human Rights Act, judges were supposed to be giving effect to it.

Article 10 starts promisingly:

Everyone has the right to freedom of expression. This right shall include freedom to hold opinions and to receive and impart information and ideas without interference by public authority and regardless of frontiers. *Article 10 (1)*

But what the law giveth, the law taketh away. Here come the exceptions:

> The exercise of these freedoms, since it carries with it duties and responsibilities, may be subject to such formalities, conditions, restrictions or penalties as are prescribed by law and are necessary in a democratic society, in the interests of national security, territorial integrity or public safety, for the prevention of disorder or crime, for the protection of health or morals, for the protection of the reputation or rights of others, for preventing the disclosure of information received in confidence, or for maintaining the authority and impartiality of the judiciary. *Article 10 (2)*

Not much that could become a potential exception to the exercise of freedom of expression is omitted. Every part of that sentence opens up the potential clash between freedom of expression and every other right guaranteed by the Convention. Nowhere does Article 10 say that freedom of expression is somehow to be given greater importance than any other rights listed in the Convention. Yet over the years, it stealthily acquired such a status, one that the Human Rights Act has now enhanced.

In practice, in the past, the UK's relationship with freedom of expression, both at government and judicial level, was one of grudging and reluctant acceptance of the European Court of Human Rights' judgements, though some English judges were more dedicated than others in following Strasbourg principles – including the apparent supremacy of freedom of expression over other rights. In 1994, the appeal court judge Lord Justice Hoffmann said: 'It cannot be too strongly emphasised that outside the established exceptions, or any new ones that Parliament may enact in accordance with its obligations under the Convention, there is no question of balancing freedom of speech against other interests. It is a trump card which always wins.'

Hoffmann's card-game analogy has resulted in a controversy that still continues and is at the crux of the question: is freedom of expression a superior right? Enter the home secretary Jack Straw, in charge of piloting the 1998 Human Rights Act through Parliament. Following weeks of pressure from media interests, he announces that freedom of expression is indeed going to get special treatment.

Section 12 of the Act suddenly creates an Orwellian concept. All rights are equal but freedom of expression is more equal than others: 'The court must have particular regard to the importance of the Convention right to freedom of expression.' The section lays down the tests a judge must apply before granting an injunction stopping publication in the press or transmission on television or radio. In theory, the exhortation to judges applies only when they're thinking about a ban; in practice it's seen as a general invitation to give free speech some sort of priority.

But what does having 'particular regard' mean? A mere reminder that judges should be careful to make sure that they take freedom of expression into account? Or does it go further, in effect stating a presumption – which can be rebutted – that freedom of expression is more important than other rights? Or stronger still, that only in exceptional cases can freedom of expression be knocked off its lofty pedestal? Judges have been arguing the point ever since section 12 came into being.

So how, on freedom of expression issues, has the judiciary behaved since the Human Rights Act actually came into force on 2 October 2000? It's been easy enough for the judges to come up with the right words. All have drawn attention to the importance of freedom of expression and of the press, and then gone on to balance against it the competing rights being claimed. But has there been a real change? Apart from issuing the usual lawyerly warning that it's far too soon to tell, the signs are on the whole positive. The new generation of judges now sitting in our higher courts are not looking for excuses and exceptions to justify weaseling out of applying freedom-of-expression principles.

The change in judicial attitude and confidence became obvious even before the Human Rights Act became law. In 1998 the law lords, in the name of freedom of expression, took a dramatic step towards giving the press a new defence when sued for libel by a political figure. The former Irish prime minister Albert Reynolds had sued the *Sunday Times* over a story alleging political impropriety; he eventually won his case, but the House of Lords laid down principles allowing the media, when publishing stories of public interest, to make mistakes without being punished for them in the libel courts – provided they weren't acting out of malice and had taken care in assembling the story.

Most freedom-of-expression cases coming before the courts, though, have lacked the serious significance of the Reynolds case. Many have been about the rights of minor celebrities to keep their names or activities out of the newspapers. Freedom of the press deserves a more elegant platform: it should be mainly about the right to criticise governments, express unpopular opinions, or expose iniquitous deeds – people have given their lives to uphold those principles – not whether or not the sexual antics of footballers or television 'personalities' should be revealed to a wider public.

But the judges cannot choose the cases that come up before them. It is not their fault that they've had to decide largely trivial disputes. But have they, in the way they've dealt with those, given any clues to how they might stand up to important challenges to freedom of expression in the future, of the kind that determines the democratic landscape of a nation?

Here, for instance, is Lord Woolf, the Lord Chief Justice, in the appeal by the *People* newspaper against a high court judge's injunction banning it from publicly revealing the identity of an adulterous footballer, Gary Flitcroft, captain of Blackburn Rovers:

> The fact that if the injunction is granted, it will interfere with the freedom of expression of others and in particular the freedom of the press is a matter of particular importance . . . Any interference with the press has to be justified because it inevitably has some effect on the ability of the press to perform its role in society. This is the position irrespective of whether a particular publication is desirable in the public interest . . . The existence of a free press is itself desirable and so any interference with it has to be justified.

Flitcroft, married and with children, had conducted short-lived but intense affairs with two women both of whom, when dumped, sold their stories to the newspaper. His attempt to keep his identity out of the story at first succeeded, the high court judge granting him an injunction on the basis that publication of his name would be a breach of confidence – even a short adulterous relationship, the judge ruled, was confidential enough to get the protection of the law. The appeal court had no hesitation in ruling that the judge was wrong; any right Flitcroft might in theory have to keep his sexual adventures secret was easily beaten by freedom of expression – not just the newspaper's but also the right of the two women to have their tales publicised.

It was expected, following the Human Rights Act, that freedom of expression would come under greatest legal threat from the newly acquired so-called right to privacy, as set out in Article 8 of the European Convention on Human Rights:

> Everyone has the right to respect for his private and family life, his home and his correspondence.

This was to be the clash of the rights titans. How would the judges behave when faced with, on the one hand, the right of people – not just celebrities but in practice usually so – to keep their private lives private and, on the other, with the media insisting on its right to tell its public about celebrities who misbehave, who are ill, who are in love, or who may just be displaying too much of their bodies? And on the outcome to that struggle would emerge the answer to the crucial question: is there really such a thing as a right to privacy?

But the expected battle hasn't really been fought, though a few skirmishes have taken place. Judges have sought and found ways of avoiding the issue. Cases involving the newsreader Anna Ford (photographs of whom on holiday on a secluded beach in Majorca were published in the *Daily Mail*), the super-model Naomi Campbell (shown in the *Mirror* leaving a drug-rehabilitation clinic when she'd always denied being a drug addict) and Gary Flitcroft were expected to raise the privacy versus freedom of the press debate, but didn't – although in all those cases the publications were, in effect, ruled justified.

High Court, London, 2003: Catherine Zeta Jones and Michael Douglas denied the right to censor. Credit: AFP / Nicolas Asfouri

Catherine Zeta Jones and Michael Douglas came to the English courts complaining that their privacy had been invaded when *Hello!* magazine managed to publish unauthorised snaps of the couple's wedding when the picture rights to the event had been sold to the competing *OK!* magazine. The judge decided the case on a legal point of commercial confidentiality, refusing to make it a privacy or a freedom-to-publish issue.

One case has pitted freedom of expression against Articles 2 and 3 of the Convention – the right to life and the prohibition of torture. Free speech was beaten convincingly. Jon Venables and Robert Thompson, the two boys – now young adults – who had killed the child James Bulger, were shortly to be released from detention, with changed names and new personal histories. They applied to the court for a perpetual injunction prohibiting the media from ever publishing any information about them that could lead to their new identities or whereabouts being publicly revealed. If the general public were to know where to find them, they argued, they would be in danger of being subjected to extreme violence; indeed, they would be at risk of their lives. Timidly, lawyers for the press argued for freedom of expression: the press could be trusted not to reveal anything that could endanger the young men's lives. But it was a losing battle. The judge, Dame Elizabeth Butler-Sloss, had no trouble granting Venables and Thompson the lifelong injunctions for which they'd asked.

Freedom of expression versus the right to a fair trial is a battle still to come. The Contempt of Court Act 1981, contains, in principle at least, stringent restrictions on the press's freedom to inform the public of what it really wants to know – all about the accused in a high-profile criminal trial. Nothing can be reported that creates a 'substantial risk' of 'serious prejudice' to a forthcoming trial – telling the jury something prejudicial about a defendant that they would not hear about in court and that might affect their verdict. Contrast that with the position in many US states, where almost nothing is banned; the absurd OJ Simpson trial is an example.

For some years, the English media, the tabloids in particular, have been pushing at the frontiers of contempt of court, giving the public more and more information about an accused, daring the attorney-general of the day to take them to court. But none has done so in recent years, not even in the case of Barry George, convicted (on sparse evidence) of the murder of television presenter Jill Dando and made the subject of a torrent of prejudicial pre-trial publicity. In the absence of any concern by successive attorneys-general to curb such excessive coverage, it may be that freedom of expression has already won a victory over the right to a fair trial, without even going to court. Even if the attorney-general stirs, believing newspaper coverage to have been prejudicially excessive (over the child murders at Soham in 2002, perhaps, or some alleged terrorists) any attempt to bring culprit newspapers to book will be resisted by a media armed with the special status of freedom of expression. Which way will the judges rule? A fair trial is a cornerstone of English justice. It will not easily yield to another right.

The courts, then, have been treating freedom of expression and freedom of the press with respect and even occasional enthusiasm. That, at least, is a positive trend. Our senior judges today are manifestly more mindful of free speech than their colleagues were even 15 years ago. I cannot imagine that today's law lords, if faced with a modern-day *Spycatcher* written by a retired member of MI5, would continue to ban publication of a book containing no secrets or implications for national security, which was on open sale in the rest of the world and its contents widely known in Britain. Nor can I envisage a judge today doing what one did only four years ago: ordering the presses of the *Sunday Telegraph* to be stopped to prevent publication of a story revealing the conclusions of the inquiry into the death of Stephen Lawrence, even though the official report was to be published four days later. Nor would the reporter Bill Goodwin be ordered by a judge, as he was in the early 1990s, to reveal his journalistic sources for a story he was writing on the financial plight of an engineering company. The list goes on. It is as much what one can no longer envisage happening in our courts as what judges have actually said and done that gives hope for the future of freedom of expression in this country – at least as far as the courts are concerned. Government is another matter. ❑

Marcel Berlins is visiting professor in media law at Queen Mary College, University of London, and lecturer in media law at City University, London. He is the legal columnist of the Guardian *and presents BBC Radio 4's* Law in Action

A new style of debate and conversation from Bob Geldof's Ten Alps Media Company and Index on Censorship.

Put some people around a table with something to drink; invite the best guests;

give them a topic and let everybody have their say on anything from

LIES & SEX TO FOOTBALL & MONEY

.....you never know who you might be sitting next to but with those ingredients you have the perfect recipe for

TALKING HEADS

The King's Head Theatre

115 Upper Street, N1 Box Office: 020 7226 1916

Tickets £10 (includes complimentary drink)

Every first Sunday of the month - Starting October 5th at 7pm

FIGHTING WORDS

ANTHONY HUDSON

WHETHER IT BE JEWS IN NAZI GERMANY,
AFRICAN-AMERICANS IN THE US OR
SLAVES IN MAURITANIA, LANGUAGE HAS
BEEN AND CONTINUES TO BE A VITAL
TOOL IN THE OPPRESSION AND ABUSE
OF MINORITIES

In August 2003, a man from Manchester enjoyed the privileged status of being the first person in England to be the subject of an anti-social behaviour order. This prohibited him from using the racist term 'Paki' and from using threatening, insulting, abusive or homophobic language in public. Should he breach the order he will commit a criminal offence punishable by up to five years in prison. He was found to have called council staff variously a 'Paki bitch' and a 'homo'.

The order is the latest in a series of orders and prosecutions in England against people using racist and offensive speech, particularly, it would seem, football supporters. Despite the right in English law to freedom of expression, as guaranteed by Article 10 of the Human Rights Act 1998, there are numerous restrictions on the use of racist and offensive words. 'Hate speech', as it is called, raises difficult questions about the extent to which speech should be protected and the extent to which words that wound should be restricted in order to protect the rights of the victims of such words.

To call a person a 'Paki bitch' or a 'homo' is clearly offensive and obviously, at the very least, distressing to the subject of the abuse (*Index* 2/ 99). In *nigger: The Strange Career of a Troublesome Word*, Randall Kennedy observes that it is often claimed that '*nigger* is the superlative racial epithet: the *most* hurtful, the *most* fearsome, the *most* dangerous, the *most* noxious'. Where, however, such speech is not accompanied by the threat of immediate violence, should it be proscribed and its use be punishable by the criminal law? Insulting and racially offensive language undoubtedly has an impact on the subject of the abuse. Does it also have, or potentially have, a wider impact? Should only offensive speech that is likely to provoke an immediate breach of the peace, 'fighting words', be prohibited? Are more far-reaching restrictions an unacceptable infringement on the fundamental right to freedom of expression?

In *Destructive Messages, How Hate Speech Paves the Way for Harmful Social Movements*, Alexander Tsesis argues that:

> Destructive messages are the main vehicles for spreading ideology. Hate speech is an essential means for popularizing hate groups. Physical persecution of outgroups ['historically oppressed racial and ethnic groups'] are commonly preceded by institutional inequalities resulting in part from the popularization of misethnic ideology.

In answer to the suggestion that racist and offensive speech are not intrinsically damaging and may be cathartic, he says:

> Hate speech is not a harmless release for misethnic attitudes. It does not mitigate threats to minorities. To the contrary, during opportune times, it inflames and recruits persons who can be catalyzed to wreak havoc on outgroups. . . . Cultural preparation for perpetrating crimes against humanity takes time and is vastly more dangerous than fighting words that lead to fisticuffs. With the aid of charismatic orators, bigots exploit social unrest to consolidate power by blaming outgroups for social ills. Misethnists then go beyond talk and back up their self-perceived superiority by brute force.

There is little doubt that racist and offensive words are damaging to both individuals and groups and may, in turn, damage society as a whole. The use of language to achieve and/or perpetuate the subordination of a group of people is well documented. Whether it be Jews in Nazi Germany, African-Americans in the US or slaves in Mauritania, language has been and continues to be a vital tool in the oppression and abuse of minority groups. The use of the word 'nigger' in the oppression of African-Americans in the US and elsewhere is powerfully demonstrated by Kennedy.

Despite the potentially far-reaching and destructive consequences of hate speech, its restriction is often vigorously opposed. Restrictions on hate speech violate the fundamental right to freedom of speech. Should, however, the right to freedom of expression take priority over the rights of those subject to hate speech? One of the reasons this is such a difficult issue is that racist and offensive speech does not always have immediate consequences. Further, laws passed to restrict speech that is generally considered to be unacceptable to vulnerable minorities can, and have been, used to

UK: racist graffiti. Credit: Nicholas Bailey / Rex Features

prosecute those very minorities. Black activist Michael X was the first person to be imprisoned in England, in 1968, for a race-hatred offence. He was convicted by an all-white jury.

Timothy Shiell, in *Campus Hate Speech on Trial*, observes that what 'may begin as a well intentioned effort to prevent harm can quickly become a weapon of speech czars'. He further argues that 'without the right to use speech considered offensive, even abusive or harmful by others, egalitarians of varying stripes will find their own speech subject to the same suppressive apparatus as anti-egalitarians. Equality needs free speech, and not just polite, sophisticated academic discourse; it needs Malcolm X, Lenny Bruce . . .' Kennedy makes the point that 'just as acute wariness of public or private censorship has long furthered struggles for freedom of expression in all its many guises, so has resistance against censorship always been an important and positive feature of the great struggles against racist tyranny in the United States, from the fight against slavery to the fight against Jim Crow'.

It is often argued that the most effective way to combat hate speech is by engaging in more speech not less (*Index* 1/98). The expression of odious and offensive ideas should be reduced or eradicated by challenging and over-coming those ideas. Suppressing the expression of such ideas and beliefs does nothing to prevent them being held and affecting conduct (albeit less vocally). This idea of a free trade in ideas puts faith in the ability of 'good' speech to overcome 'bad' speech. The importance and validity of the concept has been recognised, in a different context, by the House of Lords. In *R v Secretary of State for the Home Department ex parte Simms* in 2000, Lord Steyn listed a number of reasons for the importance of freedom of expression:

- it recognises that the best test of truth is the power of the thought to get itself accepted in the competition of the marketplace of ideas;
- it is the lifeblood of democracy; the free flow of information and ideas informs political debate;
- it acts as a brake on the abuse of power by public officials and facilitates the exposure of errors in the governance and administration of justice of the country.

It is questionable, however, whether such an approach gives much comfort and support to those, often vulnerable, minorities daily subject to intimidating and terrifying racial and homophobic abuse. The marketplace can be a very unforgiving place.

Like many other countries – Austria, Belgium, Brazil, Canada, Cyprus, Denmark, France, Germany, India, Israel, Italy, The Netherlands and Switzerland – England has legislated to restrict symbols of racial hatred and hate speech. The initial impetus for such legislation in England was the increase in anti-Semitic fascist rallies in the 1930s. The Public Order Act 1936 made it an offence, subject to exceptions, to wear in any public place or at any public meeting uniform signifying association with any political organisation or with the promotion of any political object. Geoffrey Robertson and Andrew Nicol note in the latest edition of their *Media Law* that the Public Order Act 1965 was passed 'after several years of racial violence of the most serious kind, by a Labour government whose commit-ment to freedom of speech was weakened after the infamous Smethwick by-election in which a Labour majority evaporated in the face of the slogan: "If you want a nigger for a neighbour, vote Labour".'

Part III of the Public Order Act 1986 contains a series of criminal offences involving acts intended or likely to stir up racial hatred. 'Racial hatred' means hatred against a group of persons in the UK defined by reference to colour, race, nationality (including citizenship) or ethnic or national origins. These include: the use of words or behaviour or display of written *material of a threatening, abusive or insulting nature*; publishing or distributing such material; playing recordings of and broadcasting such material; and possession of such racially inflammatory material with a view to its use in any of these ways.

The offence of inciting racial hatred may be committed by the transmission of television or radio programmes. This arguably makes it more difficult to make programmes about racism, because the offence may be committed irrespective of the producer's intention, if 'having regard to all the circumstances racial hatred is likely to be stirred up'.

The Crime and Disorder Act 1998 provides for the basic public order offences in the POA 1986 to be treated more severely where they are racially aggravated.

Several international instruments prohibit racial discrimination and prevent racist propaganda. These include: the 1945 United Nations Charter, the 1948 Universal Declaration of Human Rights, the 1965 International Convention on the Elimination of All Forms of Racial Discrimination and the 1966 International Covenant on Civil and Political Rights.

Article 10 (1) of the European Convention on Human Rights guarantees the right to freedom of expression. It is not, however, absolute. It is qualified by Article 10 (2). The right to freedom of expression may be subject to 'such formalities, conditions, restrictions or penalties as are prescribed by law and are necessary in a democratic society, in the interests of . . . public safety, for the prevention of disorder or crime, for the protection of health or morals, for the protection of the reputation or rights of others . . .'

Restrictions on the expression of racist ideas are legitimate under Article 10 (2) as being for the protection of the rights of others. They are also envisaged by Article 17 of the Convention, which emphasises that the rights guaranteed by the ECHR do not give anyone the right to engage in any activity or perform any act aimed at the destruction of any of the rights and freedoms guaranteed by the Convention. In reality, the right to freedom of expression guaranteed by Article 10 provides very little protection for hate speech.

The European Court and the European Commission have denied race-hate propaganda the protection of Article 10 of the ECHR in, for instance,

Glimmerveen and Hagenbeck v *Netherlands* in 1979, while recognising at the same time, in *Jersild* v *Denmark* in 1994, that the public exposure of racist conduct and hate speech can be protected by Article 10.

In the process of making a television documentary, Jersild, a journalist, interviewed a group of self-avowedly racist youths. As a result of broadcasting their derogatory and racist remarks about black people in general and immigrant workers in particular, Jersild was subsequently convicted of aiding and abetting the youths in making statements which insulted or degraded a group of persons on the basis of their race, colour, national or ethnic origin. Jersild complained to the European Court of Human Rights that his right to freedom of expression had been violated. The court eventually agreed with him on the grounds that his purpose in making the film was not racist and his conviction did, therefore, breach his right of freedom of expression.

JOURNALISTS SHOULD NOT BE PUNISHED FOR ASSISTING IN THE DISSEMINATION OF STATEMENTS MADE BY ANOTHER PERSON IN AN INTERVIEW

It is important to note that the European Court's decision was based, in part, on its conclusion that 'unless there are particularly strong reasons' journalists should not be punished for assisting in the dissemination of statements made by another person in an interview. To do so would 'seriously hamper the contribution of the press to discussion of matters of public interest'. The remarks made by the youths, which were 'more than insulting to members of the targeted groups', did not enjoy the protection of Article 10.

To be protected by Article 10 such programmes must provide a counterbalance to the racist speech, although the way in which that is done is a matter for the journalist concerned. It is also important that such reports do not suggest endorsement of racist views.

The restrictions on hate speech in England and the lack of protection for such speech provided by the jurisprudence of the European Court of Human Rights is to be contrasted with the significant degree of protection available in the US, where the Supreme Court has adopted a content-neutral stance in relation to the First Amendment.

In *RAV* v *St Paul* in 1992, a number of youths burned a cross they had made from wooden chair legs on the front lawn of an African-American family who had recently moved into a mainly white neighbourhood. The youths were convicted under legislation that made it an offence 'to place on public or private property a symbol, object . . . including . . . a burning cross . . . which one knows or has reasonable grounds to know arouses anger, alarm or resentment in others on the basis of race, colour, religion, or gender . . .' Their conviction was subsequently quashed by the US Supreme Court, which found that the legislation violated the First Amendment.

The reasoning of the justices in the Supreme Court differed. The majority held that the ordinance was flawed because it was a form of 'content discrimination'. To comply with the First Amendment the legislation had to ban all 'fighting words' rather than focus on hate speech. The minority held that the legislation was 'fatally overbroad' and therefore unconstitutional because it criminalised not only unprotected expression but expression protected by the First Amendment.

In his minority concurring opinion, Justice White recognised the danger of giving First Amendment protection to hate speech. He stated that the decision of the majority was a 'negative one, since it necessarily signals that expressions of violence, such as the message of intimidation and racial hatred conveyed by burning a cross on someone's lawn, are of sufficient value to outweigh the social interest in order and morality that has traditionally placed such fighting words outside the First Amendment'.

The decision of the US Supreme Court in *RAV* v *St Paul* means that legislation that seeks to protect minority groups from hate speech will be unconstitutional if it is aimed only at those minority groups.

Hate speech can, and does, cause immense harm. The criminal law may not, however, be the most appropriate way for society to combat such harm. Laws restricting speech are particularly vulnerable to abuse and to selective enforcement. At best, they arguably do no more than remove the outward signs of a much deeper problem, which may be left largely unaddressed. The challenge of protecting the right to freedom of expression while seeking to prevent the infringement of the rights of others is a difficult one. It is one that Europe and the US have confronted in significantly different ways. Unfortunately, it is a challenge that is likely to continue to have to be met. ❑

Anthony Hudson is a barrister at Doughty Street Chambers, specialising in freedom of expression and privacy

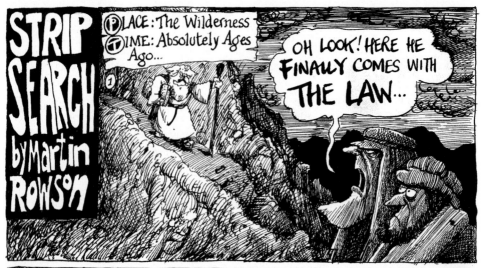

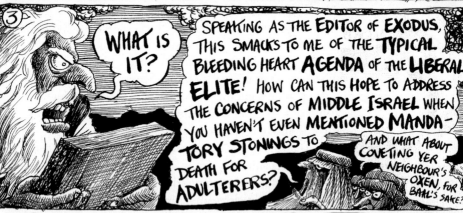

STEADY PROGRESS BACKWARDS

ANTHONY SCRIVENER

'IN ENGLAND AMIDST THE CLASH OF ARMS THE
LAWS ARE NOT SILENT. THEY MAY BE CHANGED,
BUT THEY SPEAK THE SAME LANGUAGE IN WAR
AS IN PEACE. IT HAS ALWAYS BEEN ONE OF THE
PILLARS OF FREEDOM, ONE OF THE PRINCIPLES
OF LIBERTY . . . THAT THE JUDGES ARE NO
RESPECTERS OF PERSONS, AND STAND BETWEEN
THE SUBJECT AND ANY ATTEMPTED
ENCROACHMENTS ON HIS LIBERTY BY THE
EXECUTIVE' (LORD ATKIN DURING WORLD WAR II)

The ambition of every political party in government is to retain power. This
is not always easy in a democracy. It is not just about implementing the
manifesto, that is not the problem. As Harold Macmillan explained: 'The
problem, dear boy, is events.' Before you realise what has happened, the
party of peace and internationalism is bombing the hell out of Iraq without
the sanction of the United Nations. But wars can be good news as long as
you win: they rouse patriotism and create an atmosphere of 'emergency'
that, with a bit of spin, a government can usefully turn to its advantage.
Look at what President Bush was able to achieve in the wake of 9/11,
culminating in the inspired Guantánamo regime where there are no tire-
some human rights, and 'trials' are conducted by military tribunals. Stalin
and Chairman Mao would have been proud to have invented it, and all that
was needed was an 'emergency'.

Spirits were justifiably high here as well. With the might of the US on
our side the prospect of smashing up Iraq looked pretty good. It's a pity
about those weapons of mass destruction, but we did get rid of Saddam.

There is nothing like a good emergency to get a government chipping
away at democracy and getting a tighter grip on its citizens and their freedoms. During World War II, the House of Lords held that under Regulation 18(b) of the Defence (General) Regulations, persons of 'hostile
association' could be detained without the executive giving 'reasons and

particulars'. Lord Atkin dissented and it is his words in the case of *Liversidge* v *Anderson* that the history books cite:

> In England amidst the clash of arms the laws are not silent. They may be changed, but they speak the same language in war as in peace. It has always been one of the pillars of freedom, one of the principles of liberty for which, on recent authority, we are now fighting, that the judges are no respecters of persons, and stand between the subject and any attempted encroachments on his liberty by the executive, alert to see that any coercive action is justified in law. In this case, I have listened to arguments which might have been addressed acceptably to the Court of King's Bench in the time of Charles I.

These are the fine words of principle but the other four judges in the House of Lords supported the government.

But politicians of all parties remember those words of Lord Atkin. The Anti-terrorism, Crime and Security Act 2001 allows for an appeal to the Special Immigration Appeals Commission from the Secretary of State's issuance of a certificate that he believes a person's presence in the UK is a risk to national security and he suspects the person is a terrorist.

The Special Immigration Appeals Commission Act 1997 allows for the appointment of a 'person' to represent the appellant when he and his lawyers are excluded from the hearing because of the nature of the evidence. Although well intentioned, this idea fails because the person does not have to be a lawyer and it is expressly provided that the 'person' 'shall not be responsible to the person whose interests he is appointed to represent'.

This means that the representative will not have the knowledge to contest or test the evidence and will have no idea of the case of the person he has been nominated to represent. The chances of the appellant being able to deal with evidence given in his absence is not enhanced by these provisions. However, a combination of Lord Atkin and the European Convention on Human Rights has prevented another Regulation 18(b). These provisions cover a small group of people; there is still plenty of scope for trimming.

New Labour have not waited for an 'emergency' to begin the trimming of those institutions of the state upon which freedom depends and which can cause such irritation to a government. To the uneducated and non-partisan it may look like an attack on democracy itself but it is all a matter of trust: trust New Labour. There are good reasons for messing about with these fundamental rights. Take that old chestnut – jury trials.

Juries are unpleasantly independent and unpredictable. They do not always convict when they should and they cause the government embarrassment. Clive Ponting [the whistleblower of the Falklands War *Ed*] grinning outside the Old Bailey after his inexplicable acquittal was a horrid moment for civilised government. Trial by judge alone is the answer: better control, better conviction rates.

The public will understand: jury trials are too expensive, they are used by greedy lawyers to line their pockets at the public expense. Let's start with those long fraud trials: although there is a remarkably high conviction rate in such cases, juries do not understand what is going on. The ultimate objective should be to allow the attorney-general to decide when a jury trial is necessary. He is a decent chap and a similar system has worked well in such places as Hong Kong.

The Criminal Justice Bill will begin the process of cutting down jury trials. For New Labour's bright new vision you should look beyond the bill and read the report Lord Justice Auld prepared for the government. That heralds the decline not only of juries but of lay magistrates too, in favour of professional judges: better control, better conviction rates.

But to make all this work, the government needs to control or at least influence the appointment of the senior judiciary. Happily, New Labour has this in hand too. There is good reason for this much needed reform which can be explained to the public. We need to break the traditions of public school judges. Judges should be appointed by a commission not by the Lord Chancellor who is really one of them. Lay people should have a say.

The recent consultation paper on 'a new way of appointing judges' proposes as one option the setting up of a Judicial Appointments Commission as a *recommending* body. The actual appointment of senior judges should be made by a minister or even the prime minister: guess who appoints the members of the commission under these proposals? Back to the government. Those appointed members should be able to ensure that the right kind of person becomes a judge: the sort of person who has a decent respect for elected government.

The promotion of judges once appointed is already within the powers of the government. No wonder the former Lord Chancellor, as he faded into history, remarked darkly of his fears for the independence of the judges.

Then there is the curse of judicial review which the judges have developed to quash government decisions as unlawful and which can be such a pain to elected government. The whole process needs to be reformed. One possibility could be that such cases should be dealt with exclusively by an administrative tribunal which only has advisory powers. A friendly judge and a couple of experienced civil servants on the tribunal will soon sort out judicial review. The need for reform can be easily explained to the electorate. We do not even need an 'emergency'.

Judicial review is in reality a fight between elected democratic government and a lot of public school-educated judges whose only experience of democracy is when they are elected to the Garrick Club. They should not have the power by use of judicial review to frustrate the will of the people expressed through Parliament. The will of the elected parliament should prevail: it is causing David Blunkett to get upset. Of course, as home secretary he wins most of the cases in which his department is involved but it ought to be 100 per cent. It is not for some unelected judge to rule that he has acted unlawfully. I can recall the shock felt by Chinese lawyers visiting the Hong Kong courts before the territory was returned to China, and

Rough justice: 'Struck off the Rolls' by George Morrow. Credit: Punch

PICTURESQUE ASPECTS OF OUR LEGAL SYSTEM.
A Solicitor being struck off the Rolls.

finding judicial review cases proceeding against the government. Mr Blunkett's upset is perfectly understandable.

There are no proposals yet but the corridors of power echo with murmurings. Judges who find against the government are already the subject of personal attack – a unique feature of New Labour. Watch this space!

This is not the only thing that causes Mr Blunkett upset. He wants to know what is going on. The government must be able to spy on its citizens – tap their telephones and read their emails. It is an 'emergency' situation.

Mr Blunkett, who can justly boast to be the proud successor of that other great liberal home secretary, Jack Straw, did his best to usher in Big Brother by introducing a bill that would have empowered the police, seven government departments, all local authorities, the Postal Service Commission, the Office of Fair Trading, the Financial Services Authority and the Health and Safety Executive, to name but a few, to demand your communication data from telephone companies, Internet Service Providers and post offices.

Fortunately, his son or someone mentioned the European Convention of Human Rights (which also causes Mr Blunkett upset) and this promising piece of legislation was put on hold. However, the government is still pledged to produce some similar but less ambitious legislation with spying powers because of the emergency caused by 9/11.

The argument for the electorate is simple. The government must be given exceptional powers to deal with exceptional events. It is for your safety. Local authorities and the Health and Safety Executive need to have these powers to fight al-Qaida. You do not mind them reading your emails because you have nothing to hide – you are decent and honest citizens who like your private affairs to be distributed to and read by all those officials. You do not mind. It is an emergency.

Then there are the 'media'. It is not just Mr Blunkett who gets upset by them. The obvious remedy is to introduce a system of licensing. All media should require a government licence, renewable, say, annually. But this will take time. A process of education is needed first.

On any view the media needs reform. They do not deal properly with justifiable complaints from decent citizens: they give money to witnesses and frustrate trials and the judicial system, they invade the privacy of ordinary citizens and as for 'standards' many of them just publish 'filth'. Even the BBC lie and make things up: look how they have been trying to blacken the character of poor Alastair Campbell.

The whole thing needs cleaning up. No wonder they will not reveal their sources. Perhaps we should consider a licensing system or at least the establishment of an independent Complaints Commission as a starter.

The BBC are a particularly nasty bunch as they are supposed to be independent. That is a particularly difficult concept for a political party to understand. They cannot be won over by exclusive titbits of news or by winning 'favoured son' status by publishing nice editorials. Perhaps the Hutton Inquiry will be the springboard for action.

It is sad that the fight to preserve the fundamental rights upon which democracy is based has to start at home against the New Labour government. Without the rule of law, an independent judiciary, the right to personal freedom and a free media there can be no democracy. The erosion of any of these rights can start an irreversible slide.

It is also a sad reflection of the standing of the UK that our government cannot speak out about the abhorrence of Guantánamo. The US was the greatest proponent of democracy in the free world until President Bush brushed all that to one side and invented Guantánamo. The government does not wish to risk the special relationship with the US by loudly criticising such excesses; we must tag along in silence. We cannot even do much for the two British detainees.

The problem is that the US cannot agree to them being tried in this country because the evidence obtained from them under the Guantánamo regime would probably be inadmissible under our law. Such is the influence of our government that it is considered to be some sort of diplomatic triumph to be involved in some deal under which the detainees plead guilty to something which probably could not be proved against them by evidence in a court of law, in return for some sentence considered reasonable by an unlawful military tribunal. I wonder what Patricia Hewitt and Harriet Harman think about it as ministers in the present government and as former officials with Liberty. ❏

Anthony Scrivener QC *is former chairman of the Bar Council for England and Wales*

SIX QUESTIONS IN SEARCH OF AN ANSWER

TERRY WAITE

Long before the terrible events of 11 September 2001, I held the belief that the methods adopted by the USA and Britain in attempting to deal with international terrorism were both wrong and dangerous, and would lead to increased acts of terror. I based my views on the rather old-fashioned idea that, ultimately, violence will not be defeated by violence. I am not a pacifist as I believe that in certain exceptional circumstances the limited use of force may be required. However, the reaction to 9/11 seemed to me to border on the hysterical and I became increasingly alarmed as the UK drew closer and closer to the US in adopting a 'military solution' to these complex issues of our time.

Guantánamo Bay appalled me for many reasons, not least because due process was sidestepped by legal sleight of hand. Also, to keep prisoners in the manner in which they are being kept is clearly degrading to both captive and captor and ought to be no part of civilised society. I became even more alarmed when rumours circulated that certain terrorist suspects had been transported to countries where information might be extracted from them by torture. I had no evidence for this but the rumours persisted.

My concern was heightened when one afternoon I received a phone call from the BBC *Newsnight* team inviting me to appear on the programme that evening. It was alleged that 13 prisoners being held in the UK without trial might have been arrested on the basis of evidence or information extracted under torture. It was further alleged that the suspects were appearing before an immigration tribunal where most of the proceedings were being held *in camera* under conditions of extreme secrecy. *Newsnight* had invited a government spokesman to appear on the programme to comment, but were told no one was available. As I left the set I was taken aback to meet a prominent legal spokesman for the government about to be interviewed on other political issues. Clearly, not all government spokesmen were on holiday that night.

The item shown on *Newsnight* was worrying but it was difficult to ascertain the truth of the allegations being made, given the strict secrecy surrounding the tribunal. If the central allegation that evidence obtained by the use of force was admitted, then this is clearly wrong and such evidence ought, in my opinion, to be immediately discarded.

It is wrong for several reasons. First, Article 15 of the UN Convention against Torture, to which the British government is a signatory, clearly states:

> Each State Party shall ensure that any statement which is established to have been made as a result of torture shall not be invoked as evidence in any proceedings, except against a person accused of torture as evidence that the statement was made.

That is clear and unequivocal.

It is also wrong on moral grounds, not least because the use of torture by the state signifies failure and brings the state down to the level of the terrorist. The argument is sometimes used that torture might be justified if an individual has hidden a bomb which is about to explode and possibly kill hundreds of people. In such a case, it is argued, torture might well save many lives. Unfortunately, presenting a case in this way creates a false equation. Should this method be adopted then eventually many individuals will be tortured, the majority of whom will have no information to give or power to do what their tormentor wishes them to do.

Torture is wrong because once it becomes an instrument of the state then the state begins to descend down the road to lawlessness. Due process goes out of the window; presumption of innocence falls over; the opportunity to present opposing views and present a proper defence is denied. In short, torture eventually makes the state the enemy of the people and threatens all our lives and liberty.

Since the *Newsnight* programme I have neither read nor heard anything about the so-called tribunal. Was this a case where the UK was adopting the methods of Guantánamo? Was it a trial dressed up as a tribunal? Was evidence admitted that had been obtained under duress? Who appeared before the tribunal? Who gave evidence? What was the outcome?

These, I suggest, are perfectly reasonable questions for any citizen of the UK to ask. They are more than reasonable. They are essential. ❑

Terry Waite *was at one time special envoy for the Archbishop of Canterbury. He is now a writer and broadcaster*

MAKING AN IMPACT

IMRAN KHAN

IT TOOK THE COURAGE OF ONE BLACK
FAMILY TO CHANGE THE PERCEPTIONS
OF BRITISH SOCIETY AND EXPOSE THE
RACISM AT THE HEART OF THE COUNTRY'S
MOST POWERFUL INSTITUTION

This year sees the convergence of two anniversaries which, though separated by time and distance, are intricately linked: the fortieth anniversary of Martin Luther King's famous 'I have a dream' speech in Washington, DC, on 28 August 1963; and the tenth anniversary of the death of Stephen Lawrence on the streets of south London in 1993.

Each event marked the beginning of a turning point in the life of a nation that had, until that point, slept easy in its beds in the knowledge that racism did not exist. Martin Luther King's prescient words and powerful oratory made everyone stand up and listen; the death of Stephen Lawrence brought the reality of racism into the homes and lives of everyone in Britain. The important thing today, perhaps, is how far, if at all, we have come since then.

The report on the Stephen Lawrence case produced a demarcation that some have described as a 'post-McPherson' paradise: an age, an era, when the death of a young Black man forced society to accept that racism exists within its midst; when government and public officials were finally forced to listen to the McPherson mantra of 'recognition, acknowledgement and acceptance' of institutional discrimination.

The inquiry into the Stephen Lawrence case in 1998 sat for 69 days and heard from 88 witnesses. It produced more than 12,000 pages of transcripts and finally reported in February 1999. Its chair, Sir William McPherson, was not noted for his anti-racist credentials, yet he produced, no doubt with the help of his advisers, one of the most damning indictments of the police service this country had ever seen. He concluded that the police were institutionally racist. Campaigners and community groups, lawyers and politicians had tried in vain to persuade those in power that there was something rotten at the heart of the police service and by implication society at large.

Stephen Lawrence.
Credit: Photo News Service / Rex Features

Yet it was the actions of an 'ordinary' family placed in an extraordinary situation that finally forced the issue.

It was not only the recommendations of the report that played their part in changing the public perception of its minorities, it was the inquiry itself. How often is a Black family able to force one of the most powerful institutions in the country under the spotlight and question it to the core? The fact is the process of the inquiry itself was as cathartic to society as the report's findings. It was, in essence, a kind of truth commission in which public servants previously cloaked in the secrecy of officialdom had to acknowledge their mistakes.

The Lawrence legacy could be long-lasting, despite concerted attempts to undermine it. Its achievements are manifold and it has extended its reach to parts of society that had remained untouchable. For lawyers, the clearest examples of change have come within the criminal justice system. For years before the Lawrence case, many of us had fought a losing battle with police officers and the prosecuting authorities to accept that racist attacks were being perpetrated on our communities. Rather than being protected, the victims were being persecuted and prosecuted. The number of miscarriages of justice that resulted is legion and beyond repetition here. Yet no amount of pressure or persuasion could force the pace of change in the way that minority communities were being policed.

The fact is that the cultural atmosphere of the time was impervious to the concepts that some of us now take for granted. For years, the idea that racism infected the very heart of British institutions such as the police, prisons, the National Health Service, local authorities and so on was anathema to the vast majority of the population. State-sponsored racism through immigration and asylum legislation was, and remains, a concept difficult for many to accept. It was only when a young man of 19 was killed on the streets of south London that this perception started to change. In the aftermath of the disturbances of the early 1980s, Lord Scarman rejected the idea of institutional racism, claiming that where racism did exist in the police it did so only occasionally in the behaviour of a few officers on the beat; the Lawrence report, on the contrary, made the concept of institutional racism its linchpin.

This small yet devastating shift has created real and substantial potential for change. It has reversed previous roles and stereotypes: it is no longer right to suggest that the problem lies with and within the Black communities; the problem lies with the nation and its institutions. No longer can police and public officials simply dismiss allegations of racism and racist attacks: they are forced to deal with them whether they like it or not. The real truth of our existence – on the streets, on council estates, in the workplace – has finally been accepted and given voice. Racism existed and the state had to do something about it.

The process has not stopped there, however. More generally there has been an incremental shift in emphasis from victim to protagonist; this, too, has produced a most profound change. The death of a loved one is obviously a painful experience and the failure of the state to bring those responsible for the death to account makes the reality even more painful. Grieving is put on hold as the victims' families take on the state. The concept of the 'wronged victim' fighting for justice takes shape.

Of late, unfortunately, this creature has been hijacked for political gain by the law-and-order brigade. A platform is beginning to emerge that might allow a great leap backwards. It is an issue that has caused great consternation among so-called liberal lawyers as the emphasis shifts from protecting those who are prosecuted to those who are their alleged victims. In the name of redressing the balance in favour of the victim, we are watching an attack on the ancient principle of double jeopardy and the right to trial by jury. The real, as opposed to the stated, content of concentrating on the victim now emerges as a concerted attempt to erode the rights of the defendant; and this in the context of a society still riddled with institutional racism. Black males are eight times more likely to be stopped and searched; more likely to be charged; less likely to get bail; more likely to be convicted and more likely to go to prison. It is quite clear who will feel the brunt of such measures, however they are justified.

To many who were involved in the Lawrence case, its cynical manipulation is a source of shame. The Lawrence report and its recommendations were intended to enhance the rights of individuals and not erode them. It is not axiomatic that to enhance the rights of victims we must erode the rights of the perpetrator. Yet that is the course of action proposed by the home secretary. There is a hypocrisy at the heart of this government. In the words of James Baldwin: 'What it gave, at length and grudgingly with one hand, it took back with the other.' Its commitment to anti-racism with the Stephen Lawrence inquiry and the Race Relations Amendment Act is neutralised by legislation that will criminalise Black communities even further.

While many oppose these changes, they are divided over whether the 'support for the victim' approach is a step in the wrong direction. In the course of the battle against racism in this country, the victims of injustice, who have fought in such difficult circumstances against the police and other authorities, have played a crucial role in moving the state to recognise their rights. The fights against racism and violence in the home are just two examples of the way in which the role of the 'wronged victim' has improved the lives of many in society and changed the structure of institutions.

At a time when confidence and trust in politicians and the political process were at an all-time low, the 'wronged victims' retained the moral high ground essential for the champion of a cause, a catalyst for change. They contained that one ingredient missing from lobbyists and campaigners: no one could or would impugn their motives. Their demand was a simple one: redress through a positive assertion of rights. Without a written constitution or bill of rights, the normal parameters of the English legal system were constrained. Not until the Human Rights Act 1998 could a set of positive rights be invoked by any wronged citizen. The concept of the 'impact case' fits within this new environment of the wronged citizen, asserting his or her rights and holding the institutions to account. Its basic premise is nothing new: a case that merits justice in its own right, but which, when pursued, has an impact on wider society. The Lawrence case was the most celebrated and clearest example. Others have followed.

Of particular note is the tragic case of Zahid Mubarek. On 21 March 2001, six hours before he was to be released from a short prison sentence, Zahid was attacked by his cellmate, Robert Stewart, at Feltham Young Offenders' Institution. The attack was brutal. As Zahid lay sleeping in his bed Stewart took a wooden table leg and beat him repeatedly about his head. It might have been some consolation to his family if Zahid had slept through the attack, but injuries found on the back of his forearm suggest he was woken and tried to stop the blows. He died seven days later. Robert Stewart was eventually convicted of murder and sentenced to life imprisonment.

On the face of it, this is a fairly simple, open-and-shut case, yet further examination of the facts exposed a catalogue of questions that the family wanted answered. Most pertinent of these was why Robert Stewart, known for his racist views, was placed in the same cell as a young Asian man?

The family persisted in pressing the authorities for an answer. Yet even after a police investigation, an internal prison inquiry and an investigation by the Commission for Racial Equality, it is none the wiser. In pursuing the case, however, issues about the treatment of those in our prisons have been thrown up. Changes to the prison service have been made. The National Association for the Care and Resettlement of Offenders (NACRO) says the progress of change has been impressive and has occurred in no small measure because of the actions of the Mubarek family. The case has also raised issues about the nature and effectiveness of inquests; and the House of Lords is about to give judgement on a case that will establish the precise nature of the state's obligations to protect its citizens' right to life under the Human Rights Act.

The Lawrence and Mubarek cases have obvious similarities: the death of a loved one and a failure by the authorities. Both have been described as 'wake-up' calls to the institutions concerned. From the selfless acts of the families involved, profound change – in both cases for the better – has come. The tragedy, of course, is that but for the death – but for the loss – change might never have happened.

It is a sad fact that impact cases appear to be indispensable in today's society. The price a family pays to pursue them is an unbearable one. However, as the Lawrence family know only too well, while they may not have achieved justice for themselves, society has benefited and progress for others is now more possible. ❏

Imran Khan is a human rights lawyer who represented the family of Stephen Lawrence and now specialises in impact cases

WHO DRIVES THE AGENDA?

BOB WOFFINDEN

THE UK'S TABLOID PRESS SEEKS TO
BE BOTH JUDGE AND JURY IN HIGH-
PROFILE CRIMINAL CASES; LAW LORDS
AND GOVERNMENT SEEM POWERLESS TO
SET A MORE LIBERAL JUDICIAL AGENDA

Barely a day has passed in recent years without the UK government being indicted by the media for employing those supposedly sophisticated public relations techniques characterised by that all-embracing word, spin. Indeed, the government has been lambasted so relentlessly over this that one needs to remind oneself that spin is essentially a defensive mechanism, used to enable an administration to withstand media assaults on its performance and policies. No one needs to be especially sympathetic to politicians to appreciate that many of those attacks are intemperate and ill-informed. It might bring a modicum of candour to public affairs if, instead of appearing shame-faced when caught out by the media in a particularly flagrant manifestation of spin, the government just for once retorted, 'Well, you started it.'

Developments in legal and judicial affairs provide a telling illustration of what happens when, under sustained media attack, there is no spin, or indeed self-defence, of any kind. The institutions are undermined; they become unrecognisable.

Historically, the serious press reported legal matters in the higher courts of the land. The popular press, what there was of it, covered crime. But those papers existed on the premise that they traded influence for circulation, and no one expected their reports to cause a scintilla of concern in Whitehall. Even when the notorious John Straffen child-murder case was current in 1952, the middle-ground papers such as the *Daily Mail* and *Daily Express* reserved their front pages for foreign affairs and domestic politics; the Straffen trial was reported inside.

The BBC, meanwhile, was firmly aligned with the serious press; crime was outside its ambit. Its abstemious approach had to change with the arrival of commercial television, but it was not until the early 1960s that the corporation began to carry regular reports of criminal cases. The A6 murder of

1961 – which became the celebrated Hanratty case – was the first to which BBC television assigned a reporter.

The case marked an early turning point in crime coverage because, uniquely, it featured a number of highly newsworthy developments, including the arrest and release of an original suspect prior to the nationwide search for James Hanratty, the second suspect. As the case began with a crime committed in August, the traditional silly season when genuine news material was scarce, and concluded with a controversial execution, it enthralled the public and received sustained coverage across the media spectrum. From being marginalised as a seedy and unwholesome interest – much in the way that 'true crime' books are still presented in bookstores today – crime was moving into the mainstream.

The first major point of friction, when the media confronted the attitudes and presumptions of the legal establishment, occurred in 1966, the year Ian Brady and Myra Hindley were sentenced to life imprisonment for what were known as the Moors Murders. At roughly the same time, the old trade union newspaper, the *Daily Herald*, was relaunched as the *Sun*. The relaunch was unsuccessful, and the paper, together with the *News of the World*, was sold to Rupert Murdoch's News International.

Finding it difficult to stimulate sales, the *Sun* hit on the gambit of publishing an extensive account of the Moors Murders case. The convention of the day was that once a case had run its course – and investigation, trial and appeal had all been concluded – then the verdict was final and the case consigned to history. There might be inspiration for others (the playwright Emlyn Williams wrote a notable book about the case), but the case was not news and no longer appropriate material for newspapers. The only exception was in cases where there were concerns about the safety of the conviction.

This unstated, but hitherto unbroken, rule applied above all in especially sensitive or harrowing cases, like those of child murder. The idea that such a case should be resurrected and the grief of the bereaved reawakened for naked commercial opportunism had been unthinkable. The Straffen case, for example, concerned three child murders and had been the sensation of its time. Yet in the years since its resolution (Straffen was condemned to death, but then reprieved by the home secretary and the sentence commuted to life imprisonment), no newspaper had felt the need even to refer to it. Now, here was the *Sun* reviving the most sickening of recent cases for no better reason than to boost ailing circulation. The paper was widely condemned. But, faced with this challenge to long-standing convention, the legal authorities did nothing.

It could be argued that everything that happened subsequently only proved the wisdom of the earlier approach. Having been revived in the public imagination, the case never thereafter left it. Myra Hindley turned into one of the most vilified figures in British history. The point should be reiterated: this was not because of the crime of which she had been convicted, but because of the reporting of the case in later years. (Similarly, the Mary Bell trial in 1971 attracted relatively subdued contemporaneous publicity, and only afterwards became infamous.)

Hindley then became the first British prisoner to have a whole-life tariff imposed by the tabloid press. In 1966, few would have quibbled with a recommended sentence of 30 or even 25 years. By 1996, however, the press had made her release impossible. The public outcry that would have accompanied any release would have been uncontainable and she could not have been safely released into the community.

It was the *Sun*, again, that introduced another far-reaching, and profoundly unhelpful, change. Another long-held convention dictated that those convicted were described in neutral and unemotive terms – as, for example, 'convicted murderer'. Partly because of its preference for barroom language and its impatience with words of more than two syllables, the *Sun* swept this convention aside, referring to criminals and prisoners in words that were – like Hobbes's description of the life of man – nasty, brutish and short. 'Thug', 'bully', 'killer', 'beast' and 'pervert' are but a few examples. This language was quickly adopted by the *Sun*'s competitors, the majority of the regional press and even by broadsheets such as *The Times*.

Such constant denigration of criminals meant that they could not be thought of as fellow human beings who might, in some circumstances, have been regarded with sympathy or pity and who, having served their sentences, were entitled to be rehabilitated. They were cast instead as beyond-the-pale villains who should be locked up and the key thrown away. Again, it was difficult to tell whether it was the tabloids influencing the barroom, or the barroom influencing the tabloids.

However, the real turning point in the impact of the tabloid press on the judicial process occurred with the case of Michelle and Lisa Taylor, sisters who had been wrongly convicted of the murder of Alison Shaughnessy in 1993. Alison was married to John, with whom Michelle had been having an on-off relationship. Under headlines such as 'JUDAS KISS' and 'CHEAT'S KISS', the papers used stills from a video of the wedding of Alison and John, at which Michelle had been a guest. The real cheats, however, were the press, in deliberately misrepresenting a momentary embrace between John and Michelle as something more passionate. Nor was this the only ground for complaint. The wedding video itself formed no part of the trial evidence. Trial reports should, according to contempt laws, have been restricted to matters raised during trial.

When the case went to appeal, the convictions were quashed. The appeal court judges ruled that they found it 'impossible to say that the jury were not influenced in their decision by what they read in the press'. Accordingly, they specifically instructed the attorney-general, Sir Nicholas Lyell, to examine the issue. The expectation was that several papers would have to face contempt of court proceedings.

Yet the attorney-general did precisely nothing. Even though the Taylor family tried to take forward a judicial review, he took no action. Lyell's pusillanimity in this matter had predictably catastrophic consequences. The tabloids, not unreasonably, felt they were above the law and could flout with impunity contempt laws and other reporting restrictions that they deemed inconvenient.

The media needed greater latitude to report criminal matters, not least because all outlets – across newspapers, television and radio – were becoming more dependent on crime as a staple news ingredient. For the press, television – particularly regional TV – and radio, crime provided ideal news material. It was immediate, attention-grabbing and, crucially, cheap. It required almost no journalistic input, many of the stories being taken direct from police press releases. In fact, relations between the police and tabloid newspapers became increasingly cosy. The editor of the *Sun*, Rebekah Wade, told the House of Commons select committee on culture, media and sport that the paper regularly paid police officers for stories.

It was often in the interests of both press and police to infringe *sub judice* provisions, which were meant to guarantee fair reporting of criminal cases. One of the most glaring examples occurred on 3 February 2001 when the *Daily Mail* ran a front-page headline story indicating that the police were going to charge Roy Whiting with the murder of the schoolgirl Sarah Payne in three days' time. A 'senior police source' was quoted as saying: 'The man [already named as Whiting] is due to be arrested on Tuesday and the mood among many officers is buoyant.' *The Times* also ran the story the same day, again naming Whiting.

Obviously, if Whiting were the murderer, then he was exceptionally dangerous and his arrest should not have been delayed. The actual reason for delay appears to have been to create a prejudicial pre-trial atmosphere. This was in due course complemented by the prejudicial reporting of the trial itself. The *Sun*'s front-page headline on the first day's hearing on 15 November 2001 was 'SARAH'S GRINNING KILLER'. Why go to the trouble of empanelling jurors when these matters can be predetermined by the tabloid press?

Likewise, the press pre-empted the judicial process in the case of Dr Thomas Shanks, who was accused, and later convicted, of the murder of his girlfriend. On 9 May 1998, the day following the murder, the front-page headline in the *Mirror* was 'SAS DOC EXECUTES LOVER NURSE' – which tended to obviate the need for any trial at all. When the case did go to trial, Shanks's defence was that he was a victim of Gulf War syndrome, which had affected his mental state. He was entitled to have been able to put that argument without the defence position having been undermined in advance. In fact, Shanks was convicted of possessing a firearm, but the conviction was quashed and a retrial ordered after further medical evidence was heard. At the retrial, he was convicted of murder. The tabloid press zealously covered the original dramatic incidents but had no interest in pursuing the case as it meandered through the courts. The fact that Shanks lost his second appeal in March 2003 went virtually unreported.

This approach to crime as sensational material, and the accompanying pressure on the police for someone speedily to be held accountable, but disdain for the legal complexities of the case, almost guarantees that there will be frequent miscarriages of justice. The press reports further ensure that they will be difficult to overturn. Three notable victims of wrongful convictions have suffered from gleefully malign reports of their circumstances: Sally Clark (whose conviction has now been overturned) from inaccurate reports suggesting she had a drinking problem; Sion Jenkins from entirely untrue reports suggesting he had no educational qualifications and had assaulted members of his family; and former squadron leader Nicholas Tucker from grossly exaggerated reports of a liaison with a Serbian interpreter.

There are other cases that, because of the weight of media pressure, it would be almost impossible to re-examine. Rosemary West is a sort of proxy prisoner, serving someone else's sentence. There's no proper evidence that she was involved in any of her late husband's serious crimes, yet the tabloids will keep her where she is.

AUTOMATIC ARBITRATION.

No more Exorbitant Fees ! No more Law ! No more Trials !

*Taking the easy way out:
'Automatic Arbitration' by
ET Reed. Credit:* Punch

Defence lawyers have enduring problems in dealing with the media. Their legal training encourages them to be wholly circumspect, and the overwhelming majority come to regard the media with such distaste that they run a mile in the opposite direction. Clearly, a more sophisticated approach is required. The high-profile cases have at least as much to do with PR (and, yes, spin) as with courtroom tactics or matters of evidence. One of the key rules of spin, formulated by the Clinton team that secured victory in the 1992 US presidential election, was that if there was harmful publicity, it had to be counteracted immediately. In this other adversarial contest, between prosecution and defence, the latter, far from responding immediately, rarely responds at all. The Crown wins every time by default. There have been few attempts to redress the balance, though one recalls the solicitor in the Tracie Andrews case making a public appeal for witnesses on the basis of her original story: right tactics, sir; wrong case.

If there's not enough crime around, the press can always create its own, as the *News of the World* apparently did when reporting its story about a Victoria Beckham kidnap plot. The subsequent trial of five men collapsed after it was disclosed that the paper had paid £10,000 to the star witness, a convicted conman who seemed to have instigated the supposed plot.

Having lost their opportunity to curb the tabloids' excesses, the judiciary is now frequently powerless before them. Once, judges were derided for asking apparently inane

HAVING LOST THEIR OPPORTUNITY TO CURB THE TABLOIDS' EXCESSES, THE JUDICIARY IS NOW FREQUENTLY POWERLESS BEFORE THEM

questions (albeit ones that were often necessary to establish in the court record a precise description of what might have been an ephemeral phenomenon). Now, they are taken to task on more serious issues. 'SACK HIM' headlined the *Sun* on 6 September 2003, after a Scottish judge, Lord Reed, sentenced a man who had assaulted a 13-month-old child to five years' imprisonment. Not long enough, according to the *Sun*. 'Punishment is supposed to reflect public revulsion at a crime,' the paper explained. 'The thousands of calls to the *Sun* reflect public revulsion at the judge.' Ready as ever to dance to the tabloids' tune, the judicial authorities called for a report into the case.

A few weeks earlier, on 20 July, the *News of the World* front-page headline concerned the release from prison of Gary Hart, the man found legally responsible for the Selby rail crash. Again, the paper wanted a longer sentence. However, what was truly remarkable about the paper's choice of front-page story was that, on that day, every other paper was principally concerned with the death of Dr David Kelly. There could have been no clearer demonstration of where the *News of the World*'s priorities lay.

Rarely does the tabloid press pause to examine the consequences of its drive to put people in prison, and, once there, to keep them locked up. Imprisoning people is a costly business in several senses; in other circumstances, the papers could be condemning the squandering of public funds.

With the retirement of Lord Scarman and the passing of Lord Devlin, there is scarcely a senior judicial figure of sufficient stature to inveigh against the excesses of the media. However, giving the Ditchley lecture in July, Lord Bingham, the senior law lord who is expected to lead an English supreme court, contemplated the landscape created by the media and observed: 'It must sometimes be very hard for a defendant to believe that he is . . . enjoying the fair trial which is the birthright of every British citizen.' It was perhaps significant that the report of the speech carried in the *Guardian* was coupled with another story: 'Prisons face overflow'.

Yet the problem goes far beyond this. The press has created a massively illiberal agenda. Most of the papers are contemptuous of human rights legislation and will do nothing to protect individual liberties. They are not even interested in protecting the freedom of the press itself. Over the past 20 years, as a direct result of intrusive and insensitive press reports, there has been a steady increase in the area of public life fenced off from press scrutiny. After the furore over the Ealing vicarage rape case, alleged victims in rape cases cannot be named. After the much more recent furore in the John Leslie case, similar anonymity may apply, on a more limited basis, to suspects in such cases.

Nor, in almost all cases, can the names of children involved in criminal cases be reported. Nor can any proceedings in the family courts be reported. These may well be the most unjust courts of all. However much suspect evidence is given, however many irrational judgements are reached, nothing can be reported. On this matter, the press stays silent.

The clamour of the press makes it more difficult for the government to pass liberal laws, and easier to push through hardline ones. The prime minister even knows, in appointing a home secretary, that it may be less troublesome in the end to choose someone whose social and political instincts are already attuned to the tenor of the tabloid press.

Lest there be attempts to constrain the press in ways that would really hurt – such as in the reporting of major criminal cases – an excuse is ready to hand. Any rules and restrictions that were brought in would be undermined by media outside the control of Parliament: first, the internet; second, international publicity. In August 2002, a popular French magazine appeared with a cover story devoted to the Soham murders: 'JESSICA ET HOLLY: ASSASSINEÉS PAR LEUR MAÎTRESSE D'ÉCOLE'. Of course, Maxine Carr was not a schoolteacher. Nor had she even been charged with the murders. Compared with this, the British press would doubtless argue, we're responsible and accurate.

That would be a fine example of its enduring hypocrisy. Certainly, it has taken on the judicial infrastructure and won almost all rounds. The media, and particularly the tabloid press, has taken all the liberties it wants while doing nothing to protect or enhance those of the general population. ❏

Bob Woffinden has written articles on miscarriages of justice and other legal issues for the Guardian, The Times, Daily Mail, Sunday Telegraph *and other publications. He is the author of* Miscarriages of Justice *and* Hanratty – The Final Verdict

ANYONE FOR FREE EXPRESSION?

JULIAN PETLEY

FOR MOST OF THE BRITISH PRESS, THE
RIGHT TO FREE EXPRESSION ENSHRINED
IN THE HUMAN RIGHTS ACT IS LESS
IMPORTANT THAN THE CHANCE TO BANG
THE EUROPHOBIC DRUM

That elements of the government's recent immigration legislation have been
found by the courts to run counter to Britain's obligations under the European Convention on Human Rights (ECHR) should be cause for shame.
For Britain's notoriously Europhobic newspapers, however, it's yet one
more example of Johnny Foreigner interfering with England's right to do as
it damn well pleases, and the perfect opportunity for whipping up public
indignation against a measure that many papers detest and have, from the
start, wanted to see repealed.

The provisions of the Convention were adopted by Parliament via the
1998 Human Rights Act (HRA). However, the moment the bill was
published in October 1997, the shadow home secretary, Sir Brian
Mawhinney, claimed that British judges would now be able to tell Parliament what laws they should and should not pass on the basis of the views of
foreign judges. Meanwhile, Baroness Young warned that Church of
England vicars could be forced to marry gay couples, and Conservative MP
Ann Widdecombe claimed that abortion clinics could demand to advertise
in the Roman Catholic press; moreover, church schools could be forced to
appoint atheist head teachers.

All these ludicrous claims, and more, were faithfully amplified by the
green-ink brigade in the press. Already skilled in the propagation of ridiculous Euromyths, the Little Englanders went into ideological overdrive,
raging that the HRA would outlaw fagging, compulsory cold showers and
early-morning runs in English public schools, make it impossible for
teachers to ban gay sex among under-age pupils, ensure the early release of
the murderers Myra Hindley and Rosemary West, throw Britain's motoring
laws into chaos and automatically allow the families of asylum seekers into
Britain.

Worst of all, however, this frightful Continental imposition allegedly threatened the press with a privacy law. Never mind that British judges had been developing a privacy right for some time, Article 8 of the ECHR raised their hackles by stating that 'everyone has the right to respect for his private and family life, his home and his correspondence'. Sensing in this perfectly reasonable statement a possible threat to its commercial lifeblood of kiss 'n' tell stories, the British press mounted a campaign in defence of its entirely self-appointed 'right' to pry into every nook and cranny of people's private lives. Of course, in its inimitably insular fashion, it did so in complete ignorance of how European courts had actually been interpreting Article 8. Had it bothered to enlighten itself it would have discovered that Article 8 does not create an enforceable right to privacy, although it may tip the balance in cases where courts have the discretion to weigh competing rights. As far as the ECHR is concerned, neither the right to free speech nor the right to respect for personal privacy is absolute; in practice, the two have been balanced by the principle of proportionality.

Chief among the warriors in this cause was Lord Wakeham, at that time chairman of the Press Complaints Commission (PCC), who argued that the HRA 'posed a grave threat to press freedom'. Why? Because the PCC would be regarded as a 'public authority' under the terms of the HRA, and the Act makes it unlawful for any public authority to act in a way that is incompatible with Convention rights. Wakeham, conveniently ignoring the fact that PCC decisions were already amenable to judicial review, warned that if complainants to the PCC were able to challenge its decisions in the courts or secure legal remedies for breach of its editorial code, then 'my task of seeking to resolve differences . . . would no longer be a practical proposition'. In other words, newspapers would no longer finance their creature the PCC if its activities were in any sense legally significant. As Hugo Young noted with undisguised incredulity in the *Guardian* on 12 February 1999: 'unembarrassed by the fact that the Human Rights Bill is a general law, applying to every citizen in his or her relationship with state authority, [newspapers] demand that the press be treated differently . . . They propose that the press, alone among institutions with public functions, should stand above international human rights law.' Indeed, it could be argued that the PCC's horror at being regarded as a 'public authority' amply confirmed the views of those who already regarded it as simply the incestuous spawn of the newspaper industry, and a body entirely unwilling – indeed, given the source of its funding, unable – to take on the powers and responsibilities of

Fending off the foreigners:
'John Bull' by John Leech.
           Credit: Punch

JOHN BULL GUARDS HIS PUDDING.

a fully fledged regulator. Furthermore, it seems not to have occurred to the PCC that the more it was prepared to show that it was an effective and respected self-regulatory body, the less likely would the courts be to impose their own remedies for intrusions on privacy; conversely, the more it insisted on acting as a private club, or indeed as an old-fashioned closed shop of the kind once routinely excoriated by British papers, the less would the courts be prepared to defer to its judgements.

The attitude of the press towards the ECHR is all the more extraordinary when one realises that it was not until the HRA that there was a statutory right to freedom of speech in Britain. Article 10 of the ECHR, itself based on Article 19 of the 1948 Universal Declaration of Human Rights, states that 'everyone has the right to freedom of expression. This right shall include freedom to hold opinions and to receive and impart information and ideas without interference by public authority and regardless of frontiers.' Clause 2 of Article 10 (2) includes a number of qualifications to this principle, but none the less, as Geoffrey Robertson and Andrew Nicol conclude in the latest edition of their indispensable *Media Law*, 'the Act writes into British law for the first time a presumption in favour of free speech, putting the burden on the censor to justify, as a matter both of necessity and logic, the restriction imposed.'

Although the HRA was promoted under the slogan 'rights brought home', many of the rights contained within it had never had a home here – in particular, the right to freedom of expression. Certainly Magna Carta had nothing to say on the subject in 1215, but in 1275 the first of a long line of statutory restrictions on freedom of expression appeared in the form of the offence of *scandalum magnum* which protected the 'great men of the realm' from criticism. As the law lords put it in 1936: 'free speech does not mean free speech: it means speech hedged in by all the laws against defamation, blasphemy, sedition and so forth. It means freedom governed by law.' As in other areas of British life, freedom of speech was governed by the rubric that 'everything is permitted that is not specifically prohibited'. What rights existed were purely residual ones.

The only right to free speech established by the Bill of Rights of 1688–9 was for MPs and peers. This stated that 'the freedom of speech and debates and proceedings in Parliament ought not to be impeached or questioned in any court or place out of Parliament'. This form of 'parliamentary privilege' still protects MPs and peers from libel actions over allegations they make during parliamentary proceedings. And, apart from the 1700 Act of Settlement, Britain did not review its constitutional arrangements again until Labour came to power in 1997.

According to AV Dicey, in his *Introduction to the Study of the Law of the Constitution* (1885), 'freedom of discussion is . . . in England little else than the right to write or say anything which a jury, consisting of 12 shop-keepers, think it expedient should be said or written'. However, juries often turned out to be extremely censorious. Once the property and age qualifications for jurors were lifted in 1972 and juries became more liberal, governments tried increasingly hard to avoid jury trials in cases where media freedom was involved, relying instead on various 'licensing' bodies, on creating offences that could be tried only in magistrates' courts, and on civil rather than criminal law as a means of curtailing publication on the grounds of copyright, confidentiality, official secrecy and so on.

Of course, injunctions, whether interim or permanent, run directly counter to the famous 'publish and be damned' principle and to the notion

that prior restraint is incompatible with free speech, not to mention democracy. As William Blackstone put it in his 1765 *Commentaries on the Laws of
England*: 'the liberty of the press is indeed essential to the nature of a free
state; but this consists in laying no previous restraints on publications, and
not in freedom from censure for criminal matter when published. Every free
man has an undoubted right to lay what sentiments he pleases before the
public; to forbid this is to destroy the freedom of the press; but if he
publishes what is improper, mischievous or illegal, he must take the consequences of his own temerity.' This, however, did nothing to stop judges
throwing around injunctions like confetti; as Robertson and Nicol put it:
'in civil cases, judges have routinely suppressed the publication of newsworthy information on the ground that it is property which belongs in
confidence to governments and corporations.' In other words, property
rights have traditionally trumped any residual rights to free expression.

That numerous newspapers wish to see the destruction of a measure that
will make these various restrictions on freedom of expression a great deal
more difficult to obtain in the future speaks volumes about the peculiar
nature of the British press. Their hostility to the HRA is all the more
extraordinary given that it actually includes a special section which, as Lord
Wakeham explains in his contribution to the recent Institute for Public
Policy Research (IPPR) publication on privacy, *Ruled by Recluses*, goes 'a
long way to protecting freedom of expression and ensuring the continued
effectiveness of tough and independent self-regulation'. This was actually
proposed by Wakeham himself in a bid to dampen press hysteria over the
apparent threat of a privacy law posed by Article 8 of the ECHR, and
provides that a court must have particular regard to the importance of the
right to freedom of expression in any action against the media. In spite of its
dubious origins it does have merit, in that it gives Article 10's presumption
in favour of free speech extra force, places particular emphasis on the notion
of the public interest in publication, inhibits prior restraint by making it
more difficult to obtain interim injunctions against the media and requires
courts to pay particular regard 'to the extent to which the material has, or is
about to, become available to the public'.

For most of the British press, however, freedom of expression counts for
far less than the chance to bang the Europhobic drum, whip up hatred
against asylum seekers and poke its snout into people's private lives. But
there's a more profound reason for this hostility, one that takes us back into
history and deep into the atavistic heart of most British newspapers.

Lord Wakeham put his finger on the matter when he noted that, when the Convention was drawn up in 1953, Britain 'was unprepared to import alien legal concepts into its sovereign parliamentary and judicial system'. He might also have quoted Dicey, for whom it was a source of much pride that 'there is in the English constitution an absence of those declarations or definitions of rights so dear to foreign constitutionalists'. In those countries, 'individual rights are deductions drawn from the principles of the constitution, whilst in England, the so-called principles of the constitution are inductions or generalisations based upon particular decisions pronounced by the courts as to the rights of given individuals'. So although Britain was the first country to ratify the Convention it did not actually incorporate it into British law, as it was felt that English common law already offered sufficient protection to people's rights.

Much has been made of Britain's role in drafting the Convention, but it could be argued that, as in so many matters involving continental Europe, British politicians and civil servants were motivated chiefly by the desire to water down a measure they saw as a threat to British sovereignty. Significantly, it was not until 1966 that Britain even permitted its subjects to petition the European Court of Human Rights in Strasbourg.

Certainly the post-war Labour government was largely hostile to the ECHR. As Britain's leading human rights lawyer, Lord Lester, has argued: 'the Convention had a painful beginning, barely surviving the strenuous efforts of the Attlee government to stifle or cripple it at birth.' The Chancellor Lord Jowitt stated that he was not 'prepared to encourage our European friends to jeopardise our whole system of law, which we have laboriously built up over the centuries, in favour of some half-baked scheme to be administered by some unknown court'. In particular, he was worried that emergency powers of detention without trial, or judges' peremptory powers to commit people to prison for contempt, would not pass muster. The senior judiciary agreed. The attorney-general, Sir Hartley Shawcross, said that 'any student of our legal institutions . . . must recoil from this document with a feeling of horror'; in particular, the right of individual petition was 'wholly opposed to the theory of responsible government'. The colonial secretary, James Griffiths, was strongly opposed, on the grounds that 'emergency powers' taken in the colonies to deal with anti-colonial uprisings would be judged incompatible with the Convention. (In fact, Britain applied for, and was granted, several 'derogations' from the

Convention in just these circumstances.) In short, the Labour government saw its duty as the protection of the constitution, the common law system and the British Empire from 'subversive' European influences and the legal equivalent of 'fancy foreign food'.

Undoubtedly the HRA *does* introduce significant changes into the way in which Britain is governed, changes for which liberal opinion has long argued and which it has generally welcomed.

In particular, it enables the judges to build up a corpus of constitutional principles in the area of human rights. This will obviously alter the balance between Parliament and the judiciary. Dicey's famous dicta – that 'there is no law which Parliament cannot change. There is no fundamental or so-called constitutional law', and that there is no body 'which can pronounce void any enactment passed by the British Parliament on the ground of such enactment being opposed to the constitution' – are now no longer valid. The HRA means that the European Convention is now the 'fundamental law'. Parliament cannot alter it (although it can 'derogate' from specific articles and could, in theory, repeal the HRA), and while judges cannot actually strike out any laws that run contrary to the Convention, they can pressure Parliament to alter them. To this extent, Britain's constitutional arrangements have indeed changed, but this is hardly cause for national nervous breakdown. As Tocqueville put it in *Democracy in America*, 'in England, the Parliament has an acknowledged right to modify the constitution; as, therefore, the constitution may undergo perpetual change, it does not in reality exist', a point echoed more recently by Lord Sedley in his observation that 'our constitutional arrangements have never been much more than a matter of convention, and what passes for constitutional law has generally been a Panglossian description of the way things are'. In other words, up until the HRA, Britain's constitution was largely what those in power said it was.

That this pre-modern state of affairs has now begun to come to an end should be cause for profound rejoicing. None the less, mindful of the extraordinary power of conservative opinion wielded by the press in Britain, Labour's introduction of the HRA was constantly hedged about by endless assurances that it 'must not disturb Parliament's supremacy', as a much-beleaguered Lord Irvine put it. To which Anthony Barnett responded in *This Time*: 'as if that historic supremacy is as fine and dandy as it ever was. The supremacy to which Irvine refers is formulaic. Already the Commons is the site of the submission of the legislature to the Executive. The claim of the "supremacy" of Parliament therefore raises rather than resolves the issue of democracy. A strong party system has knee-capped the power of MPs to hold ministers to account. With the Lords otiose, the supremacy of the Commons means the supremacy of party. In modern conditions, the supremacy of party means the supremacy of the leader.' What we have had, therefore, is the supremacy of the central government in Parliament or, in Lord Hailsham's phrase, an 'elected dictatorship', a situation all too easily exploited by those who believe that the purpose of being in power is regularly to administer 'the firm smack of strong government', and who have not the slightest truck with any nonsense about the separation of powers.

But although this situation may gradually be changing, it is still ludicrous to argue, like the *Mail* for example, that the HRA has turned judges into 'dictators in wigs'. In the real world, the Act simply requires the courts to interpret legislation in a way compatible with Convention rights. The courts will thus develop law in line with the Convention. In the case of legislation they deem incompatible with Convention rights, all they can do is to issue a declaration of incompatibility and leave it to Parliament to amend the legislation accordingly. Equally ludicrous is the charge that laws, including a privacy law, will be introduced by the 'back door of the Human Rights Act', as Lord Wakeham habitually puts it.

This is simply constitutional illiteracy. As the Chief Justice, Lord Woolf, has made perfectly clear, the law now includes the Human Rights Act, and judges are simply ensuring that the laws made by Parliament are upheld. Parliament makes the law, the executive ensures that it is carried out under law, and the judiciary interprets and applies the law. By enacting the Human Rights Act, Parliament requires the courts to interpret and apply both statute law and common law compatibly with the rights and freedoms protected by the European Convention. To argue that the courts are exceeding their authority in this matter, or that we are seeing a 'wholesale erosion of parliamentary sovereignty', simply beggars belief. It also completely ignores the fact that over the past 30 years the decisions of government officials, including ministers, have been subject to judicial review. If the primacy of Parliament is threatened by Britain's current constitutional arrangements, it is not by the judiciary but by overweening executive and ministerial power.

These, however, are the antediluvian and anti-democratic arrangements that most British newspapers want to preserve at all costs, including the abolition of the only measure that offers a statutory right to freedom of expression. One is irresistibly reminded of Mr Podsnap's remark to a benighted foreigner in Dickens's *Our Mutual Friend* to the effect that 'We Englishmen are Very Proud of our Constitution, Sir. It Was Bestowed Upon Us By Providence. No Other Country is so Favoured as This Country.'

Of course, as we have already seen, commercially motivated hostility to any measure that might limit their ability to pry into people's personal lives also plays a key role in this bizarre pantomime. Consider the *Guardian*'s ill-fated 1998 attempt to garner press support for a Privacy and Defamation Bill that would establish a legal right to privacy while also setting out defences to actions and against prior restraint. In particular, it aimed at reforming the libel laws by placing the burden of proof in libel on the plaintiff, and providing the media with a 'qualified privilege' to publish statements of public importance that are reasonably believed to be true and are not motivated by malice. Such was his fellow editors' obsession with privacy legislation and their complete lack of interest in all the other myriad restrictions on press freedom that, at the start of 1999, a battered Alan Rusbridger pronounced the project 'doomed'.

As Robertson and Nicol argue: 'if those who work in the media wish to enjoy the freedom promised by the right to publish facts and opinions that are in the public interest, they may have to forgo some of the comparative freedom they enjoy to publish facts and opinions that are not.' Thus far, most of the British press has resolutely set its face against such a deal. Instead, newspapers have terrified successive governments into refusing even to countenance privacy legislation; in so doing they have denied Parliament the opportunity to frame a sensible and workable privacy law, and thus, paradoxically, have left the matter to the hated and despised judges who, as the anti-juridical *Mail* now routinely asserts, 'have it in for Britain'. In so doing, they have also concocted and propagated absurd and alarmist myths about both the European Convention and the Human Rights Act – measures which, should they choose to stop abusing and start using them, could play a key role in sweeping away many of the anachronistic restrictions on freedom of expression that still exist in this country. ❏

Julian Petley is chair of the Campaign for Press and Broadcasting Freedom and professor of film and television studies at Brunel University

MEDIA POWER

JOHN LLOYD

BIG MONEY, POLITICS AND TELEVISION: THE
CONNECTIONS BECOME CLOSER, AND THE
PUBLIC INTEREST WEAKER, THROUGHOUT
MUCH OF THE WESTERN MEDIA. IN THE UK,
WHERE A GREAT PUBLIC BROADCASTER IS
POWERFUL ENOUGH TO WITHSTAND THE
TREND, THE AIR HAS BEEN NOISY WITH THE
SOUND OF WOUNDS BEING SELF-INFLICTED

This past summer, the British have been privy to a gargantuan demonstration of the power of the media in the political arena. The Hutton Inquiry into the death of David Kelly has been an object lesson on the matter. Dr Kelly was a Ministry of Defence weapons expert who committed suicide after being revealed as the source of a BBC report broadcast by one of its defence correspondents, Andrew Gilligan – a report that claimed that aides to the prime minister had knowingly falsified a document on the weapons situation in Iraq.

If a government, up to its prime minister, can become so engaged in denying an allegation – aired in its pure form, though it was later slightly modified, at 6.17 in the morning – that it reveals, to its own embarrassment, its inner workings and vast amounts of detail on its own secret services, then the broadcasters must be mighty indeed.

They are. The media is now among the first powers in the world. Its power is the greater for being disguised, including from itself. Its own estimation – that it is the medium through which power is held to account – obscures, most of all from journalists, its huge ability to give out versions of the world that deeply affect the actions of leaders and followers at every level, from a local planning decision to global movements of capital, people or terror.

Media power is often discussed in terms of ownership, and that is a reasonable prism through which to view it. But it is only reasonable if it is recognised that in most cases, at least in advanced and also in many developing countries, 'ownership' is never a purely a matter of an owner enjoying his own and being able to dictate the terms under which he owns it – in the case of the media, to dictate what it prints or broadcasts. Media are nearly always the object of three kinds of ownership: by private owners, by the state, and by the journalists and others who ceaselessly create and re-create the media's versions of the world, 24 hours a day, almost everywhere.

This is still a largely unexplored universe – unexplored in the sense that we are at a primitive stage of our knowledge on what the media do to our societies, since it is only fitfully in the interests of the owners of the media to enquire into these effects. There is much name-calling across the divides between these owners, a species of argument that both defines and constricts the debate and the enquiry. Owners tend to think journalists are too liberal and irresponsibly radical. Journalists view owners, both the state and private, as repressive. The state sees journalists and owners as prejudiced against the public sphere . . . and so on.

It is not that these arguments are always, everywhere, wholly wrong: they often have considerable force. It is that they do not rest on the fact of the matter: that all owners – state, private and professional – strive for increased power and tend to see the correct balance of power as that which favours their own position. Yet at the same time they present themselves as the victims of the machinations of the other powers: the state libelled by the journalists and the owners; the owners at the mercy of the power of the state; the journalists' quest for the truth quashed by both public and private power.

The key matter is that the media are a field for competing powers – and that, when these powers strive to aggrandise themselves and most of all when they conflict on the proper borders of their power and on the balance between and among them, what suffers is the aim to which they all pay fulsome lip-service: the 'public's right to know'. All publics suffer from this at times: though it must also be said that the public constitutes itself a sepa-rate power, which often demonstrates its influence by refusing to be inter-ested in what the media have to say, especially when the subject is politics. And all national publics are very different: for while it is true that news can be available globally, the media, like politics, are organised largely in national clusters, and their characters differ greatly from state to state. So we can illustrate the nature of the interplay of powers from state examples: the UK, Russia, the USA and Italy.

United Kingdom

The British are undergoing a deeply educative experience. The Hutton Inquiry into the death of David Kelly shows us something of what modern media are, how they operate and how they seek and gain power. It shows them, on a careful reading, how our reality is constructed, and how the world is made up for us day by day, hour by hour.

It does this in two ways – first, by the revelations the inquiry itself produces; and, second, by the way in which these revelations are themselves reported. The first is showing us – spasmodically, confusingly, contradictorily – how the media and the state deal with each other. The second shows us how bad much of the British media have become, and how they are likely to stay that way.

The inquiry has also produced its first undoubted victim: the *Today* programme defence correspondent, Andrew Gilligan. Gilligan backed away from the central assertion of his report: that the government knew the claim that Iraq could launch weapons of mass destruction within 45 minutes to be wrong. In doing so, he destroyed the stance he had taken, and the stance the BBC had taken, since the affair began. The massed ranks of the Corporation stood by his story: Gilligan, the *Today* programme, the head of news and current affairs, the director-general and the Board of Governors.

They asserted that what he had broadcast was the truth: the government it was that lied. And then Gilligan said: well, no, not exactly. Not quite like that, perhaps. No better lesson could have been devised for showing us the standards of truth, accuracy and balance that were deployed in his reporting for the prime current affairs slot in the whole of the Corporation's output, including TV, radio and internet.

One can see Gilligan as a British equivalent of Jayson Blair, the *New York Times* reporter who, through systematic falsification of his reports and the indulgence he received from his editors, brought the world's best newspaper into disrepute, and ultimately caused the resignation of its two top executives. But Gilligan is not a destroyer, as was Blair. He is a victim.

He is the product of a culture, a mindset and a practice. He comes from that part of the BBC (it is too big and sprawling and diverse and, in parts, magnificent to have one overall approach – a fact that may yet save it) that sees the government as a bunch of spinners, obfuscators and, ultimately, liars. He was taken on because he was 'edgy': when at the *Daily Telegraph* he had a reputation for being a man who would stick it to the government. That is what made him attractive to the heads of current affairs at the BBC.

He was hired as an attack dog and proved instantly and constantly worthy of his hire. Were the BBC to produce an anthology of his reports during the Iraq invasion – which would be a service – we could hear again the tenor of his reporting. It was a style that took the fact or event most embarrassing or inconvenient to the government (there were many to choose from) and made it into the explanatory vehicle for the conduct of the war. The fact itself would be 'right' in the sense that something like it had happened, unlike the 'sexing up' of the dossier. But its treatment would be of his own making.

This is what we might call laser journalism: the opposite of journalism-in-the-round. Laser journalism shines a bright and relentless light on one spot in the chaos of detail and riot of opinion that makes up real events. It isolates the fact, preferably the 'killer fact', the matter that so clearly and fatally exposes the wickedness or mendacity at the heart of the state machine that heads must roll.

It operates on the unstated belief that such mendacity is the rule, not the exception, and thus all that is needed is aggressive, directed investigation. In this diabolic account of our state, such figures as Alastair Campbell, the prime minister's chief press secretary, naturally become vastly important. They are the liars-in-chief, the gatekeepers of vaults of dirty big secrets that wait for the deployment of journalistic diligence and courage to be uncovered.

This is not what British government is. Composed as it is of men and women, it has liars, fantasists and self-publicists in its ranks. But we know enough – all of us, from observation and reading and listening – to know that such an assumption is unwarranted. The ills of our society do not include a state that systematically twists reality. Reality, or what version of it we wish to live in, is available to be discovered.

Why did the BBC fall for this malign vision of the British state? For the worst of reasons: it did not think about it. It saw, in the newspaper culture, a journalistic practice of attack. It came to share the view that this was the way true journalists should behave. It took the position that since the government had an unassailable majority, and the Conservative Party was weak and badly led, that it must thus substitute for the opposition.

In this, the *Today* programme was the vanguard. The one programme almost everyone in high public life was sure to hear something of, broadcast at an hour when daily agendas were being set, it has unrivalled influence. It embraced Gilligan because it had already embraced his values.

It wanted lasers because it regarded journalism-in-the-round as boring. Journalism-in-the-round is conscious that there are at least two sides to a story. In the old-fashioned BBC version, it did not go too far. It said what the government said, what Her Majesty's Opposition said, and left it at that. It could, indeed, be boring.

But at its best, journalism-in-the-round is an attempt to come to grips with the complexity, nuances and constant shifts of public life. In constructing that part of reality called 'the news', it seeks transparency for itself: to allow the reader or viewer to see that the facts assembled at high speed and printed or broadcast under constraints of time, lack of full knowledge and competitive pressure, are a first and almost certainly imperfect draft of what will become history.

It is what the BBC should be doing, and what it sometimes, in other parts of its dense forest, does do, though rather more about foreign events – such as the Norma Percy/Brian Lapping account of the fall of Milosevic broadcast last year, which was a beacon of care and real journalistic courage. But it did not think it through and, with Greg Dyke as its director-general, it will not. Dyke, who believes the myth of the lying state, has always preferred the sensational to the careful. For him, as for those he employs to do the news, 'boring' is, first and last, the greatest crime the BBC can commit.

The Hutton Inquiry unfolds, and will continue to unfold, through the media: that is how we learn of everything outside our restricted personal circles. And the media now are taking sides: against the government, or against the BBC – or, on good days, against both. The spin in the headlines, in the writing of the stories or bulletins, in the selection of images and comment is relentless. We see a culture of media spin revealed through a culture of media spin.

Russia
Russia presents the picture of media that enjoyed a frolic of freedom, and are now experiencing a reaction – in part from the public, in larger part from the state. The TV networks are now all either in state hands or, as NTV ('N' is for *nezavisimiye*, meaning independent, now something of a satire), controlled by the gas corporation, which is controlled by the state. This does not mean that nothing critical appears: journalists who have learned some of the lessons of independence do not give up easily. But it means that little comes on the screen that properly explains the nature of power, or that

questions the actions of those in the public or private arenas who wield power. 'This is a real change for Russia,' said Yasen Yasursky, the dean of the faculty of journalism at Moscow State University in a recent interview. 'In the last few years we have lost all four private TV channels.'

Andrei Norkin, an anchor for Ekho TV – a channel that produces programmes in Moscow for export only to the Russian diaspora in Israel – told the *Baltimore Sun* this month: 'In the Kremlin, they believe that to achieve some real results you have to be in control of the mass media.' Ekho TV is owned by the expatriate oligarch Vladimir Gusinskii, currently in Greece and fighting an extradition demand from Russia. Gusinskii, who would face charges of tax evasion if he is brought back to Russia, is the former owner of NTV (*Index* 4/95, 4/00).

A volatile figure, Gusinskii financed the broadcast and newspaper outlets that employed the best of the independent Russian journalists. His baton has

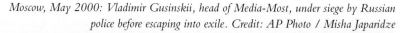

Moscow, May 2000: Vladimir Gusinskii, head of Media-Most, under siege by Russian police before escaping into exile. Credit: AP Photo / Misha Japaridze

been picked up by a fellow oligarch, Mikhail Khodorkovskii, the owner of the vast Yukos oil company, who is financing opposition newspapers and has employed Yevgeny Kiselyov, NTV's chief news anchorman, as an editor of one of these, *Moskovskiye Novosti*. At the same time, Khodorkovskii has put Yegor Yakovlev, a veteran of the period of Mikhail Gorbachev's perestroika, at the head of the paper's supervisory board.

Khodorkovskii, a fabulously wealthy man, is now the largest barrier to a general state control that Russia presently has. Andrei Piontovskii, one of the foremost of Russia's political analysts, said of the appointments to *Moskovskiye Novosti* that they were 'very good news. It is Yukos's way of saying it will not surrender easily to the advancing Chekists' (meaning the KGB, a reference to the past employer of President Vladimir Putin and of many of his aides).

Yukos is, however, itself under attack: a senior executive, Platon Lebedev, has been imprisoned on charges of stealing state property. Yukos's financing of opposition parties has also attracted Kremlin displeasure. Media freedom is not snuffed out, but it is in danger, and only big capital is presently able to pose at its saviour.

United States of America

The US is disturbing in European eyes because it is a more raucously democratic state than any in Europe. Its practice of electing people for public office rather than appointing them, as Europe does with judges and sheriffs, is one aspect; the other is the spread of its news media, from left liberal to libertarian right. The recent appearance of Fox News, the news division of the Rupert Murdoch-owned Fox Network, has caused much mockery from Europeans (and from liberal Americans). But it is important to recognise the difference between the nature of these criticisms, for they illuminate a difference between the two cultures.

For non-Fox-viewing Americans, the station is reprehensible because it does not adhere to balance and distance. Its coverage of the Iraq war, which won it millions of viewers, was patriotic in the extreme: in being so, it eschewed most of the accepted canons of objectivity, balance and explanation. For Europeans, it is reprehensible because it's right-wing: Europeans have been accustomed to broadcast media that are obliged to be balanced between political positions.

The larger issue, however, is US TV's inextricably close relationship to politics. Candidates for political office need TV to reach the masses: to do so, they must buy time – and the less the networks cover politics and public affairs, the more money they must spend bringing public affairs, and the candidates' positions on them, to the viewers.

The US commentator Mark Damner has put this best:

> American politics subsidises American television – to the tune this year [2000] of US$600m for the networks and broadcast stations alone (not counting cable). With the decline of local party organisation, TV has long since become the essential way – virtually the only way – to reach voters. And as TBV time has become more and more expensive, the American political world has come increasingly to resemble Republican Rome, in which the wealthy and powerful expend their largesse to make it possible for their chosen candidate to reach and thereby seduce the masses. American politicians have been forced to become a species of bagmen who collect money from the wealthy and deliver it to television in order to sell themselves to the voters.

This is a privatisation of politics that benefits TV and is in tune with a general trend that sees politics, public affairs and debate as tedious, corralled into off-peak times, or 'sexed up' by aggression and confrontation. When TV provides decreasing amounts of news; when TV's owners increase their profits; when candidates go into debt to pay their TV bills; when politics ceases to be a central concern of the most powerful medium – then voters become not only alienated, but increasingly uninformed.

Italy

The prime minister of Italy controls almost all the TV channels watched by Italians: the three channels operated by Mediaset, owned by Silvio Berlusconi (there is one other private TV channel); and the three channels of Radio Televisione Italiana (RAI), which Berlusconi controls by virtue of holding the political majority in the country. This involves him in two differing, and enormous, conflicts of interest: one, that his political power can directly benefit his commercial interests, as in his manipulations of the judicial system (see p93); and, more seriously, that his near monopoly of the most powerful communication medium in the state directly contradicts liberal assumptions about both politics and media's role in a democratic society.

Berlusconi built up Mediaset through the acquisition of hundreds of local TV stations (at their peak in 1980 there were 1,300); he strung them together into a national network to get around legislation that protects the RAI national monopoly. The capstone was set by the state: the Mammi law, named after the then minister of telecommunications, was passed by the Socialist government and cemented the RAI–Mediaset duopoly, which remains to the present day (the Maccanico Act of 1997 changed little of fundamental importance). By the beginning of the decade that saw his rise to supreme, and presently largely unchallenged, political power, Berlusconi had control of three channels of national television. They gave him the huge cash revenue generated by their advertising; and they gave him far more influence than any other media mogul in the world had or has within his own state.

Many Italians of the left compare Berlusconi to Mussolini, but it mis-states his importance. He is not a haranguer but a seducer; and one of the means of his seduction is to pose as the underdog and the champion of underdogs – one who, himself intolerably oppressed, lifts the weight from the oppressed. Thus he and his associates constantly point to the domination of RAI, especially its news and cultural programmes, by leftists: a charge in which there is some truth. This is because, as in most states, current affairs and cultural journalists tend to be liberal left and in Italy that often meant supporting the Communist Party; and also, more pertinently, because RAI is as politicised as any other major institution of the state, with carve-ups of the channels and managerial posts accorded to political interests.

Alexander Stille, writing in the *New York Review of Books*, encapsulates Berlusconi's importance:

> As a country that was late to unify and industrialise, Italy is a place where all the strains and problems of modern life are present but with few of the safeguards that exist in older, more stable nations: ideas get taken to their logical extreme. The increasingly close relations between big money, politics and television are important every-where, but in Italy, thanks to Berlusconi's domination of the networks and the press, they have achieved a kind of apotheosis. ❏

John Lloyd *is a freelance journalist*

FIVE SHAMEFUL LAWS

GULLIVER CRAGG

SILVIO BERLUSCONI BEGAN HIS
PRESIDENCY OF THE EU IN JULY BY
CALLING GERMAN MEP MARTIN SCHULZ
A NAZI. NOT A GOOD START, MANY FELT

Silvio Berlusconi's outrageousness 'gaffe' in his first session as president of the EU provoked widespread condemnation, but proved a hugely successful diversion from the more serious issue posed by German MEP Martin Schulz: why had Italy just passed a law protecting its prime minister from prosecution, just as the prime minister in question was staring at a guilty verdict in his last outstanding corruption trial for allegedly bribing a judge to block the sale of food giant SME to Carlo De Benedetti in 1984?

Invoking the hope that Italy might host the signing of the European Constitution this year, Berlusconi appealed to his fellow statesmen's desire to 'make a good impression' in Europe when he assumed the presidency. It simply *wouldn't do* for the prime minister to be involved in a corruption trial. Italy's ever-cautious president, Carlo Azeglio Ciampi, was convinced, and approved the law. Silvio was off the hook.

Which is not to say that Berlusconi has always been absolved. Indeed, many of his associates, including best friend Cesare Previti, have been found guilty of crimes committed on behalf of Berlusconi's business interests. His own cases have simply expired – often thanks to the PM's gleeful willingness to change the law as it suits him. However, not all his attempts to do so have had quite the desired effect. So, perhaps taking inspiration from France's President Jacques Chirac – another major European leader who has escaped the law thanks to immunity legislation (in Chirac's case a somewhat debatable application of existing rules) – he decided to have done with it and simply put himself above the law.

All the same, some of this stuff can get pretty hard to spin. Berlusconi famously owns half of Italy's television and has considerable influence over the rest, plus the unequivocal support of at least one national newspaper: Paolo Berlusconi's *Il Giornale* reported his brother's recent declaration that judges were 'mad' and 'anthropologically different' from the rest of humanity, which provoked a fierce written reprimand from Ciampi and was front-page news across Italy.

The fact is, even without having to face trial, every suggestion of corruption in Berlusconi's business history damages his image as the self-made man whose business acumen will make a success of 'Italy plc'. Clearly, a little more help would not come amiss. Hence the proposed Gasparri Law designed to enable the PM to extend his media influence still further.

Writing in *La Repubblica,* Massimo Giannini has described the Gasparri bill as the 'fifth shameful law' of Berlusconi's government. In summary, the five go as follows:

False accounting September 2001
The crime of false accounting was downgraded and effectively legalised in many cases. Notably, it became statute-barred after four and a half years rather than 15, with retrospective effect. Berlusconi was then defending three charges of false accounting, one of which concerned the cover-up of US$12 million paid to the then prime minister Bettino Craxi, who later fled to Tunisia to avoid prison. Under the new law, all three charges expired and Berlusconi was able to avoid false accounting charges in the SME case.

An investigation is under way at the European Court of Justice as to whether these changes contravene an EU requirement that member states set appropriate penalties where firms fail to publish accounts.

Rogatorie October 2001
A clause was inserted into an agreement between Italy and Switzerland ruling that evidence obtained under *rogatorie* (judicial requests for information from abroad) was inadmissible unless it bore a stamp of authenticity on every page. This would clearly be unworkable in the case of the digital archives of Swiss banks, as the banks were quick to point out. Unsurprisingly, key evidence in many of Berlusconi's and his associates' corruption cases is held by Swiss banks.

Again, Rogatorie has particular bearing on the SME case. Swiss bank records are believed to contain evidence of the bribes Berlusconi is alleged to have paid. Berlusconi's lawyers in the SME case immediately appealed to have certain pieces of evidence thrown out under the new legislation. The Milan courts refused, choosing to adhere to existing international codes.

Cirami Law on 'legitimate suspicion' November 2002
This rules that a trial can be moved from one jurisdiction to another if the defendant(s) can claim 'legitimate suspicion' of judicial bias. It is widely regarded as a transparent attempt to stall the SME trial in order to buy time for further laws to be passed and to bring its expiry date nearer. Berlusconi

immediately demanded that the SME trial be moved from Milan to Brescia under the new law. But the final appeals court ruled that there were no grounds for suspicion in Milan.

Schifani Law (aka Maccanico Law) June 2003

This provides for immunity from prosecution for the holders of the five highest offices in the Italian government, and the suspension of any judicial procedures currently in progress. This is the law that finally freed 'Il Cavalieri' from the SME case, which is now highly unlikely ever to resume as it will probably be statute-barred by the time Berlusconi leaves office. Moreover, there is no clause preventing him from seeking another of the five immune positions.

Crusading judge Antonio Di Pietro has collected 1 million signatures calling for the law's revocation, which theoretically means a referendum must be held. It remains to be seen whether this will work in practice; even the centre left are lukewarm about the idea.

Gasparri Law September 2003

Reform of Italy's television, increasing governmental power to name the board members of state broadcaster RAI and envisaging an eventual privatisation of RAI that would allow no individual to hold more than 1 per cent of the shares. It also allows the owners of broadcast media to own newspapers as well; Berlusconi is rumoured to have his eye on Italy's largest daily, the *Corriere della Sera,* whose editor resigned earlier this year complaining of government pestering. Berlusconi can delay until 2006 switching his Rete4 channel to satellite, which he has been legally required to do for 15 years and had promised to complete by 2004.

Due to be passed in July 2003, the bill was delayed. At the time of going to press, Ciampi was expected to rule it unconstitutional in its current form. As Ezio Mauro put it in his editorial in *La Repubblica* on 5 September: 'The semblance of institutional normality surrounding Berlusconi's government is a sham' – an assessment that may well be connected to Berlusconi's latest 'gaffe' in which he describes Mussolini as 'benign' because he 'didn't kill people, he sent them on holiday'. ❏

Gulliver Cragg *is a freelance writer and a research assistant at* Index

LEGAL EVIL

JONATHAN RÉE

ORDINARY JUSTICE FOCUSES ON GUILT
AND THE CRIMINAL'S MIND; VICTIM'S
JUSTICE IS INTERESTED IN EVIL AND
THE STATE OF THE WORLD

It is the received wisdom of legal theory that the point of any system of laws is that it takes the functions of vengeance and retribution out of the hands of individuals and entrusts them to the state instead. And the state, like the deity, must be no respecter of persons. It has to treat similar offences in similar ways: an assault is an assault, even if one victim is a saintly Christian determined to turn the other cheek and another an enraged fanatic demanding vengeance a thousand times over. The idea that individual victims have 'rights' that need to be kept in some kind of equilibrium with those of alleged criminals shows a complete misunderstanding of the objectivity and impartiality that are essential to any sustainable system of law.

But that is quite a narrow way of looking at it. The purpose of the overall movement for 'victim's justice' is not so much to make room for vengeful sentences as to shift attention from the punishment of criminal guilt towards the remembrance of innocent suffering – and not just the special sufferings endured by particular individuals, but the systematic sufferings of groups, societies and collectivities of all kinds. Victim's justice is broad where ordinary justice is narrow: it is concerned not only with holding individuals to account but also with shaping communal memory and forging political traditions. While ordinary justice focuses on guilt and the criminal's mind, victim's justice is interested in evil and the state of the world.

Evil is a hard word of course, and apt to make the boldest lawyer nervous. The Nuremberg War Crimes Tribunal of 1945–6, which was conducted from the point of view of victors rather than victims, gave it a very wide berth, and the judges concentrated on breaches of the laws of peace and war rather than so-called 'crimes against humanity'. Half a century later, in 1995, the South African state took a bold initiative by setting up an inquiry into the injustices of apartheid – a process that would be concerned not so much with the guilt of criminals as with the sufferings of victims. The South African Truth and Reconciliation Commission, which has since been imitated by similar inquiries in East Timor, Sierra Leone and Peru, owed its success to the fact that it recognised that victim's justice may be better served by an open judicial investigation than by a conventional court. It was more interested in documenting injustices than in laying blame, and it is notable that its final report did not shrink from describing the apartheid regime as 'evil'.

These victim-centred processes have learned some of the lessons, it seems, of the controversial trial of Adolph Eichmann. Eichmann was a Nazi functionary who took an interest in 'the Jewish question' and had special responsibility for implementing the 'final solution'. In 1960 he was kidnapped in Argentina by the Israeli secret police and brought to Jerusalem to face accusations of crimes against humanity and against the Jewish people. The trial started in April 1961, and the chief prosecutor, Attorney-General Gideon Hausner, a close associate of Prime Minister David Ben-Gurion, immediately made it clear that he was not going to confine himself to the activities of the bald and bespectacled defendant sitting before the court in a bulletproof glass cage. 'Here with me at this moment stand six million prosecutors,' he began, 'but alas they cannot rise to level the finger of accusation in the direction of the glass dock and cry out *j'accuse* against the man sitting there.' Addressing himself not to the three judges who were trying the case, but to the members of the public who crowded into the courtroom and the tens of thousands of Israelis who were listening to continuous live coverage on Israel radio, Hausner spent months putting together the first really comprehensive survey of the Holocaust. He relied on the testimony of scores of 'sufferings of the Jewish people witnesses', seeking to prove that they had been so worn down by Europe's perennial anti-Semitism that they had no choice but meekly to accept their fate. He also suggested that one of the main proponents of the Final Solution was an Arab – Haj Amin el Husseini, the former Mufti of Jerusalem – and implied that the poison of Nazi anti-Semitism, far from being destroyed with the defeat of the Axis powers, had been lovingly preserved throughout the Arab world. These arguments obviously had as much to do with the legitimacy of the Israeli state as with the activities of the man who was supposed to be on trial, and when Eichmann was hanged in May 1962 (his guilt had never been in doubt), no one was very interested.

The Eichmann trial had the privilege of entering history together with an extraordinary running commentary by a great political thinker. Hannah

*Jerusalem 1961: Adolf Eichmann
on trial. Credit: Misha Bar-Am /
Magnum*

Arendt was born to Jewish parents in Hamburg in 1906 and received an
education in the highest traditions of German philosophy before emigrating
in 1933 and eventually settling in New York. She came to Israel to cover
the trial for the *New Yorker*, and her reports were gathered together in *Eichmann in Jerusalem* in 1963. Arendt was very critical of the entire legal
process, especially Hausner's digressive and self-indulgent conduct of the
prosecution, but she supported both the verdict and the sentence. Eichmann
himself was vain and ridiculous in her opinion – indeed his pompous and
inept use of the German language was sometimes 'quite hilarious' – but
however stupid he was, he had taken part in 'the greatest crime in recorded
history' and no one could be expected to continue to share the earth with

him. His trial, according to Arendt, had been a long demonstration of the nature of evil, and she was as keen as anyone to see him sentenced to death.

Eichmann in Jerusalem is a great book, even a great Jewish book, but it was loathed by leaders of Jewish opinion in Israel and New York. Arendt's descriptions of Eichmann's pettiness were seen as attempts to excuse or justify him, and her summaries of trial evidence about Jewish collaborators and about non-Zionist Jews and their role in the resistance were treated as attempts to blame the Jews for the Holocaust and undermine the Zionist cause. Arendt was subjected to a campaign of vilification by the Anti-Defamation League and other Jewish defence organisations, and had to get used to being called an anti-Semite and even a Nazi. In an open letter published in *Encounter*, her former friend Gershom Scholem denounced her as 'heartless', 'malicious' and lacking in 'love of the Jewish people'. Her calm and brilliant reply – surely one of the best public letters of the century – elicited no response. In Israel itself, she was effectively silenced. A publisher who had procured a Hebrew translation of the book was persuaded not to issue it, and Scholem's denunciation was reprinted in Hebrew many times over, but always without Arendt's reply. (A fresh translation of *Eichmann in Jerusalem* was eventually made, and appeared in Israel in 2000.)

Arendt had used a brilliant phrase to sum up the philosophical conclusion she drew from the trial as a whole: 'the lesson of the fearsome, word-and-thought-defying *banality of evil*'. The words 'banality of evil' were incorporated into the subtitle of the book, and readers seem to have had extraordinary difficulty in seeing what they meant. In particular, Arendt's invocation of banality has been repeatedly interpreted as if it were a rough and indirect way of saying that Eichmann's offences, and perhaps the horrors of the Holocaust as a whole, were really rather trivial, and not worth making a fuss about. But Arendt was a philosopher, and she did not express herself in approximations. Her reason for speaking about banality was, as she patiently explained to Scholem, not to minimise evil in general, still less that of the Holocaust, but to suggest that it is always wrong to see evil as 'deep' and 'demonic'. Evil may be devastating and extreme, but it can never be profound: hence its essential banality. And in insisting on the word 'evil', Arendt was deliberately reaching back to pre-modern concepts, particularly biblical ones: concepts that, she thought, would allow people to face up to their disasters and calamities with ruthless but unaccusing calmness, instead of impotent, vindictive rage.

Arendt's philosophical training in Germany (particularly with her mentor Martin Heidegger) had made her suspicious of the modern obsession with private subjectivity. She saw the drive to psychologise every problem as a threat to clear thinking not only in philosophy but in public life as well, especially in matters of crime and punishment. Public deliberations needed to be kept separate from private emotions, including the emotions of victims and offenders involved in legal processes. Arendt concluded *Eichmann in Jerusalem* by lamenting the fact that the trial had got hung up on 'the subjective factor', or in other words on 'the assumption current in all modern legal systems that intent to do wrong is necessary for the commission of a crime'. She preferred the old-fashioned notion that a crime is a crime simply because it 'offends nature', regardless of all the subtleties of motivation and personal circumstance that will inevitably attend it. Her conception of evil was designed to be sombre without excluding hope, and pitiless without excluding love. It is a shame that so many people would not or could not listen. The banality of evil is no excuse. ❑

Jonathan Rée is a freelance writer and a member of the Philosophers' Group of the British Humanist Association. He recently edited (with Jane Chamberlain) The Kierkegaard Reader *(Blackwell)*

we are everywhere

the irresistible rise of global anticapitalism

edited by
Notes from Nowhere

we are everywhere is a whirlwind collection of writings, images and ideas for direct action by people on the frontlines of the global anticapitalist movement. This is a movement of untold stories, because those from below are not those who get to write history, even though we are the ones making it.

we are everywhere wrenches our history from the grasp of the powerful and returns it to the streets, fields and neighbourhoods where it was made.

VERSO

FORGING THE SOCIAL CONTRACT

IRENA MARYNIAK

**THE HIGHLY PERSONALISED CODES OF
LOYALTY AND MORALITY THAT WERE THE
MAINSTAY OF LIFE IN COMMUNIST EUROPE
COME UP AGAINST EFFORTS TO IMPOSE A
MORE FORMAL RULE OF LAW**

Even in the days when Central Europeans talked about books, politics and ideas, entering into an argument was a perilous kind of undertaking. To bellow your despair was more forgivable because feelings have a dynamic of their own, but it was improper and foolish under most circumstances to address a problem by raising questions or trying to make a better case. Any longer conversation already implied that you were on the same side and shared an inside knowledge of the Right and the True.

Those who like to take the longer view may refer to moralistic, predominantly Roman Catholic, cultural traditions in Poland, Hungary or Slovakia; to stifled ethnic, economic or industrial tensions in the Hapsburg, Prussian and Russian Empires before 1918; to 40 years of Soviet-style communism, and to its cruel petrification of language. In all these systems, law was synonymous with central command and choice boiled down to collaboration with unprepossessing regimes, or withdrawal underground into conspiracy and resistance. The oppressed create cultures of glaring moral clarity. God is offset by the Evil One; the Cause – Freedom, Independence, say – is highlighted by the emperor, party or State. The actors may lose their glossy sheen, of course, acquire shades of grey, switch sides, do rather well in the opposing camp. But that need not affect the strength of the moral culture itself, or the law by which oppressed communities survive.

Visiting Krakow for the first time in the 1970s I felt envious of other teenagers I met. They lived in two-room flats with parents and siblings, and the cream cheese and paprika every night was a bit samey, but everyone had so many friends. Friends who fixed things and brought sausage, lemons, tights and jokes; friends who appeared with medicines, scarce periodicals or theatre tickets; friends who could arrange a job, a car, a few extra metres of living space. The rules of exchange and association by which people operated under communism were political – as observers always liked to point out – but they were also intensely personal. Formal organisations to protect interests, resolve problems or engage in economic initiatives were forbidden. So it was often a moment of empathy, a sense of being shackled to the same galley, that forged links that made life more tolerable. Friendship networks lasted for decades; they became institutions more robust than bonds of kinship. They had their own laws and formed self-sufficient emotional and economic havens in a political order that was unpredictable, impersonal, paternalistic and sometimes dangerous. The Czech dissident Milan Simecka described what he called a 'special kind of social contract' between the party and the population by which citizens were guaranteed a minimum of social welfare in exchange for ritualised loyalty and non-interference. Politics was for the party – that ladder for the ambitious, the opportunistic, the power-hungry and the competent. Everyone else took refuge in intimacy.

Outsiders were not easily accepted. They might have mistaken loyalties, and their presence couldn't satisfy cravings for the strengthening affirmation of real group solidarities and shared meanings. For out there was the Beast that measured and threatened everything you did and thought. If people lived by the rule of their friendship network, they lived within the rule of the party. There was legislation on the stability of the state and the security of its citizens, there were constitutions, but law was never conceived as a medium of communication between people or an independent check on government power. Lenin, like Marx, considered legal constraints inapplicable to the revolutionary vanguard. And even once communist regimes stabilised and sought international legitimacy, their legal systems – though conventional on paper – remained subordinate to the party, its decrees, secret instructions and telephone calls. In the eyes of the public, written law had neither legitimacy nor relevance. It was a 'door in the middle of an open field', the Bulgarian saying went. You could walk through it, but why bother? Connections and the black economy were far more effective for practical purposes and offered additional personalised protection. Crime was contained by police enforcement, of which there was plenty, but the assumption was widespread that there existed an inverse relationship between law and morality.

One difficulty the eight Central and East European countries joining the EU in May 2004 now face is the transition from localised cultures, which emphasise the moral imperative, to internationally orientated state cultures, which encourage responsibility and competence. This is something of which Wiktor Osiatynski, professor of legal studies at the Central European University, is acutely aware. 'Legal cultures deal in debate, controversy, the search for a grey in-between. Moralistic cultures rest on the Curse, the threat of expulsion, with no defence, no due process, no appeal, nothing,' he says. 'They may serve well under occupation or oppression, when times are hard, but they are based on the premises of criminal law: their currency is guilt and punishment. Legal culture addresses relations between members of the community, the premises of civil law, and prefers the notions of damage and responsibility. No one calls me evil because I caused an accident or a tile fell off my roof, though I may have been negligent. But they do say I must make redress for the damage done and pay a hefty fine. Next time I'll make sure the roof is fixed.'

New constitutions have been drawn up to codify the principles of democratic political, administrative and legal orders, but intimate lives have been only mildly affected. The rules of association that count pertain to personal loyalty, rather than any internalised sense of civil legislation. Friends and family carry out many roles that in more complex and varied societies would rest with formal organisations. The broader community does little to encourage public trust and there is an instinctive preference for working with the devil you know. Rules for dealing with strangers are not well understood and no code of honour applies. After a cyanide spill three years ago into the River Tisza in Baia Mare, Romania, market stalls were found selling poisoned fish; transactions to buy a flat or car are made for cash, into a suitcase, with no guarantees; taxi drivers charge arbitrary and hugely inflated rates if they hear an unfamiliar intonation; tenants can be evicted without notice. And just as under communism no one expected the law to vindicate their rights or restrain officials, so now people expect to have to absorb any losses. Courts are overburdened and under-resourced, cases may not be resolved for years, recourse to the law is frightening and in bad taste. 'People assume that to be better off they must break the law,' Hungarian legal sociologist Zoltan Fleck says. 'This is as true of attitudes to taxation as it is of road traffic. There is a mystic uncertainty in the economy. It's time we got to know one another better.'

The social infrastructures of former communist states are not yet bound by the impersonal associations and interests that underpin Western 'civil societies' where relationships are negotiable and easily severed. In Birmingham, Brussels or Berlin, people find their identities not with one group

Prague, Czech Republic, 2002: the comfort – and security – of friends.
Credit: Stuart Franklin / Magnum

or hierarchy, but many: a sports club or union bar, an office or prayer meeting; with business contacts, the rock band, a parents' association, a political party. And they stay only as long as they want. In more traditional societies, to break the Rule that commands and protects a friendship network is to Do Wrong and face excommunication. This is as true of dissident groups under communism as it is of the communist *nomenklatura*, of Polish insurrectionists in Poznania and Galicia in the 1840s, or of mafia groups smuggling petrol from Hungary to Serbia during the Yugoslav war in the 1990s.

The post-communist order has not built the trust necessary for people to accept looser forms of bondage. It is marked by insecurity, pauperisation, crime, disappointment, resentment and failure. 'We wanted justice, we got the rule of law,' the aphorism goes. 'We wanted civil society, we got NGOs.' The communist state was a monopoly welfare provider and dependency has proved a hard habit to shake off. People may hunger for legal protection, yet thirst for power, freedom and natural justice. How do you square what you want with everything else you want? Ildi, a young mother from a southern province of Hungary, is studying law. It sets precedent and example, she says piously, it defends people. After a while, more subversive thoughts begin to crawl out of the woodwork. Educated people are sharks, especially lawyers. Officials, the judiciary and police are unaccountable and corrupt, white-collar crime is all-pervasive, former apparatchiks and secret police have won the day. 'I'd like to push these clever people out and make the life of the poor better. The government says there are no funds for education and health yet money flows constantly from pocket to pocket. It creates bad feeling among people who work in factories ten to 12 hours a day for a pittance . . . The law is political,' she says finally, 'it serves insouciant elites and is an obstacle to what most people want.'

Corruption is widely denounced, but there is greater tolerance of mafia-style entrepreneurs than gays, and more intolerance of minorities than of threats to civil rights. In Hungarian politics, Fleck says, it takes little to persuade people that a reduction in rights is worth the material benefits it might bring. And the desire for a prosperous, holistic community, which politics exploits, is as strong in Central Europe as it is in the USA. The Hungarian right argues that a social consensus on moral values is needed before democratic institutions or the constitution can gain legitimacy. The pre-industrial village is a living memory, and throughout the Central European plain people yearn to recreate the rituals of collective belonging in an alienating, apparently anarchic and rootless market order. Public institutions seem to have little value, and the notion that they could create more effective bonds in the community seems absurd or threatening.

There has been some successful institutional grafting, however. The Polish ombudsman and the Hungarian Constitutional Court are effective and widely respected. But even though law appeals more to the public imagination in Central Europe than in Yugoslavia, Albania or Belarus, Hungarian estimates indicate that 40 per cent of the economy still operates through black and grey market exchanges. In Poland, polls suggest that only 42 per cent of the population think it right to abide by written legislation.

Yet in all post-communist countries words such as 'constitutionalism', 'democracy', 'law' have an almost symbolic status. The principles of social and political order are broadly agreed even though parliaments, political parties, judges and elections are sneered at. Democratisation is a way of escaping what Milan Kundera once called the sense of being victims and outsiders, of representing 'the wrong side of European history'. People like to talk about a transition from 'abnormality' to 'normality'. And to gain perceived 'normality' they have been prepared to conform to standards existing outside their own societies and histories. Democracy means reintegration into the community of nations, a recovery of self-respect and – in all likelihood – prosperity, if only the cringe, the anxiety that there is so much to learn that Westerners already know, can be overcome.

There are unprecedented tensions in the twin process of recovering sovereignty, with its emphasis on nationhood and tradition, and integration into international organisations such as the EU or NATO, with concomitant pressures to 'harmonise' and modernise. Rapid constitutional and legal changes have been requested and served up. But these are changes in texts. Lives are less easily rewritten. The process of cultural and institutional transformation is necessarily constrained by social practices, habits, fears and mindsets. The idea that a flourishing private life, not sustained by government, cannot be 'legal', for example; the habit of thinking in terms that are rule-bound and rule-negating at once; opting for conformism and lip-service, rather than discourse and questioning; favouring a negative conception of legality, thinking of law solely as a restraint. The letter seems easier to grasp than the spirit. Any idea that law may contain in-built values that should be actualised not just protected (such as ensuring the dignity and integrity of minorities) is viewed with scepticism. And anxiety persists that any authority, particularly the state, is an enemy and its institutions are suspect.

> RAPID CONSTITUTIONAL AND LEGAL CHANGES HAVE BEEN REQUESTED AND SERVED UP. LIVES ARE LESS EASILY REWRITTEN

This is where cultural pundits pessimistic about prospects for a fragmented region with a small middle class and an erratic work ethic come into their own. Civil societies are based on mutually restraining institutions that protect people, they say. Laws should mesh with the intuitive rules by which people organise their lives; institutions must be supported by consistent conduct and belief. Yet in Central–Eastern Europe law is dysfunctional and institutions are quarrelsome and corrupt. Former Soviet states – some, such as Estonia, about to join the EU – boast glittering new constitutions that are implemented only in part. Czech legislative texts (six massive tomes in 2000) have been criticised for being improvised and poorly translated. External structures may seem to 'harmonise', but can the goodwill of government elites be enough? Are the underlying social and political cultures of East and West Europeans compatible?

There are 27 countries and 400 million people in the former communist region. If language is like a city – a maze of ancient streets surrounded by new boroughs, as Wittgenstein wrote – so is cultural context in all its variety. It impinges on the present but needn't rule the future. In Central–East Europe confidence is highly personalised, true. Organisations lack credibility though individuals may acquire it, which can make a difference. The Hungarian ombudsman is trusted, so is the institution. But most post-communist countries have given no priority to building effective consultation and negotiation channels between public institutions and voters. And, as Stephen Holmes of New York University has pointed out, despite EU involvement in the development of justice systems, judicial education and decision-making practice, the Union has done little to encourage responsive governance or active citizenship in Central Europe for fear of derailing economic reform.

If anything is to make democratic institutions credible and a civil society possible, it has to be public trust and public involvement. But these are dangerous times, when levels of participation in Western Europe are also under question – which could encourage non-consultative government further east. Marginalised communities are likely to have little incentive to participate helpfully in a *Rechtsstaat* or community of *états de droit* and to internalise the shape of international legislation. On the other hand, things many Westerners take as read – operating in legal loopholes, colluding in inequalities, spinning the story, living with loose connections – often provoke seemingly naive outrage among East Europeans. If effective channels of communication were allowed to develop, a slow merger between democratic organisations and the personalised, morally coded, loyalty-bound modes of association already existing in Central Europe might bring prospects that are more creatively energising and, perhaps, culturally or economically innovative than anyone dares anticipate. ❏

IM

Radio Free Maine

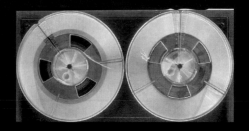

VOICES OF THE LEFT
UNEDITED & UNCENSORED

Radio Free Maine is an unparalleled living archive
of audio and video tapes featuring some of the
United States' most critical and dissenting voices.
NOAM CHOMSKY, HOWARD ZINN and **RALPH NADER**
recorded live at conferences and public appearances.

AUDIO TAPES
$11 each post paid to US
Canada and Mexico, add $1 postage per tape; all other countries, add $3

VIDEO TAPES
$20 each post paid to US
Canada and Mexico, add $2 postage per tape; all other countries, add $5

Payment in US funds must accompany order
Allow two weeks for delivery
Free catalog with every order

For a catalog of **Radio Free Maine** audio and video tapes, please send
a self-addressed envelope, stamped with $1 postage

Please make check/money order payable to ROGER LEISNER and send to
RADIO FREE MAINE, P.O. BOX 2705, AUGUSTA, MAINE 04338

For more information go to www.radiofreemaine.com

AFTER THE WAR IS OVER . . .

ANDREW PUDDEPHATT

THE CENTRAL ROLE OF THE MEDIA IN
CONFLICT RESOLUTION IS INCREASINGLY
BEING RECOGNISED BY GOVERNMENTS.
BUT THEY HAVE A LOT TO LEARN, SAYS
THE DIRECTOR OF ARTICLE 19

As conflicts in our modern, globalised world proliferate, the international community – predominately governments operating through international institutions but also international agencies and NGOs – increasingly focuses on the importance of the media in conflict or post-conflict zones. The way to end conflict is by providing security and the rule of law. Fear drives violence and overcoming that fear must be the prime objective of any international intervention. The media can help overcome that fear and provide stability.

But the media will not do this by pretending that the issues that caused the conflict do not exist. Conflict is an essential part of any society and cannot be avoided. Iraq, is a good example. After years of repression, the collapse of the Saddam Hussein regime has led to a free-for-all in the media. In many parts of Iraq engineers and technicians who worked for the Iraqi national station have taken over relay stations and started their own stations. Over 100 newspapers have sprung up. Such diversity can channel conflicts into non-destructive forms: encouraging competition between political parties and interests, public debate and discussion, and subjecting government – or in this case, the occupying authority – to scrutiny and criticism. This does not undermine the basic structures of the state; the absence of physical security does that. A diverse media can take the dry fabric of public administration, the legal system, electoral politics, and give them life.

The media also provides information, acts as a watchdog on all those who have power and offers a forum for intense public debate about the choices facing a society. This is why an independent media has long been seen as an essential element in the making of a democratic society. This often creates a tension between a new administration in a post-conflict society and the emerging independent media. A fragile government fears loss of control. So, in Afghanistan, after years of Taliban repression, dozens of newspapers and broadcast media flourish. But there are tensions between them and the government, even more so with many of the provincial warlords. There have been persistent attempts to control both the media and the independent journalists' association, attempts that mostly pass without comment from the broader international community.

It is, of course, important that the media is not partisan in a conflict to the point that it exacerbates tensions. As Mark Thomson analysed in *Forging War*, the war that engulfed what was Yugoslavia was in no small measure fuelled by the inflammatory state-controlled media in each of the country's component parts. Independence and objectivity are hard to achieve but they are vital to strive for. They are particularly so in the face of humanitarian catastrophes; this has led many to call for 'peace' journalism, or a journalism of 'attachment' that identifies and supports the victims of conflict.

But the media must be wary of identifying themselves too closely with any side – even the apparent victims. Modern paramilitary groups have an immense level of media sophistication and will use any partisanship in their interests, as they demonstrated so ably in Bosnia and Kosovo. Even peace journalism begs the question of whose 'peace' and in whose 'interest'. The independence of the media from any political interest, including the international community, is essential if it is to contribute to the stability of a post-conflict society.

If we look back on the interventions by the international community that have given priority to the media, four elements recur time and time again:

- Great emphasis is always placed on journalists' training. This includes the fostering of journalists' unions, assuming the government allows them to be independent.
- Much effort is directed to developing private and independent media. In Bosnia this profusion of independent radio stations and TV stations became ludicrous: while every village or faction had its own media outlet, what was needed was a national, non-ethnic voice.
- In some cases there has been support for reforming the state media, to make of them genuine public service broadcasters.
- There has been substantial support for the drafting of new media laws, regulations and policies, following recognised international norms.

These elements are present in most conflict or post-conflict interventions. The most important lesson learned from the last ten years has been the need to foster a powerful local dimension to media development; without local ownership and control of the various initiatives media are doomed to fail. If the international community or its agencies, whether IGOs or NGOs, try to develop a media climate without this involvement they will misunderstand local conditions, fail to utilise local expertise and lose legitimacy. Simply having the money and wanting a quick fix designed by outsiders, however good, is not enough.

The second lesson is the need to improve coordination and cooperation between the various agencies. Too often they compete, even within the UN family. It proved very difficult in the Balkans for the different actors to achieve any coherence in their approach. However, they – the UN, the OSCE and the EU – are learning from their mistakes. The multilateral approach, for all its weaknesses, is likely to prove more successful in the long run than rule by one dominant power.

Part of the problem with interventions in the last ten years is that they have not been guided by any clear philosophy. The underlying debate about the nature of media support has been between what have been called the 'institutionalisers' and the 'liberalisers'.

Institutionalisers argue that investment must be made in the structures that support the media, not just the obvious legal and regulatory aspects, but deeply rooted political and economic institutions that can cope with the immense stress of transformation. Institutionalisers will place a high priority on the creation of a public service broadcaster capable of representing the nation as a whole.

Liberalisers are more wary of state institutions and tend to believe that the market should be encouraged to let rip – as much media as possible, as quickly as possible. But the problem is that where their views held sway, lawlessness and corruption undermined their best efforts. As a result, it is the instutionalisers who have won the argument. Even the US-dominated plans for the media framework in Iraq reflect more the views of the former, although US policy has been consistently on the liberaliser wing.

The most difficult challenge facing the international community comes from societies where, through state repression or state collapse, there is no history of journalism or independent media to build on. Iraq is a good example: full of technically skilled journalists and broadcasters but, except in the Kurdish north, with little experience of a journalist culture.

In the past, the first approach has been to create a media environment by establishing media under international control, to try to bypass local

Khartoum, Sudan, 2001: 'Whose news?' Credit: Sven Torfinn / Panos

combatants – as in Cambodia, for instance – or unreliable local actors. This may not be necessary in all circumstances. In Iraq, for example, people have access to a wide variety of international media – from Al-Jazeera to the BBC World Service – that provide coverage that is not connected to locally opposed factions. The key task is to create domestic media that can help stabilise the post-conflict situation and provide an environment in which conflicts can be argued and resolved, or at least channelled by non-violent means. Media policy should therefore make the stimulation of the local media sector a priority. In turn, media policy itself should be made a high priority; it is not an optional add-on to the aftermath of a conflict but an essential building block of a new society.

It has proved particularly difficult to achieve a high level of donor and international cooperation over the last ten years. In Iraq, if only for political reasons, this will require another UN resolution that provides for a clear progression to Iraqi self-rule and lays the basis for a more systematic international intervention.

It will also require a complete overhaul of the international bureaucratic arrangements for managing the post-conflict intervention. All too often, key international agencies – whether the different UN agencies, the OSCE or the EU – do not have the capacity to react rapidly to the challenge on the ground and are afflicted by national rivalries. NATO has a better record than most in this respect, because of its long history of integrated working.

At the heart of the problem is the 'politicisation' of the structures and appointments to international institutions. Far too often people are appointed to key positions in international institutions on grounds other than merit: either from the pressure of dominant powers and diplomatic niceties or through personal relationships with existing officials. While this might be simply embarrassing in some contexts, in those of post-conflict societies it can be disastrous. Inexperienced, overbearing international staff are posted to these countries, on salaries beyond imagining to the local communities. Young people with no experience whatsoever of institution-building lecture communities where elders are respected and wisdom valued.

At the same time, staff are often given little scope for independent action and the corresponding confusion can be exploited ruthlessly by unscrupulous local forces, which threatens to bring the entire intervention into disrepute. A good example was that of UNMIK in Kosovo which, under pressure, introduced a regulation out of line with international standards to jail people for hate speech and, as a result, exacerbated local tensions.

These criticisms have been aired widely, and many hoped that clear US control in Iraq would at least lead to a more coherent policy approach. Such hopes were sadly mistaken: the State Department's rivalry with the Pentagon is worthy of any institutional feud at international level. I firmly believe that we should persist with a multilateral approach.

Success requires consistent commitment over time. It is no use promising vast sums of money for reconstruction and delivering nothing. It is a scandal that Afghanistan was promised US$7bn in aid and has received US$200m. We can scarcely complain if the Northern Alliance show contempt for internationally promoted democratic values.

Nor should international NGOs and media organisations be exempt from criticism. Far too often, there is an unseemly and competitive scramble for international funds which ends with the international community looking like a permanent occupying power, presiding over demoralised communities and institutionalised crime.

Organisations such as UNESCO, which carry the policy brief for the media in the international arena, have a crucial role to play in developing the right planning mechanism for post-conflict intervention. Of course, many governments will prefer to work bilaterally, where they can control the disbursement of their funds, rather than hand them to agencies they don't trust. But there is a growing willingness among governments to think hard and deeply about how best to intervene and use what resources they have in the most productive way. This is an opportunity to learn from past mistakes. If we don't, we are condemned to repeat them. ❑

Andrew Puddephatt is the director of Article 19

AND GOD CAME DOWN FROM THE MOUNTAIN

PHILIPPE SANDS

AMERICA'S 'À LA CARTE MULTILATERALISM' – A POLITE TERM USED IN THE STATE DEPARTMENT FOR ITS SELF-SERVING SUPPORT FOR ONLY THOSE INTERNATIONAL LAWS THAT SUIT IT – IS UNDERMINING THE INTERNATIONAL LEGAL ORDER AND US LONG-TERM INTERESTS

In recent years, the popular media has portrayed the USA as having turned its back on established international rules, in particular on the use of force, the protection of individual human rights and the conduct of warfare. To a certain extent this is true.

In the aftermath of 9/11, the 'war on terrorism' has resulted in large numbers of prisoners being detained indefinitely and unlawfully at Guantánamo Bay, and an illegal war has been waged in Iraq. But even before 9/11 the US had been taking active measures to block new international rules tackling climate change (Kyoto Protocol) and rules seeking to end impunity for the most serious international crimes (International Criminal Court).

But the story is more complicated. Not all international rules are under attack: the US remains strongly committed to international law in key economic areas, notably where international rules are seen to promote commercial interests and economic liberalisation in a globalising world (free trade, WTO, NAFTA, foreign investment protection, etc).

The US has played a leading role – if not the leading role – in the construction of a rules-based system of international governance. Before World War II, international rules were minimal in content and addressed only limited areas. By 1944, the US and its allies – known then as the 'United Nations' – published a blueprint for new international institutions and laws that would serve as the foundation for a new rules-based approach to international order. The immediate result was the United Nations and the Bretton Woods institutions (World Bank, IMF, etc). These bodies emerged in 1945 as the centrepiece of a visionary world order based on common values and minimum international rules in three areas: the protection of individual human rights, the promotion of economic liberalism, and the prevention of war and armed conflict.

Since 1945, a growing body of international rules have been put in place, largely in the form of treaties, many of which have received widespread support: the 1948 Universal Declaration of Human Rights provided the benchmark for a set of regional and global treaties establishing minimum standards of protection around the world; the Genocide Convention, also adopted in 1948, was the first of a series of new conventions adopted over the following 30 years that criminalised acts such as torture, discrimination, apartheid and terrorism; in 1949, states adopted the first international conventions establishing universal rules on the conduct of war and armed conflict, including the treatment of prisoners of war. That same period also saw the creation of the General Agreement on Tariffs and Trade (GATT), putting in place the system of free trade that has now been incorporated into the World Trade Organisation. A few years later, the World Bank adopted complementary rules to encourage foreign investments in developing countries. And in the early 1970s, a systematic effort began to put in place rules for the protection of the global environment, including biodiversity, the ozone layer and the climate system.

By the 1980s, the vision of a 'rules-based' international system was an emerging reality. The US had provided leadership and active support because it saw international rules as a means of bringing stability and promoting its economic and social interests.

But in the 1980s and 90s a new perception emerged. With the rise of neo-conservatism in the US many of the rules were seen as imposing unjustifiable limitations on sovereign power. Even before 9/11 the US had turned against many of the new rules, including some that had attracted widespread support. The US was the only country – alongside Somalia – not to have become a party to a human rights Convention on the Rights of the Child, because it limited the right to carry out the death penalty on juveniles. The 1997 Kyoto Protocol (aimed at combating climate change) was seen as a threat to the US economy and to US values (gas guzzlers in particular). And the 1998 Statute of the International Criminal Court (ICC) was seen as a threat to US power, subjecting military personnel (and other individuals) to the risk of prosecution by an independent international prosecutor. Like any state, the US was entitled to choose not to become a party to these and other treaties. But its reasons for not doing so marked a change of perspective. There emerged a presumption against international rules; instead of creating opportunities, they were seen as imposing constraints.

That context provided the backdrop for a sustained and unprecedented effort to refashion international law to promote economic rules but to abandon or undermine rules promoting human dignity and welfare – human rights, humanitarian law, environment, etc. The attack on the World Trade Centre was the catalyst for the systematic disregard of well-established international rules – reflected, for example, in the treatment of combatant prisoners and the use of force against Iraq. The US barely even sought to justify the invasion of Iraq in terms of law; and its treatment of prisoners at Guantánamo Bay was widely recognised as violating long-established norms.

The US, it seems, is embarked on an approach that threatens significant damage to the rules-based system put in place after World War II. Moreover, the US has not proposed a viable alternative and may be undermining its own long-term interests by alienating many of its allies and de-legitimating its actions.

The US has been selective in its approach to the enforcement of international criminal laws: they may be applied to foreigners but not to Americans. So the US played a leading role in creating the Yugoslav war crimes tribunal (ICTY) in The Hague, and threatened to withhold financial aid if the new Yugoslav government failed to hand over former President Milosevic to the ICTY (which it then did). On the other hand, it has embarked on an active campaign to undermine the new ICC and, in violation of the ICC statute, is seeking to persuade every country in the world not to extradite any US national to the ICC under any circumstances. This selective approach undermines the universality of the system of international criminal justice and its traditional commitment to a rule-of-law based approach. The approach is also inconsistent with historical US support for an international criminal court.

The development of international rules for the protection of the environment dates back to the 1972 UN Conference on the Human Environment, when the US, under President Nixon, proposed a new set of rules based on the US Environmental Policy Act 1970. Over the next 15 years, the US played a leadership role, culminating in the adoption of the 1987 Montreal Protocol on ozone-depleting substances, which the EU and UK initially opposed.

Yellowstone National Park, Montana, USA, 2000: fire-ravaged landscapes in an environment the US refuses to protect.
© Peter Marlow / Magnum

Since then, US involvement in new multilateral environmental agreements has declined. It has refused to become a party to many of the more important recent instruments, including conventions prohibiting international trade in hazardous wastes and the conservation of biodiversity. The US contributes 25 per cent towards annual greenhouse gas emissions. However, in 2001 George W Bush announced that the US would not become a party to the Kyoto Protocol on climate change and it has subsequently engaged in sustained diplomatic efforts to dissuade other countries from joining the Protocol, most notably Russia. The Protocol commits industrialised nations to reducing their emissions of greenhouse gases by 2012; the US decision to stay out was based on fears that the Protocol would impose unacceptable economic costs and give economic advantages to developing countries, which are not required to undertake reduction commitments. There are reports that the same arguments are now being made by the US in relation to proposed new obligations on ozone under the Montreal Protocol.

The treatment of detainees at Guantánamo Bay suggests that the US is also well on its way towards abandoning its historic commitment to international human rights law. It claims the right to hold the detainees indefinitely and without charge, although it has indicated that charges may be brought in a prosecution before a US military tribunal. The US also argues that international human rights rules do not apply because the detainees are 'illegal combatants' and are being held outside US territory. In November 2002, the Court of Appeal in London rejected these arguments, ruling that Ferroz Abbassi, a British detainee, was being held in a 'legal black hole' in violation of his fundamental human rights.

America's behaviour violates international standards and will make it more difficult for the country to rely on these rules in respect of the treatment of its own nationals abroad. By failing to take active measures to bring the US into compliance with international law, the UK may also be seen to undermine these well-established international rules.

The United Nations Charter outlaws the use of force with only two exceptions: individual or collective self-defence in response to an armed attack; and action authorised by the Security Council as a collective response to a threat to the peace, breach of the peace or act of aggression. In March 2003, the US, with the UK and a few other states, used force against Iraq.

The US government made virtually no effort to justify its actions as lawful within the bounds of the UN Charter. In contrast, in the face of growing public concern – and a possible Cabinet revolt – the UK went out of its way to make a case for its legality. In the absence of a Security Council resolution explicitly authorising the use of force, the UK justified its actions on the grounds that the force had been authorised by a series of earlier Security Council resolutions dating back to 1991, in which Iraq was said to be in 'material breach' by reason of its continued development of weapons of mass destruction (WMD). The UK did not claim that the use of force was justified by way of self-defence, an argument intimated by the US.

The UK's legal arguments have won virtually no support from other states or from independent legal commentators. Kofi Annan said the use of force was of doubtful legitimacy; the great majority of opinion is that the use of force by the US and the UK was illegal and undermined the foundations of the UN system. The absence of a clear Security Council mandate for the use of force – and consequential concerns about legality – have also made it more difficult to involve other states in the reconstruction of Iraq.

In contrast to its recent positions on the rules relating to human rights, humanitarian law and the use of force, the US remains an active proponent of international law on international trade and the promotion of foreign investment, as well as in other economic areas such as the protection of intellectual property rights. The US remains a strong supporter of the WTO and its binding mechanisms for the resolution of disputes. This stems from its concerns that without such mechanisms those states that do not comply with WTO rules will gain unfair economic advantages vis-à-vis the US and its corporate sector. The US supports and uses only those rules that are perceived to provide clear economic advantages. It has been equally active in promoting international rules to protect the overseas investments of its corporations. In the 1960s, it played a leading role in creating the World Bank's International Centre for the Settlement of Investment Disputes (ICSID), and since then it has entered into hundreds of bilateral treaties with other states to prohibit them from nationalising, expropriating or otherwise interfering with American investments.

These international rules are intended to encourage investment in developing countries by protecting the economic rights and interests of the investors. But there is increasing concern that the rules are being used to limit the ability of developing countries to adopt and enforce effective social and environmental standards – for instance, labour and human rights standards, rules prohibiting pollution and so on. Recent case law suggests that these international rules may be used to undermine social efforts in developing countries.

Selective support for international rules – described as 'à la carte multilateralism' by an official in the US State Department – undermines the legal order and US long-term interests. It alienates allies, particularly in the developing world, and challenges the legitimacy of other US actions. There is no evidence that it assists the 'war on terrorism'. It also brings into question the long-term stability and viability of the established international legal order, premised on a set of rules intended to prevent the use of force, promote the dignity of the individual, and encourage economic integration and development.

The consequences of the illegal war on Iraq – in particular the inability to persuade other states to contribute to reconstruction without a UN mandate and leadership – illustrate the dangers of ignoring international law. It remains to be seen whether the post-WWII settlement will be undone by neo-conservative US activism, as is plainly intended, or whether the backlash will, as I think necessary, reinforce the sense that international legal rules provide the minimum necessary for international solidarity and intercourse, in the economic fields and elsewhere. ❏

Philippe Sands QC *is professor of laws at University College, London, and a barrister at Matrix Chambers*

LIES, AND THE LYING LIARS WHO SUE

JOANNE MARINER

In what passes for irony in some parts of the USA, a fat man may be known as Slim and a St Bernard may be called Tiny. It's always been tempting to understand Fox News' use of the slogan 'Fair and Balanced' in this light. Its cheerleading coverage of the Iraq war, to cite just the most glaring example, set a new standard for ideological bias and emotional manipulation.

But Fox's absence of fairness and balance has not stopped it from taking a proprietary interest in the phrase. The network registered 'Fair and Balanced' as a trademark in 1998, giving it a legally cognisable interest in maintaining the phrase's value. And to those who fail to take its ownership of the trademark sufficiently seriously, Fox has a ready response: to sue them.

In August, Fox filed suit in federal court against Al Franken, a comedian and political satirist and author of a book due for September release, *Lies, And the Lying Liars Who Tell Them: A Fair and Balanced Look at the Right*.

Franken's use of Fox's trademark phrase, the Fox court papers averred, was likely to 'blur and tarnish' the phrase. Adding to the injury, in Fox's view, was the fact that a photo of Fox news commentator Bill O'Reilly was featured on the book's cover. According to Fox's attorneys, readers seeing the photo might mistakenly believe that O'Reilly had endorsed the book.

The reference to O'Reilly as an aggrieved party hinted at the suit's origins. A blustering bully of the American right, O'Reilly had fallen into a shouting match with the unabashedly liberal Franken at this year's BookExpo America, telling him to to 'shut up' (and foreshadowing what was to come).

In the book world, there is no more effective way to muzzle one's political opponent than via a court order. Fox thus sought an injunction to stop Franken from selling the book in its existing form and demanded unspecified punitive damages. They took it very personally. 'Franken is neither a journalist nor a television news personality,' charged the complaint papers. 'He appears to be shrill and unstable. His views lack any serious depth or insight.'

While Fox's expertise in this department went unquestioned, outside commentators thought the lawsuit ill-advised. The *New York Times* called it 'frivolous'; the *Chicago Tribune* said it was 'fair and balanced baloney'. Dozens upon dozens of 'Fair and Balanced' spoof websites popped up on the internet.

O'Reilly could not stand by and came back with a self-pitying screed. 'Liberal ideologues' and their allies, the 'elite media', were angered by Fox's success, he complained. Fox was compelled to respond in court to their unfair attacks, slander and defamation.

But in a telling omission, O'Reilly's repeated references to defamation were not reflected in Fox's legal complaint. Why? Because defamation, as a legal matter, looks to the facts. Under the relevant constitutional rules, Fox would have to prove Franken wrong. It would have to show that O'Reilly was not a liar – let alone a lying liar.

A trademark case hinging on the ownership of words rather than on their accuracy must have been a more inviting option for the Fox lawyers. It is difficult to squelch unwanted criticism via a claim of defamation, yet it may still be possible to misuse trademark law to achieve the same ends.

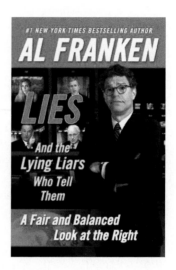

But the Fox News attorneys still had to persuade a federal judge of their position. At a hearing in late August, a Fox attorney struggled to explain how Franken's use of the 'Fair and Balanced' slogan would confuse consumers.

The judge, sceptical from the outset, asked, 'Do you think that a reasonable consumer, seeing the word "lies" over Mr O'Reilly's face, would believe Mr O'Reilly is endorsing this book?' Ignoring the laughter in the courtroom, Fox's counsel responded that the cover's message was 'ambiguous'. 'It does not say "parody" or "satire",' she explained, straight-faced.

The judge was unconvinced. 'This case is wholly without merit,' he concluded. 'Mr Franken is clearly mocking Fox.'

And, indeed, it is Al Franken who has had the last laugh. The publicity drove his book to the top position on Amazon.com's sales chart and it currently stands at number one on the *New York Times* non-fiction bestseller list.

The dismissal of Fox's suit was a clear victory for freedom of expression. Chalk one up for fairness. And with the release of Franken's book into a market otherwise saturated with such right-wing diatribes as Ann Coulter's *Treason*, chalk one up for balance. ❏

Joanne Mariner *is deputy director of the Americas division of Human Rights Watch and a contributor to the Findlaw's Writ legal commentary website, http://writ.news.findlaw.com. Her comments here are her own.*

A censorship chronicle incorporating information from Agence France-Press (AFP), Alliance of Independent Journalists (AJI), Amnesty International (AI), Article 19 (A19), Association of Independent Electronic Media (ANEM), the BBC Monitoring Service Summary of World Broadcasts (SWB), Centre for Human Rights and Democratic Studies (CEHURDES), Centre for Journalism in Extreme Situations (CJES), the Committee to Protect Journalists (CPJ), Canadian Journalists for Free Expression (CJFE), Democratic Journalists' League (JuHI), Digital Freedom Network (DFN), Glasnost Defence Foundation (GDF), Human Rights Watch (HRW), Indymedia, Information Centre of Human Rights & Democracy Movements in China (ICHR DMC), Institute for War & Peace Reporting (IWPR), Instituto de Prensa y Sociedad (IPYS), the United Nations Integrated Regional Information Network (IRIN), the Inter-American Press Association (IAPA), the International Federation of Journalists (IFJ/ FIP), the Media Institute of Southern Africa (MISA), Network for the Defence of Independent Media in Africa (NDIMA), International PEN (PEN), Open Media Research Institute (OMRI), Pacific Islands News Association (PINA), Radio Free Europe/Radio Liberty (RFE/ RL), Reporters Sans Frontières (RSF), The Southeast Asian Press Alliance (SEAPA), Statewatch, Transitions Online (TOL), the World Association of Community Broadcasters (AMARC), World Association of Newspapers (WAN), World Organisation Against Torture (OMCT), Writers in Prison Committee (WiPC) and other sources including members of the International Freedom of Expression eXchange (IFEX)

AFGHANISTAN

On 25 June, Transitional Administration chairman Hamid Karzai ordered the release of *Aftab* newspaper editor **Mir Husayn Mahdawi** and his deputy **Ali Riza Payam**. The two had been jailed on 17 June for blasphemy over articles on 'crimes committed in the name of Islam by prominent Northern Alliance members'. (RSF, CPJ, UNAMA)

Copies of the 20 July issue of *Payam-e Mojahed* were confiscated, reportedly on the order of defence minister Mohammad Qasim Fahim. It reportedly called Hamid Karzai 'powerless' and claimed that real power rests with 'the US, Britain and the UN'. (RFE/ RL)

On 18 August, a 24-hour FM station called Radio Kelid began broadcasting in Kabul. The radio station covers about 30 kilometres and will air news, educational, cultural and sports programmes. (RFE/RL, Afghanistan Television)

Justice minister Abdul Rahim Karimi said on 20 August that under a proposed new Afghan law on political parties, communist parties will be banned, citing the requirements of 'the Afghan Constitution', taken as meaning the 1964 version, currently in the process of redrafting. (RFE/ RL)

Recent publications: *Afghanistan: Re-establishing the rule of law*, Amnesty International, 2003

ALGERIA

Media groups called for the immediate release of the managing editor of the daily *Le Matin* **Mohamed Benchicou** and cartoonist **Ali Dilem**, of the daily *Liberté*, after their arrest by police in Algeria on 9 September. *Le Matin* and *Liberté* are accused of insulting Algerian Minister for the Interior Moulay Guendil in articles making reference to his Jewish and Moroccan ancestors. (*Le Matin*)

Foreign correspondents covering the 2 July release of Islamic Salvation Front (FIS) figureheads **Abassi Madani** and **Ali Belhadj** were ordered by Algerian officials not to report the event. Visiting reporters were confined to their hotels and several were expelled. (CPJ, RSF)

On 31 July, the government announced plans to add lessons in Tamazight, the language of the country's Berber minority, to the state school curriculum. Tamazight was recognised as a state language last year after Berbers pressed for greater cultural and political recognition. (BBC online)

After the state printing house demanded immediate settlement of the printing bills of seven newspapers, five failed to appear on 18 August. One, *Le Matin*, was further banned for nine days after it reported that the orders were politically motivated. (AFP)

ARGENTINA

Indymedia Argentina photographer **Alejandro Gordín** was attacked by police on

9 June while outside a factory in Buenos Aires where staff continue to work despite the owners' bankruptcy. (CPJ)

On 23 June, Judge Juan Carlos Codello ordered the arrest of reporters **Silvio Valenzuela** and **Manuel Ibarra** of LT7 Radio Corrientes and Canal 13 TV and the confiscation of film shot during their investigation into abuse of government vehicles. The two were later released and are suing Codello. (*Periodistas*)

Clara Britos, director of *La Tapa* newspaper in the city of Guernica, Buenos Aires province, received new threats on 28 June in connection with her paper's identification of a policeman facing prosecution over the death of two demonstrators in June 2002. (*Periodistas*)

Ulises Caballero, editor of the newspaper *Artículo 14*, received death threats by phone on 9 August. The threats are connected to his broadcasts on FM La Porte Radio in Buenos Aires province and an investigation into corruption during the construction of a city hospital in the town of Quilmes. (*Periodistas*)

ARMENIA

On 18 July, the applications of opposition radio stations A1+ and Noyan Tapan had their bids to recover their broadcast licences refused for a third time since failing to retain their existing frequencies in April 2002. Both stations were critics of President Robert Kocharian's government. (RFE/RL, RSF)

AZERBAIJAN

Journalist **Rauf Mirqadirov** of the newspaper *Zerkalo* was fined 82,500 manats (US$18) on 7 July after angering Baku mayor Hacibala Abutalibov with questions about problems with the city's roadworks. When Mirqadirov asked who was in charge of road repair, the mayor replied: 'I am in charge of everything here, and you had better mind your own business.' Policemen standing nearby seized Mirqadirov and assaulted him — then charged him with 'hooliganism'. (RFE/RL, RSF)

The journal *Monitor* was suspended again on 9 June, when printers broke their contract with the paper, says founder and editor-in-chief **Elmar Huseynov**, under pressure from the national tax authority. The tax body has led the state's war on the paper in election year, says Huseynov. (RUH, CJES)

Since 25 June, the National Council for Television and Radio requires that a minimum of 75 per cent of all programmes, announcements and advertisements on both state and private broadcasting must be in Azeri and cover events that the state decides are of 'national and special state importance'. (RFE/RL)

Civic Solidarity Party presidential candidate **Sabir Rustamkhanli** accused the authorities of deliberately triggering a power cut during his pre-election TV broadcast. On 27 August, Rustamkhali lodged a formal protest with the country's Election Commission. (RFE/RL, zerkalo.az)

BAHRAIN

Editor **Mansour al-Jamri** and reporter **Hussein Khalaf** of *al-Wasat* face prison sentences of six months or a fine of 1,000 dinars (US$2,650) for violating a gagging order imposed on the release on bail of three suspected terrorists in March. Their trial began on 21 June. (RSF)

BANGLADESH

Mahfuz Anam, editor of the *Daily Star*, **Matiur Rahman**, editor of the daily *Prothom Alo,* and **Abdul Jalil**, secretary-general of the opposition Awami League, were charged with criminal defamation on 11 June after publishing a letter from Jalil on 3 June criticising the choice of a senior government official for an executive position in an international organisation. (AI)

Journalists **Tipu Sultan** (*Index* 2/01, 3/01, 4/02, 3/03) and **Bakhtiar Islam Munna** of the daily *Ittefaq* were threatened by men responsible for a brutal attack on Sultan in January 2001. Sultan, who now works in Dhaka, had been in the Femi area to visit his family. (AI)

On 19 June, **Abul Bashar** of the daily *Janakantha* was kidnapped and beaten up by members of the pro-government student group Jatiyatabadi Chhatra Dal (JCD). He had been blamed for attacks on Shariatpur residents. Bashar also came under threat while in hospital. (CPJ)

Hasan Jahid Tusher, a correspondent for the English-language *Daily Star*, was beaten by 20 JCD student activists with iron rods, outside his dorm room at Dhaka University on 31 July. Since the incident four of Tusher's attackers have been expelled from the JCD. (CPJ)

On 5 August Reporters sans Frontières reported that this year to date there had been 51 physical attacks, including ten attempted murders of Bangladeshi journalists. Some 50 faced death threats, 13 were arrested, 14 were prosecuted or faced law suits and five had been kidnapped. (RSF)

Hiramon Mondol, local correspondent for the daily *Dainik Prabartan*, was attacked on 8 August by members of a police special unit and ended up seriously injured in Khulna prison hospital, charged with theft. Mondol had accused the unit of stealing fish from Baroyariya market. (RSF)

A year after the country's first private terrestrial broadcaster ETV was closed down and its equipment seized (*Index* 4/02, 1/03), the High Court ruled on 20 August that the closure was illegal, ordering the state to consider ETV's bid for a new licence and return its equipment within 30 days. (*Daily Star*)

Recent publication: *Ravaging the Vulnerable: Abuses Against Persons at High Risk of HIV Infection in Bangladesh*, HRW, 20 August 2003, 51 pp

BELARUS

On 3 June, the satirical newspaper *Navinki* was suspended without official notice, only learning of the closure order

from the state distributor Belsajuzdruk. The magazine had received two warnings from the information ministry in May about its publications. (RSF/RL)

The new opposition weekly *Ekho*, which has only come out once since opening this year, was again barred from publication on 4 June when it announced that it planned to include articles from the independent daily *Belorusskaya Delovaya Gazeta*, closed for three months on 28 May. (RSF)

On 4 June editor **Viktar Ivashkevich**, sentenced to two years' internal exile in December 2002 for libelling President Aleksandr Lukashenko, had his sentence halved and awaits release from a detention camp in Baranovichy on 16 December. (*WiPC*)

On 28 June, **Pavel Selin**, Minsk correspondent for Russia's NTV network, was expelled for allegedly 'biased' reports on the funeral of opposition writer **Vasil Bykov** and banned from returning for five years. After more threats, NTV's Minsk bureau was shut down on 8 July. (RSF, IFEX)

The ministry of foreign affairs refused visas to Organisation for Security and Cooperation in Europe (OSCE) media freedoms commissioner **Freimut Duve**, scheduled to visit the country on 1 September and meet local journalists before his term of office expires at the end of this year. (RFE/RL)

BELGIUM

The European Court of Human Rights in Strasbourg has ruled against the Belgian government and declared illegal (*Index* 3/95) a series of police raids on media organisations and journalists' homes in 1995. (IFJ)

BOTSWANA

On 16 July, the *Botswana Gazette* was sued for damages of 10 million pula (US$2.07 million) by ten Chinese construction companies after publishing an article entitled 'Protect citizen contractors against Chinese', quoting Botswana Confederation of Commerce Industry and Manpower's vice-president, Mogolori Modisi. (MISA)

On 8 August, Gabz FM radio host **Jacob Kamodi** was kicked in the groin by freelance sub-editor Charles Kidega, supposedly representing *Business and Financial Times* magazine, after Kamodi refused to broadcast the magazine's advert. Kidega later apologised. (MISA)

BRAZIL

Brazilian journalist **Alvanir Ferreira Avelino**, of the Rio de Janiero daily *Dois Estados*, began serving a ten months and 15 days' 'part-time' jail sentence on 29 September under a 1967 law passed by the former military dictatorship to restrict expression of opinion. Avelino had been sentenced in 2001 for 'expressing an opinion' under the military regime's 1967 press law, which had been otherwise forgotten. (RSF)

On 3 June, journalist **Melyssa Martins Correia** of the daily *Oeste Notícias*, São Paulo state, was shot in the head at point-blank range. Martins Correia's murder appears to have been prompted by the newspaper's coverage of criminal organisations. (RSF)

The co-owner of the weekly *Boca do Povo*, **Edgar Ribeiro Pereira de Oliveira**, was killed on 9 June in Campo Grande city in north-western Brazil. His weekly was known in the region for its reporting on public corruption. (IAPA)

On 30 June, journalist **Nicanor Linhares Batista**, owner of Radio Vale do Jaguaribe in the city of Limoeiro do Norte, was shot dead in the studio by unknown gunmen who fled on a motorcycle. Batista's controversial and hard-hitting commentaries had angered many local politicians and public officials. (CPJ)

Freelance photographer **Luiz Antonio Costa** was shot on 23 July as he was preparing a report for the weekly *Apoca* on land belonging to a Volkswagen plant in São Bernardo do Campo, São Paulo state, occupied by members of a movement of homeless people. (RSF)

BURMA

Aung San Suu Kyi, leader of the National League for Democracy (NLD) and writer, was taken into 'protective custody' on 1 June following clashes between NLD and pro-government supporters on 30 May. (PEN, Article 19)

Chief editor **U Zaw Thet Htwe** and journalists **Than Htut Aung**, **U Zaw Myint** and **Soe Pa Pa Hlaing** of the sports weekly *First Eleven* were arrested on 17 July, apparently for reporting that organisers of the Asian Champion Club tournament had fined a Burmese football team for failing to participate as planned. (RSF)

Recent publications: *Myanmar: Justice on Trial,* Amnesty International, 2003; *Burma Issues*, Vol. 13 No. 7, July 2003

CAMBODIA

On 13 June, in a press release, Human Rights Watch said the government must act immediately to allow opposition parties access to broadcast media and to repeal restrictions on public demonstrations and party meetings in the weeks before the 27 July national election. (HRW)

Khiev Kagnarith, Secretary of State of the Ministry of Information, threatened to shut down FM 105 Sambok Khmum Radio (Beehive Radio) on 7 July for re-broadcasting news from Radio Free Asia and Voice of America. Kagnarith claimed that a special licence was needed, though observers argued that no such regulation existed. (Article 19)

CAMEROON

Remy Ngono, host of satirical programme *Konde Chaud* on Radio Television Siantou, was fined US$360 and jailed for six months for criminal defamation after he mocked embezzlement allegations made against local businessman Ketch Jean. It was reported that the case had been brought over a year ago, but Ngono had not been informed. (RSF, CPJ, AFP)

CANADA

Reporters sans Frontières called on the Canadian courts to cancel warrants granted to Quebec City Police to search the offices of three media outlets – TQS, TVA, and Radio Canada. Police officers claim it is necessary to enable them to conduct an investigation into a juvenile prostitution ring. (RSF)

In another case, the Toronto Police Association lost its claim that articles in the *Toronto Star* alleging racial bias on the part of the police were libellous. Canadian Journalists for Free Expression (CJFE) executive director Joel Ruimy said libel law 'should not be used to try and silence investigative journalists'. (CJFE)

CENTRAL AFRICAN REPUBLIC

On 26 June, a La Lobaye court sentenced **Michel Ngokpele**, publication director of *Le Quotidien de Bangui*, to six months' imprisonment for defamation and provocation of ethnic hatred over an article claiming that deaths at a local hospital had increased after the arrival of the new head doctor. (JED)

Ferdinand Samba, director of the daily *Le Démocrate*, was arrested on 11 July and detained for four days before being released on 15 July without charge. Samba had published reports of violence by soldiers north of Bangui.

PRAYER TO A LABOURER

VICTOR JARA

Stand up
look at the mountain
source of the wind, the sun, the water –
you who change the course of rivers,
whose soul flies like the seed from a sower's hand.

Stand up
look at your hands
take your brother's hand
so you can grow.
We'll go together, united by blood,
the future can begin today.
Deliver us from the master who keeps us in misery.
Thy kingdom of justice and equality come.
Blow, like the wind blows, the wild flower of the mountain pass.
Clean the barrel of my gun like fire.
Thy will be done, at last, on earth
give us the strength and courage to struggle.
Blow, like the wind blows, the wild flower of the mountain pass.
Clean the barrel of my gun like fire.

Stand up
look at your hands.
Take your brother's hand so you can grow.
We'll go together, united by blood.
Now and in the hour of our death. Amen. ❏

Victor Jara was a Chilean singer, guitarist and songwriter. Throughout his working life – except for the short period of the Allende regime – he was subject to various kinds of political censorship, personal smears and even physical attacks. He was 40 when he died, on 14 or 15 September 1973, murdered by Pinochet's military in the Estadio Chile in Santiago.

This lyric was one of four specially translated for publication in Index on Censorship *in 1974 by the poet and playwright Adrian Mitchell in collaboration with the author's widow, Joan Jara. It is reprinted here as a tribute to his memory, 30 years after his death.*

'They that can give up essential liberty to obtain a little temporary safety deserve neither liberty nor safety' Benjamin Franklin

NOAM CHOMSKY ON
ROGUE STATES

EDWARD SAID ON
IRAQI SANCTIONS

LYNNE SEGAL ON
PORNOGRAPHY

... all in  INDEX

SUBSCRIBE & SAVE

UK and overseas

○ **Yes! I want to subscribe to *Index*.**

❑ 1 year (4 issues)	£32	Save 16%
❑ 2 years (8 issues)	£60	Save 21%
❑ 3 years (12 issues)	£84	**You save 26%**

Name

Address

B0B5

£ _____ enclosed. ❑ Cheque (£) ❑ Visa/MC ❑ Am Ex ❑ Bill me
(Outside of the UK, add £10 a year for foreign postage)

Card No.

Expiry   Signature

❑ I do not wish to receive mail from other companies.

INDEX

✉ Freepost: INDEX, 33 Islington High Street, London N1 9BR
☎ (44) 171 278 2313   Fax: (44) 171 278 1878
e tony@indexoncensorship.org

SUBSCRIBE & SAVE

North America

○ **Yes! I want to subscribe to *Index*.**

❑ 1 year (4 issues)	$48	Save 12%
❑ 2 years (8 issues)	$88	Save 19%
❑ 3 years (12 issues)	$120	**You save 26%**

Name

Address

B0B5

$ _____ enclosed. ❑ Cheque ($) ❑ Visa/MC ❑ Am Ex ❑ Bill me

Card No.

Expiry   Signature

❑ I do not wish to receive mail from other companies.

✉ Freepost: INDEX, 708 Third Avenue, 8th Floor, New York, NY 10017
☎ (44) 171 278 2313   Fax: (44) 171 278 1878
e tony@indexoncensorship.org

He was accused of spreading panic and publishing false information. (RSF, JED)

CHILE

On 23 July, the Televisión Nacional de Chile network withdrew a documentary re-creating the murder of Santiago lawyer **Patricio Torres Reyes**, stabbed to death by two prostitutes in his office. The prostitutes, sisters **Nancy** and **Marcela Imil**, were jailed, but the documentary producers believe that one, Marcela, may have been wrongfully convicted. But the murdered lawyer's widow, Eugenia Hevia, petitioned the Court of Appeals to bar the programme as a violation of her and her children's constitutional right to honour and privacy. (CPJ)

CHINA

Huang Qi, the founder of a dissident website www.4-6tianwang.com in Chengdu, Sichuan Province (*Index passim*), was sentenced to five years in prison on charges of subversion at a closed hearing on 9 May. Huang established the site with his wife **Zeng Li** in June 1998 to help people trace missing family members. It also carried articles increasingly critical of the government, none of which were actually written by Huang. Former cellmates report that Huang was repeatedly beaten during his three years of detention. (BBC, CPJ, RSF, HRIC)

Four other internet writers, **Xu Wei**, **Jin Haike**, **Yang Zili** and **Zhang Honghai** (*Index* 3/01), were sentenced to jail terms ranging between eight and ten years on 28 May

by a court in Beijing, also on charges of subversion. The men, arrested in March 2001, established an internet forum to discuss political and social reform and circulate essays and articles. (BBC, CPJ, RSF, HRIC)

Luo Yongzhang, a freelance writer from Changchun, Jilin Province, was reportedly detained by police on 13 June. Luo is credited with writing and publishing some 150 essays on the internet, many critical of China's human rights record and restrictions on free speech. His whereabouts are not known. (BBC, CPJ, RSF)

Human Rights in China (HRIC) reported on 7 July that **Hua Huiqi**, a known Christian dissident from Beijing, had been refused the right to send his six-year-old daughter to school. Hua was reportedly refused household registration documents and thus access to basic services. (HRIC)

The Cardinal Kung Foundation (CKF) reported the arrest of six underground Catholic clergy in China. **Father Lu Xiaozhou** was arrested on 16 June in Zhejiang Province as he prepared to administer the last rites to one of his congregation. **Fathers Kang Fuliang**, **Chen Gouzhen**, **Pang Guangzhou**, **Joseph Yin** and **Li Shujun** were arrested on 1 July in Hebei Province while on their way to visit another priest, **Lu Genjun**, just released from a three-year term in a labour camp. CKF reported on 4 July that ten bishops are either imprisoned or under house arrest in China, 15 priests are either in prison or

labour camps, and the status of a further four priests is unknown. (HRIC, CKF)

The press in China continues to come under political pressure as part of an ongoing 'review' of the media industry. It was reported on 2 June that up to 500 staff in the international section of the official Xinhua news agency had their housing allowances and other benefits cut in April as punishment for revealing information about the Sars outbreak to the world media. A senior editor, **Yang Zidi**, was dismissed. *Beijing Xinbao*, a weekly news tabloid, was closed down and its editors dismissed after running a story on 4 June entitled 'Seven disgusting things in China', one of which was the National People's Congress. 'Why is it so surprisingly amateurish and unprofessional? . . . Who elected these delegates, and how?' asked the article. *Caijing*, a bimonthly business magazine, was banned in late June, apparently after publishing stories on Sars and a bank loan scandal allegedly involving top government officials and their children in its 20 June edition. It was reported on 20 August that the Publicity Department, formerly known as the Ministry of Propaganda, issued a circular to official publications, universities and think tanks banning public debate on ongoing reforms of the party constitution. The reforms are expected to focus on including Jiang Zemin's political theory into the party's constitution and ideological canon. (CPJ, *The Hindu*, RSF, *Washington Post*)

China passed legislation in June that prepares for the

issuing of electronic ID cards to the majority of Chinese citizens. Limited official discussion on the introduction of the cards focuses on the need to avoid forgery of the current plastic cards, but avoids debate on the nature of information to be stored on the electronic version. Trials will reportedly be carried out in 2004 with as many as 800 million cards predicted to be in circulation by 2006. The cards will be issued and administered by the Ministry of Public Security. (*Dow Jones*)

Around 500,000 people in Hong Kong demonstrated on 1 July against proposed legislation that it was feared could severely limit freedom of expression in the territory. Article 23 of the Basic Law, supported by Beijing, would have banned groups affiliated to groups similarly banned in China, given police emergency powers to conduct searches and seizures without a court warrant, and created an offence of 'handling seditious publications' which was of particular concern to journalists in the territory. Hong Kong Chief Executive Tung Chee-hwa postponed passage of the bill through the Legislative Council in the wake of the demonstrations, but a redrafted version is likely to be presented later this year. (SCMP)

Three Chinese writers were among 28 from 13 countries who received Hellman/Hammett grants awarded in July 'in recognition of their courage in the face of political persecution', reported Human Rights Watch on 29 July. **Liao Yiwu** (*Index* 2/03), a poet, novelist and film-maker, has been arrested and detained on numerous occasions since 1990. His most recent reported detention was in December 2002 after he signed a petition to the 16th Party Congress calling for a reversal of the verdicts against the 1989 demonstrators. **Liu Binyan**, a journalist, fell foul of the communist authorities as early as 1957 when he was prohibited from writing for 20 years, but became a special correspondent for the *People's Daily* from 1978 to 1988. He has been in exile in the US since 1989 when he was refused entry back into China, and has since written extensively about social and political reform in China. **Wang Lixiong**, a Tibetologist who has written on Tibetan and Uighur nationalism, was detained in Xinjiang in 1999 while researching social issues among the Uighur population, and dismissed from an environmental NGO in February 2003 because of his views. His writings are banned in China. (HRW)

Dr Yang Jianli, an academic based at Harvard University, was tried in Beijing on 4 August on charges of espionage and illegal entry into China. His sentence has not yet been announced. Dr Yang was detained on 26 April in Yunan Province having entered China with a fake passport. The charge of espionage apparently relates to the allegation that Dr Yang once received a research grant from a Taiwanese organisation, and was in China to research labour protests. (AP, AI, HRIC)

Zhao Changqing (*Index* 2/03), who drafted a petition to the 16th Party Congress calling for a reversal of the verdicts against participants in the 1989 Tiananmen demonstrations (see **Liao Yiwu** above), was sentenced to five years in prison on 4 August by a court in Xi'an, Shaanxi Province, on charges of subversion. Zhao was suffering from TB prior to his arrest in December 2002 and his condition is thought to have worsened. (HRIC, Reuters)

The 2003 Tucholskii Award has gone to the Chinese poet and writer-in-exile **Jun Feng**, award organisers from the Swedish PEN writers' rights group announced on 6 September. Jun, presently living in exile in Odense, Denmark, was driven from his home by police harassment in 1988, then imprisoned in Laos for two years. Now he is a Danish citizen, editor of several literary magazines on the internet and a co-founder of The Independent Chinese Pen Centre. (Swedish PEN)

Chinese Premier Wen Jiabao has urged television programmes to focus more on the lives of ordinary people, and should reflect public demands – but at the same time publicise China's achievements in reform and opening-up. Speaking on 26 August he said: 'TV programmes should serve the people as well as the work of the CPC and the government,' underlining TV stations' role in inspiring people and unmasking social problems. (*People's Daily*)

China has taken a step towards loosening state con-

WHEN ELEPHANTS FIGHT, IT IS THE GRASS THAT SUFFERS

INFORMAL SECTOR SERVICE CENTRE

The announcement of the collapse of the peace talks, unilaterally by the Maoists, is a serious setback to resolve the problems by peaceful means. The announcement is a dangerous attempt to revive abduction, intimidation, extortion, violence and murder. The fragile hope for peace of people is crashed. They are unsure what goes the next. All they receive from the ugly call is a psycho-pain that they have to go through day and night.

Not a single party is responsible to call for this day. Both the government and the Maoists were contributing equally to prove the prospect and significance of code of conduct irrelevant. The seven-month-old ceasefire and the subsequent peace process were not completely calm. During the period of arms-halt, 122 persons lost their lives in the collision of two arms, where the Maoists shared 44 lives.

The recent development of the incidents overstepped the people's expectation to retrieve the rights nullified in course of armed conflict. The break up of ceasefire still creates social and political unrest cultivating violence. Time undoubtedly steps against the will of the people giving birth of their new perpetrators. Now people have to go through the coercion, subversion, chaos and pain. But ultimately, people overcome the pain, suffering and cut apart the net of chaos. People need peace and want to be a party of the peace process. They are committed to solve the problems by peaceful means. Any Hercules, which comes to undermine the people's wills, will be taken to pieces and the history never excuses them. People know only the peace has a breast to suck. People are determined to outlive the sound of war drums and the exploits of brave fingers. So, we appeal the parties to be sincere to the people's will and resume peace talks. ❏

Taken from the website of Informal Sector Service Center (INSEC),
www.insec.org.np, in the immediate aftermath of the Maoist rebels pulling
out of peace talks with the government of Nepal on 27 August 2003

trol over its television production industry, approving a batch of eight private companies that can make TV series without being shadowed by a state-run corporation. The approval from the State Administration of Radio, Film and Television, the industry regulator, illustrates a wider push by the administration of China's president Hu Jintao to introduce commercial reforms to its bloated state media machine. (*Financial Times*)

COLOMBIA

On 6 June, investigative editor **Fabio Castillo** was asked to resign by the Bogotá-based weekly *El Espectador*. Castillo noted in his letter of resignation that the weekly's decision was linked to his investigation into irregularities implicating Interior and Justice Minister Fernando Londono Hoyos. (PFC)

In August, *El Tiempo* columnist **Roberto Posada**, also known as **D'Artagnan**, was prosecuted for comments published in his column in connection with businessman Pedro Juan Moreno Villa. The journalist was accused of libel for claiming that Moreno has been involved in paramilitary activities. (FLIP)

On 18 August, camera operator **Jorge Real Castilla** of RCN TV in Valledupar, northern Colombia, was assaulted by members of the Colombian army's La Popa battalion. Castilla was reporting on the death of alleged members of the National Liberation Army (ELN) guerrilla group and the seizure of military equipment. (FLIP)

On 22 August, **Juan Carlos Benavidez**, radio journalist for Manantial Eastereo, was killed by rebels from the Revolutionary Armed Forces of Colombia (FARC) while travelling in Putamayo State. Benavidez was shot and his colleague **Jaime Conrado** injured when they failed to halt at a roadblock on their way to cover a meeting between President Alvaro Uribe and regional officials. (IFJ, CPJ)

Radio journalist **Emiro Goyeneche** was arrested in Arauca on 20 August on suspicion of collaborating with ELN guerrillas and accused of 'rebellion'. Like others recently arrested by the military – including human rights activists and trades unionists – he was accused by unnamed 'informers' as an alleged supporter of leftist guerrillas. Goyeneche, one of the main presenters with the radio station Sarare Estereo in the town of Saravena, was arrested during a military operation while he was doing his morning show. (RSF)

Amnesty International has condemned the recent detention of about 42 social activists and human rights defenders in the city of Saravena. A reported 28 remained under arrest on 27 August. Amnesty condemned what it described as 'an ongoing coordinated campaign' to expose trade unionists and human rights activists to increased attack from army-backed paramilitaries. (AI)

Julio Cesar Ardila, the mayor of Barrancabermeja, was charged on 11 July with ordering the murder of a radio journalist who had accused him of being corrupt and having links to outlawed paramilitary groups. The bullet-riddled body of **Juan Emeterio Rivas** and the body of an engineering student were found in April outside Barrancabermeja. Three other officials from city hall were detained over the killing. (RSF)

DEMOCRATIC REPUBLIC OF CONGO

Romain Kambala Bilolo, director of the privately owned Kasaï Radiotélévision (KHRT), was arrested on 7 June and accused of broadcasting false information instigating rebellion. His arrest was linked to the station's reports on the conflict over the property rights of a diamond mine in Lungudi. (JED)

Radio Mandeleo was allowed to resume broadcasting in the town of Bukavu on 7 July after being banned for more than six months. State communications chief Jean-Pierre Lola Kisanga agreed to the lifting of the ban if the station resumed operation under a different format. (JED)

The Lubumbashi-based correspondent of *La Tribune*, **Donatien Nyembo Kimuni**, was sentenced to five years' imprisonment on 11 July for an article criticising the dangerous working conditions of miners. (JED)

Etienne Bwande Bwana Pua, local radio director for the town of Kisangani, was suspended on 6 August by Alimasi Mayanga, his provincial director from the Radio-Télévision Nationale

Congolaise (RTNC) network. Mayanga had been summoned by regional vice-governor Floribert Asiane and told to take action after Pua failed to include pro-government programming in his schedules. (JED)

REPUBLIC OF CONGO

Radio France International and Reporters sans Frontières correspondent **Alain Shungu** was allegedly threatened on 27 June by Police Services Director General Colonel Jean François Denguet. Shungu had reported that Denguet had banned a meeting organised by opposition leader Andre Milongo in Makelele. (RSF)

CROATIA

On 10 June, the editor of the weekly *Nacional*, **Ivo Pukanic**, was summoned to the police, and quizzed about the paper's interview with fugitive war crimes suspect General Ante Gotovina. He refused to reveal the paper's sources, citing the country's press laws. (*Feral Tribune*)

On 9 July, the Croatian parliament voted to amend the criminal code and excise an article that protects journalists from libel prosecution if the defamation was unintentional. Other amendments in power allow for the jailing for a year of journalists who publish an opinion about on-going trials. (*Feral Tribune*)

CZECH REPUBLIC & SLOVAKIA

The Slovak government has asked Czech authorities to investigate Czech journalist **Jiri Kominek**, author of articles about the Slovak Intelligence Service's links to arms smuggling and former communist security service officers, published in the British *Jane's Intelligence Digest* defence magazine. (RFE/RL)

CÔTE D'IVOIRE

Abahebou Kamagate, a human rights activist with the organisation SOS Exclusion, has been forced to flee to exile in the US, after criticising stringent new citizenship restrictions that may remove citizens' rights for up to 40 per cent of the population. (DFN)

CUBA

New restrictions on 26 jailed journalists arrested in March 2003 limit family visits to once every three months instead of every three weeks, as normally allowed. Some have been transferred to prisons hundreds of kilometres from their homes. The Russian news agency Prima News reported that journalist **Adolfo Fernández Sainz** and other jailed dissidents had begun a hunger strike to demand the right to see their families more often. (RSF)

The International Federation of Library Associations and Institutions (IFLA) raised concerns that US efforts to isolate Cuba were limiting Cuban rights of freedom of information. It spoke out after **Marcia Medina Cruzata** of the country's national library was refused a visa to attend a meeting of the Association of Caribbean University, Research and Institutional Libraries in Puerto Rico. (IFLA)

On 7 August, jailed journalist **Oscar Espinosa Chepe** was taken ill and removed to a military hospital in Havana, according to his wife, journalist Miriam Leiva. Espinosa Chepe, 62, was jailed for 20 years on 7 April for actions against 'the independence or the territorial integrity of the State', and suffers from a number of medical conditions, including liver failure and high blood pressure.

In response to a crackdown on dissident artists in Cuba that has seen 75 Cuban cultural and social activists jailed for up to 28 years, The Netherlands' Prince Claus Fund has withdrawn its funding from the 8th Havana Biennial, scheduled for November 2003. The Prince Claus Fund was a key financier of the 7th Havana Biennial in 2000, contributing €90,000 (US$98,600) to the event in recognition of its 'high quality' and 'the emphasis on intercultural exchange with artists in Latin America, the Caribbean, Asia and Africa'. (Prince Claus Fund)

DJIBOUTI

On 9 July, the Appeals Court resentenced **Daher Ahmed Farah**, editor of the independent newspaper *Le Renouveau* and head of the opposition party Movement for Democratic Renewal and Development, to three months' imprisonment. He was sent back to Gabode prison, from where he had been released on 23 June by a lower court. Farah was also given an additional three-month suspended sentence and fined 13 million Djibouti francs (US$75,000) for libel and undermining the 'army's morale'. (HRW, RSF)

DOMINICAN REPUBLIC

State security officials questioned journalist **Marino Zapete Corniel** for five hours on 11 June, accusing him of insulting President Hipólito Mejía in a series of articles on his handling of the collapse of the Banco Intercontinental bank.

Horacio Emilio Lemoine and **Carlos Martínez** of Radio Montecristi were detained for two days after polling listeners on their choice of possible presidential candidates. One caller said on air that she would 'rather vote for the devil' than President Mejía, others called in to concur. The police were listening too.

EGYPT

Editor **Mustapha Bakri** and journalist **Mahmoud Bakri** of the weekly *al-Ousbou* had their one-year jail sentences for libel confirmed by an appeals court on 1 June. They had accused Mohammed Abdel Aal, head of the opposition Social Justice Party and editor of the newspaper *al-Watan al-Arabi*, of corruption. But Aal had been jailed for ten years by another court six days previously for taking bribes from businessmen. The Bakri brothers were freed on 25 June. (RSF, arabicnews. com)

The government organised the delivery of identical sermons in 88,000 mosques across Egypt from 1 August as part of extensive new censorship of mosques and inde-

pendent imans that do not toe the official line. According to the Awaqaf (religious endowments) ministry, no preacher will be free to deliver his own sermon and sermons will now be written by government officials. New imans will only be appointed after clearing an examination and passing a security test. (IPS)

The film *The Matrix: Reloaded* was banned in Egypt, said state director of artistic censorship Makbur Thabet because the film deals with religious subjects like 'human existence and creation'. But the film was also largely set in a place called 'Zion', raising other concerns. (*Cairo Times, Middle East Times*)

The **Egyptian Organisation for Human Rights** (EOHR) was legally recognised as an NGO by the Ministry of Social Affairs after 18 years of work on 24 June. Two other human rights groups – the **New Woman Research Group** and the **Land Centre for Human Rights**, a peasants' rights group – were refused. (*Al-Ahram*, metimes.com)

On 4 June, four of the 21 men jailed in the 'Queen Boat' homosexuality case (*Index* 1/02, 3/03) were released from prison, their sentences reduced from three years to one. (*Cairo Times*, meonline.com)

ERITREA

Voice of America Asmara stringer **Aklilu Solomon** was arrested on 8 July after reporting criticism of the state media's unsympathetic treatment of families of soldiers killed in the 1998–2000 war

with Ethiopia. Despite holding discharge papers, he was sent to an army base to 'finish his national service'. (CPJ)

ESTONIA

Argo Riistan, 21, published around 12 interviews with celebrities in various Estonian papers, but all but two of them were false – most of them concocted out of interviews conducted by other journalists for foreign journals. However, in the case of Czech author **Milan Kundera**, who had not given an interview for some ten years, Riistan, who claimed to have met Kundera in Paris, simply invented the whole thing. Riistan, who was exposed by the cultural weekly *Sirp*, which decided to check whether his claimed interview with philanthopist George Soros was genuine, explained his conduct by saying that he had wanted to see 'stories about stars' in the press with his byline. (*Baltic Times*)

EUROPEAN UNION

The European Commission organised a meeting of 'some of Europe's best experts, psychologists, sociologists, criminologists and education specialists scientific experts' in Brussels in September to progress its debate on ways and means to 'protect' young people against violence on TV, the internet and video games. The Commission will draft an outline policy on EU audiovisual issues, including a view on whether there is a need for new Community measures on the protection of minors. (EJC)

Recent publications: *Response to the Council of Europe's Draft Recommendation on the Right of Reply in the New Media Environment,* Article 19, 22 August 2003

FRANCE

Activist **Jose Bové** was jailed on 22 June for destroying samples of genetically modified rice and maize. He was freed by presidential order in August after five weeks of a ten-month sentence but his movements were severely restricted, a ban that kept him from attending the September Cancún WTO summit. (Reuters)

Reporters sans Frontières has called for the abolition of a 1881 press law that still allows the state to ban selected publications and ban 'disrespect' to a foreign head of state. The law allowed Moroccan King Hassan II to successfully sue the daily *Le Monde* over reports linking him to the drug trade in 1995. (RSF)

Diana Diaz Lopez, daughter of the photographer who took the famous image of Latin American guerrilla leader Che Guevara, petitioned a Paris court on 11 June to prevent RSF using the image in its campaigns for press freedom in Cuba. RSF said the ban 'plays into the hands of the Cuban authorities'. (RSF)

THE GAMBIA

Ten soldiers searched the offices of the *Independent* newspaper on 21 June, after it reported the arrest of Kanilai Camp commander Lt Yankuba Badjie on charges of misappropriating presidential funds. Editor-in-chief **Abdoulie Sey** and managing editor **Alagi Yorro Jallow** were questioned about the article. (Allafrica.com)

The Gambia's controversial National Media Commission, empowered to ban papers, jail journalists and force them to reveal sources, has been inaugurated by the government in the face of strong objections from the Gambian Press Union and media rights groups. The Gambian Bar Association has withdrawn its participation, questioning the commission's constitutionality. (Allafrica.com)

GEORGIA

On 9 July, a Tbilisi court jailed Grigol Khurtsilava for 13 years after he confessed to the killing of prominent investigative journalist and political talk-show host **Giorgi Sanaya** two years ago. He claimed he shot Sanaya after he made sexual advances. Sanaya's widow dismissed the trial as 'a farce'. (*RFL/RL*)

GUATEMALA

Jose Ruben Zamora, publisher of the daily *el Periódico* was attacked at home on 24 June by a group of men who held him and his family for two hours. One attacker asked why Zamora had a problem with the 'people at the top'. Zamora had written articles exposing the military's continuing influence in Guatemalan politics.

CERIGUA news agency journalist **Carmen Judith Morán Cruz** received an anonymous threat on 29 June: 'I'm giving you 24 hours to resign from CERIGUA because I've run out of patience with what they publish,' said the caller. 'If you don't, your children and your family will suffer the consequences.'

The home of **Luis Eduardo de Leon** of the daily *el Periódico*'s investigative unit was burgled on 3 July. The raiders took a computer, tapes, notes for an article on official corruption and papers belonging to his wife, formerly with the Archbishop of Guatemala's Human Rights Office, but nothing else of value, including cash and jewellery.

On 8 July, **Angel Martín Tax**, *Prensa Libre* correspondent in Alta Verapaz region, found a vase of flowers in his home doorway of his house — symbolic of a funeral in Guatemala. The day before he had been assaulted and robbed of his notebook by unknown men.

GUINEA

Members of President Lansana Conte's guard assaulted **Azoca Bah**, reporter for *Le Lynx–La Lance*, and **Aboubaka Akoumba**, managing editor of *l'Aurore*, on 27 June. The assaults followed reports raising questions about the president's health and the chances of his re-election in December. (MISA, IFJ)

Officials banned a planned election campaign conference on democratic change and the role of political parties, organised by the opposition Rassemblement Guinée (RPG) party. Five foreign politicians arriving to attend were refused entry to the country. (IRIN)

HAITI

Government officials agreed on 15 August to respond to Committee to Protect Journalists (CPJ) requests for information on the status of judicial investigations into press freedom abuses documented by the group. The agreement came during a five-day visit to Haiti by a CPJ delegation. (CPJ)

HONDURAS

On 24 June, TV journalist **Renato Álvarez** listed several public figures, including police, judges and politicians, allegedly linked to drug trafficking. Security Minister Óscar Alvarez, a guest on his programme, did not dispute the report, but since then journalist has been threatened with violence unless he reveals his source and two of the named seek his jailing on criminal defamation charges.

INDIA

On 4 June, 186 supporters of the Save the Narmada Movement were detained after peacefully resisting efforts by police to move hunger striking protest leader **Medha Patkar** (*Index* 1/00, 3/01, 4/01) to hospital. All 186 face charges of rioting, unlawful assembly and acts prejudicial to maintenance of harmony. The group had demanded a halt to construction of the Sardar Sarovar dam until all the families affected by the project are resettled. (AI)

India's Supreme Court held on 6 August that government employees had 'no fundamental, legal or equitable right' to go on strike. Ruling on a challenge to the dismissal of 170,000 Tamil Nadu state employees for striking in July, judges MB Shah and AR Lakshmanan also held that trade unions 'cannot claim to have a guaranteed right to an effective collective bargaining or to strike, either as part of collective bargaining or otherwise'. (IANS, *Frontline, The Hindu*)

Indian Information and Broadcasting Minister Ravi Shankar says his government will speed up the establishment of an independent broadcasting sector regulatory body, it was reported on 29 August. Shankar said his pleas for self-regulation of television content and advertising have not had the desired results and that he was under pressure to bring in more stringent regulations. Industry representatives urged him in turn to include public broadcasters Doordarshan and All India Radio under any such regulatory body. (Radio Netherlands)

The government deferred a bill to ban the slaughter of cows, revered by the country's Hindu majority, after opposition protests that the 2003 Prevention to Cruelty to Cows bill, if passed, would unconstitutionally deny non-Hindus the right to their choice of staple diet. (*Straits Times*)

On 22 August, it was reported that nine separatist groups in India's north-east had called for a ban on both local filming and screening of Bollywood popular films after 15 November. The groups allege that the films undermine social and cultural values, especially among the young. (ScreenIndia.com)

Two years after its exposés of corrupt defence deals made it a global name, the online news service www.tehelka.com (*Index* 3/01, 2/02, 4/02, 1/03, 2/03) launched a print weekly on 23 August. Dubbed *Tehelka (The People's Paper)*, it will also concentrate on investigative journalism, said CEO Tarun Tejpal. (*Times of India*)

Activists of the Bharatiya Janata Party (BJP) clashed on 24 August with opponents of the party's campaign against *Ponga Pandit Jamadarin*, a play by **Habib Tanvir**. BJP, Shiv Sena and other Hindu extremist activists claim the play depicts Hinduism in a bad light. (IANS)

Recent publication: *Compounding Injustice: The Government's Failure to Redress Massacres in Gujarat*, HRW, 1 July 2003, pp 70

INDONESIA

On 16 June, Muslim activist **Muhammad Iqbal Siregar** was jailed for five months for defacing a picture of President Megawati Soekarnoputri during an anti-government protest on 15 January. Siregar had been in detention awaiting trial since 24 January. (Article 19)

The body of Indonesian TV (RCTI) cameraman **Mohamad Jamal** was recovered on 17 June from a river in Banda Aceh, capital of strife-torn Aceh. His eyes and mouth had been covered with tape, his hands bound and a rock tied to his neck. Gunmen kidnapped him on 20 May, the day after martial law was imposed in Aceh. (CPJ)

On 3 August, US freelance journalist **William Nessen** was sentenced to 40 days in jail and barred from the country for a year for breaking visa conditions while working as a journalist in Aceh, during which time he spent several weeks with Acehenese rebels. He was released on time already served. (CPJ, IFEX)

On 4 July, **Alif Imam Nurlambang** of private Radio Namlapanha was assaulted in a village in south Aceh by Indonesian security forces. He had been interviewing local residents about a recent exodus of area villagers.

RCTI journalists **Ersa Siregar** and **Ferry Santoro**, their driver and two local guides, who went missing on 29 June, were found to be in detention in a rebel camp in east Aceh's Peureulak District, according to a statement by the rebel Free Aceh Movement (GAM). On 6 July, RCTI representatives met with Siregar and Santoro and confirmed that the journalists were in good health.

Recent publication: *Indonesia: Old laws – new prisoners of conscience*, Amnesty International, July 2003

IRAN

Student protests against the privatisation of Tehran University in June were interpreted by conservatives as heralding demonstrations to mark the anniversary of the brutal suppression of student protests in July 1999. On 12 June, 40 protesting students were injured and ten held by conservative vigilantes. On 27 June, the authorities reported the arrest

of more than 4,000 students, 2,000 of whom remained in custody. Among them were **Abdullah Momeni** and **Mahdi Amin Zadeh**, leading members of the student movement Takim-e-Wadat. (BBC Online)

As tensions deepened state prosecutor Saeed Mortazavi ordered the arrest of journalists trying to report the protests. The first – **Taghi Rahmani** of the weekly *Omid-e-Zangan*, editor **Reza Alijani** and journalist **Hoda Saber** of the monthly *Iran-e-Farda* – were arrested on 14 June. The next day **Mohsen Sazgara**, editor of the www.alliran.net website and the banned reformist daily *Jameh*, and **Amin Bozorgian**, editor of *Golestan-e-Iran*, were both arrested. And on 16 June **Ensafali Hedayat**, of the Tabriz-based newspaper *Salam*, and **Ali Akrami**, of the reformist daily *Nedat Eslahat*, were seized by vigilantes and disappeared until 2 July when their arrest was confirmed by Iranian authorities. (RSF, BBC Online, *Daily Telegraph*)

A joint declaration was issued by 248 reformists on 15 June declaring the right to criticise the conservative leadership. Among the signatories were **Hashim Aghajari**, then under sentence of death for apostasy (*Index* 1/03, 2/03) and **Ayatollah Hossein Ali Montazeri**. On 14 July, the death sentence for apostasy handed to Professor Aghajari was commuted on appeal to four years in prison. (*Financial Times*, BBC Online)

Four reformist MPs began a 48-hour sit-in in the Iranian parliament on 28 June to

protest against the clampdowns. Tehran MPs **Fatemeh Haqiqatjoo**, **Ali Akbar Musavi-Khoeini** and **Maysam Saeedi** and Shiraz city MP **Reza Yousdefian** may face prosecution and ejection from parliament for their defiance. (CNN.com, BBC Online, RSF)

On 23 June, Canadian freelance photojournalist **Zahra Kazemi** was arrested after photographing notorious Evin Prison, which holds most of Iran's reformist prisoners. Kazemi later died on 12 July after falling into a coma due to head wounds received during her interrogation. (*Guardian*)

On 6 July, broadcasts by US-based Persian language satellite TV stations including VOA TV, Pars TV, Channel 1 TV and Azadi TV were jammed by signals reportedly originating from the Iranian embassy in Cuba, which blocked signals from the Telstar-12 satellite relaying the broadcasts. (Iran Press Service, RFE)

Mohammad Mohammadi, father of imprisoned student activist **Manuchehr Mohammadi** and his sister **Simin**, were themselves arrested and held in solitary confinement in Evin Prison on 8 July after they visited the jail to see him. Mohammad Mohammadi suffered a heart attack and was hospitalised after his arrest. (RSF)

After the arrest on 12 July of journalists **Hussein Bastani** and **Wahid Ostad'Pour** of the moderate daily *Yass-e No*, and **Shahram Mohammadi**, director of the weekly *Wakht*, on 15 July Iranian

President Mohammad Khatami ordered his justice and interior ministers to investigate the campaign against journalists and reformists by Iran's hardline judiciary. (Shianews.com, RFE)

On 12 August, Iran's conservative Guardians Council rejected a parliamentary bill on Iranian membership of the Convention on the Elimination of All Forms of Discrimination Against Women, claiming that the bill violated both Islamic law and the Iranian constitution. (RFE/RL)

Authorities have drafted a list of 'immoral' and 'political' sites that 'make fun of religious and political figures in the country'. Internet Service Providers could face court action if they do not comply. **Sina Motallebi**, online journalist and the proprietor of www.rooznegar.com, was arrested over interviews he had posted on his website, and for defending another journalist who ran a cartoon in a newspaper that offended the government. (RFE/RL)

IRAQ

The US-appointed director of the coalition-backed Iraqi Media Network TV, **Ahmad al-Rikabi**, resigned on 8 June amid continuing criticism of the project, which is directed by a US defence contractor, notably its failure to attract Iraqi viewers and meet agreed budget and development targets. (www.arabicnews.com)

The Coalition Provisional Authority (CPA) issued Order No. 14 to Iraq's fledgling media on 10 June making it an offence to broadcast, publish or syndicate material that incites violence against any group or coalition forces or advocates support of the outlawed Baath Party. Journalists who violate the order face one year in prison, or a US$1,000 fine. (CPA)

Iraqi police closed down the offices of *al-Mustaqillah* newspaper on 21 July, arresting the newspaper's office manager. '*Al-Mustaqillah* newspaper has chosen to threaten the basic human rights of Iraqi citizens, especially the right to life and the right to live without fear or threat,' stated a CPA press release, citing the paper's article entitled, 'Death to all spies and those who cooperate with the US; killing them is religious duty.' (AFP)

US troops raided the offices of the Shia newspaper *Sadda-al-Auma* on 12 June after it carried an article urging resistance to the coalition occupation of Iraq in violation of Order No 14. Four employees of the paper were taken into custody, one of whom, **Ali Chiand**, was held bound and hooded for four days while the other staff were interrogated. (Boston Globe)

On 27 July, US troops detained four Turkish journalists – **Yalçin Dogan**, **Özdemir Ince**, **Faruk Balikiçi** and **Ferit Aslan** – and deleted digital camera files. The same day, al-Jazeera cameraman **Nawaf al-Shahwani** was arrested in the northern city of Mosul after filming an attack on US soldiers. His film was confiscated and he and his driver were held until the following evening. (IFJ)

On 28 July, US soldiers in Baghdad assaulted **Kazutaka Sato**, a reporter for the independent news outlet *Japan Press Weekly*, and briefly detained him while he was filming a raid on a house in a search for ousted President Saddam Hussein. (RSF)

On 29 July, US forces reported that Iranian state TV journalists **Said Abu Taleb** and **Soheil Kareemi** had been detained for 'security violations' in Diwaniyah on 1 July while working on a documentary film for Iran's Channel 2 television. No evidence for the alleged offence was provided. (IFJ/CPJ)

On 6 July, British freelance journalist **Richard Wild** was killed by an unknown assassin outside the Iraq National Museum. The following day, **Jeremy Little**, a freelance soundman for the US network NBC, died of complications from injuries received during a grenade attack in Fallujah a week before. (CPJ, *Sydney Morning Herald*, BBC Online)

A Palestinian cameraman working for Reuters, **Mazen Dana**, died of wounds received after he was shot by US troops on 17 August outside Baghdad's Abu Gharib Prison. (RFE/RL)

Recent publications: *Iraq: On whose behalf?*, Amnesty International, June 2003; *The US in trouble in Iraq*, Middle East International, 27 June 2003; *Impetus for Reform?*, Cairo Times, 14–20 August 2003; *Iraq, neither safe nor free*, Middle East International, 11 July 2003; *Hand-picked for government*, Middle East International, 25 July 2003; *A litany of setbacks in Iraq*, Middle East International, 22 August

2003; *Iraq and the Kurds: In the wake of liberation*, KHRP Newsline, Summer 2003; *Covering the Iraq war*, Dangerous Assignments, Summer 2003; *Banipal*, magazine of modern Arabic literature, Summer 2003

IRELAND

Irish Finance Minister Charlie McCreevy set the cost of a request under the Freedom of Information Act (FOI) at €15 and €240 for an appeal against refusal. McCreevy claimed the real costs ran into hundreds of euros; Information Ombudsman Emily O'Reilly said the charges will discourage inquiries. (Irish Times)

Police were reported to be seeking access to journalists' phone records in a bid, it was said, to progress an inquiry into reports that the son of the Minister for Justice had been assaulted in Dublin. (Irish Independent)

A new report on Ireland's defamation laws proposes a statutory press council and a right to claim right to 'reasonable publication' (*Index 3/02*) as a legal defence. (Irish Independent)

Approximately 5,500 people demonstrated in the town of Sligo against the state Broadcasting Commission of Ireland to revoke the licence of local North West Radio and award it to rival Ocean FM. (*Irish Independent, Irish Times*)

ISRAEL

The 'Nationality and Entry into Israel (temporary order)' law passed its first reading in the Knesset on 18 June. It

seeks to prevent Palestinian spouses of Israeli citizens from assuming Israeli citizenship, and from living in Israel with their spouses. (HRW)

UK journalist and teacher **Sean O'Muireagáin** was arrested on 12 July by Israeli security forces and wrongly accused of being a member of the IRA training Palestinian militants. O'Muireagáin, who was deported, was on an exchange trip run by the Ireland–Palestine Solidarity Movement. (BBC Online)

ITALY

Journalists and press workers called a strike in June to protest against increasing government influence over the national media following the resignation of **Ferrucio de Bortoli**, editor of the daily newspaper *Il Corriere della Sera*, a critic of media magnate and Prime Minister Silvio Berlusconi's government. (IFJ)

Pending bills before parliament aim to ease the rights of Italian MPs to transfer business interests to family or associates without risking censure for conflict of interest, and to ease rules on cross-ownership of media and controls on advertising volume. Both would, if passed, significantly benefit Berlusconi's business operations, say media rights groups. (RSF)

JAPAN

It was reported on 31 July that the Post and Telecommunications Ministry is planning a ratings system for web pages accessible from mobile phones. Manufacturers could be required to install filters

which could then block access to sites deemed unsuitable for minors. (www.asahi.com)

JORDAN

The Jordanian parliamentary elections on 17 June saw the number of seats increased from 80 to 110, the voting age reduced by one year to 18, and six seats reserved for women. A record 54 female candidates included the first Bedouin woman candidate **Fayza Nueim**. (*Times*, BBC Online)

KAZAKHSTAN

On 2 June, editor-in-chief **Ermurat Bapi** of the opposition paper *SolDat* resigned after the newspaper was fined an unpayable US$350,000 for alleged tax evasion in a judicial ruling characterised as 'questionable' by media rights groups. (RFE/RL)

On 19 June, lawyers for jailed journalist **Sergei Duvanov** said the Almaty Oblast Court had refused to review the case against their client, sentenced in January to three and a half years' imprisonment for statutory rape. (RFE/RL)

On 21 August, president Nursultan Nazarbaev called upon the media to report events objectively and responsibly, act to bring society together, preserve harmony among ethnic groups and mobilise the people behind his leadership's programmes to raise living standards. (RFE/RL)

KYRGYZSTAN

On 11 June , the opposition Russian-language newspaper

Moya Stolitsa was forced to close under the weight of punitive fines for libel suits brought by state employees. Staff planned to start a new paper called *Advokat* to continue their independent journalism. (RFE/RL, RSF, Freedom House)

An international printing house funded by the US NGO Freedom House was scheduled to open at the end of October 2003 to serve the needs of the independent and state press in Kyrgyzstan and across Central Asia. (CJES, IRIN)

Bekmamat Tagaev, editor of the newspaper *Osh sadosi*, said his staff would be allowed to moonlight in other jobs from 30 August onwards, to 'keep qualified journalists in the profession'. (CJES)

KUWAIT

Kuwaiti Information Minister Ahmed Fahad al-Ahmed al-Sabah granted licences to three new satellite TV stations to broadcast from Kuwait on 3 July. The stations must comply with local regulations, including a ban on broadcasts seen to threaten Kuwait's relations with other Arab states. (www.arabic news.com)

As male Kuwaitis went to the polls on 5 July to elect representatives to the semi-parliamentary Ummah council, Kuwaiti women denied the right to vote held a parallel mock election on 5 July in protest. (www.arabnews.com)

On 7 August, over 50 Kuwaiti intellectuals, businessmen and political figures petitioned for changes to Kuwait's hitherto unamended 1962 constitution, to recognise political pluralism, the rights of women and lower the voting age from the present 21 years. (www.arab news.com)

LAOS

In June, Belgian reporter **Thierry Falise** and French cameraman **Vincent Reynaut** were arrested while reporting clashes between Hmong rebels and the armed forces. On 30 June, both men and their translator **Naw Karl Mua** were sentenced to 15 years in prison on unspecified charges but then released on 9 July. (RSF, CPJ)

LEBANON

The studios of Lebanon's Future TV, owned by Prime Minister **Rafiq Hariri**, were damaged in a rocket attack on 15 June. (IFEX)

Human rights activist and lawyer **Muhamed Mugraby** was arrested on 8 August on the charge of 'impersonating a lawyer', which carries a sentence of between six months' and three years' imprisonment. It was the latest attempt by the Lebanese authorities to censure his activities. (HRW)

LESOTHO

Radio MoAfrika, owned by veteran dissident **Candi Ratabane Ramainoane**, shut down for two days in June to protest against outstanding punitive fines and compensation orders totalling 105,000 maloti (US$14,250), awarded against the station in December 2002 in a defamation case brought by MP Moeketsi Sello. (MISA)

On 15 and 16 July local media were reportedly denied access to cover parts of the visit of Britain's Princess Anne to Save the Children and Skillshare International charity programmes, even though South African media were allowed in. (MISA)

On 23 July, the weekly *Mohahlaula* was ordered to pay 200,000 maloti (US$27,100) in damages in a case brought on behalf of trade and Industry Minister Mpho Malie over a story alleging that his department had allowed selected businessmen to build factories that did not meet legal standards. (MISA)

LIBERIA

Broadcasting chief official Emmanuel DS Todo closed down six amateur radio broadcasters alleging that their 'motives . . . were not clear'. The Association of Amateur Radio Stations (AARS) has appealed against the decision, claiming that all were officially registered. (MISA)

Lyndon Ponnie, former editor of the *Concord Times*, was attacked and robbed at home on 12 June by armed men, the same day **Bobby Tapson** and **Bill Jarkloh** of the *News* and **Joe Watson** of LBS radio were briefly abducted by LURD rebels. A week before, another *News* reporter, **Stanley McGill**, had also been attacked. (MISA)

Sygma Corpis photographer **Patrick Robert** was seriously wounded in the chest and arm on 19 July during clashes between government and rebel forces. Two days later journalist **Tom Mas-**

land of *Newsweek* was injured in crossfire in the capital Monrovia. (RSF, www.all africa.com)

LIBYA

On 24 July, **Reporters sans Frontières** had its consultative status with the United Nations Commission on Human Rights suspended on July 24 for one year at the request of Cuba, after RSF activists protested against the appointment of Libya as the commission's chair. (BBC online)

MALAWI

On 2 June, **Gen. Evans Namanja**, the National broadcasting chief, banned community radio stations from transmitting news bulletins, limiting news programming to the official Malawi Broadcasting Corporation and Television Malawi. (MISA)

After the 21–22 June edition of the *Weekend Nation* commented on the food supplied at President Bakili Muluzi's public speeches, the president warned of unspecified action if the media did not stop 'rubbing their nose' into his business. On 21 July, one of Muluzi's United Democratic Front (UDF) officials warned the *Nation* against covering the party's August convention. *Nation* photojournalist **Daniel Nyirenda** was beaten up and robbed, apparently by UDF supporters, at a party meeting on 7 July. (MISA)

MALAYSIA

Journalist and film-maker **Hishamuddin Rais**, among six Reformasi ('Reform')

activists sentenced in June 2001, was transferred from Kamunting Detention Centre on 1 June. After bail hearings on several outstanding charges, including illegal assembly, Rais was eventually freed on 4 June. (WiPC)

A Malaysian teenager was given a forced haircut by Muslim authorities who deemed his punk-style 'Mohican' un-Islamic. It was reported on 23 August that the unnamed 17-year-old – described as a high school dropout – was caught by the Islamic Development Unit of Kota Baru, Kelantan, a northeastern state controlled by the Islamic political party PAS. (BBC Online)

Recent publication: *Memorandum on Malaysian Sedition Act 1948,* Article 19, 29 July 2003

MALDIVES

Ibrahim Luthfee (*Index* 2/02, 4/02, 2/03), jailed for life in July 2002 for publishing the *Sandhaanu* e-mail bulletin, escaped his police escort on 24 May while in Sri Lanka for medical treatment. The two National Security Service officers who escorted Luthfee to Sri Lanka were jailed on their return home. (AI)

On 20 June, Luthfee's *Sandhaanu* colleagues **Mohamed Zaki** and **Ahmed Ibrahim Didi**, also jailed for life, were taken away for interrogation in the wake of his escape. Amnesty feared that the two were tortured or ill-treated. (www.maldivesculture.com, AI)

Mohamed Nasheed (*Index* 2/02, 3/02, 4/02, 1/03, 3/03), historian, activist and

former reformist politician, continues to be harassed by the government. On 13 June, two days after its publication, all copies of the book *Dhandikoshi*, a history of the capital city's Dhandikoshi clan, were confiscated and the permit for its publication was revoked. (www.maldives culture.com)

On 3 July, journalist **Adam Haleem** of the daily *Haveeru* and its Dhivehi-language magazine *Huvaas*, was placed under indefinite house arrest. The order is linked to a story by Haleem alleging that Adam Saeed, chief of the archipelago island of Dhiddhoo, had illegally buried a human foetus. (www.maldivesculture.com)

Recent publication: *Republic of Maldives: Repression of peaceful political opposition*, AI, 30 July 2003, 20 pp

MAURITANIA

On 1 June, the Islamist weekly *Raya* was banned and its offices closed. The newspaper had previously been told to stop publishing in early May and editor-in-chief **Ahmedou Ould Mohamedou** and the chairman of the newspaper's board, **Mohamed Mahmoud Ould Mohamed**, fled to Belgium after the ban was announced. (RSF)

In early June, just before an attempted coup later blamed on Islamists, the government declared mosques to be 'public institutions' and claimed powers to appoint imams and regulate the content of their sermons. On 25 August, 41 Islamist leaders and activists seized during an April–May sweep were freed on bail. (AI, IRIN, arabicnews.com)

The 24 July edition of the newspaper *Le Rénovateur* was banned from distribution, said managing editor **Cheikh Tijane Dia**, due to an article about the fall of the national currency, the ouguiya, on the black market in the capital, Nouakchott. (RSF)

The 20 August issue of the weekly *Le Calame* newspaper was impounded by officials, apparently in reaction to an interview with presidential candidate **Ahmed Ould Daddah**. *Le Calame* has been seized 32 times by the Ministry of Interior and was suspended for three months in 1999. (Media Foundation for West Africa)

MEXICO

State Prosecutor Pericles Namorado Urrutia resisted calls to investigate the disappearance of journalist **Jesus Mejía Lechuga** of Radio MS-Noticias in Martínez de la Torre on 12 July, after interviewing Alfonso Alegretti, an opposition Institutional Revolutionary Party (PRI) local councillor, despite appeals from international media groups. Mejía had recently accused PRI federal deputy Guillermo Zorilla Pérez of links to drug cartels. Urrutia alleged Mejía had gone on the run after stealing a car. (WAN, RSF)

MOROCCO

Ali Lmrabet (*Index* 3/03), editor of the now-banned satirical weeklies *Demain* and *Douman*, had his sentence reduced from four to three years on appeal on 17 June.

Lmrabet, a diabetic with a heart condition, ended his hunger strike on 23 June after seven weeks. The end of the fast was announced by the king's cousin, Prince Moulay Hicham, who had apparently persuaded Lmrabet that he could better serve the cause of freedom alive than dead. (RSF, BBC, El Mundo)

On 11 July, **Mustapha Alaoui**, managing editor of the Arabic-language weekly *al-Ousboue*, was given a one-year suspended prison term and a fine of US$53 for publishing a letter from a hitherto unknown group on 16 May claiming responsibility for bombings in Casablanca. He was convicted of 'hiding a document likely to help in an ongoing investigation on offences' and 'publishing wrong information likely to disturb public order'. The paper was banned for three months. (RSF, www.arabicnews.com)

Three journalists were sentenced on 4 August to prison terms ranging from one to three years for 'incitement to violence'. **Mohammed el Hourd**, managing editor of the weekly *Asharq*, based in the north-eastern city of Oujda, was sentenced to three years, while editor-in-chief **Abdelmajid Ben Tahar** and managing editor **Mustapha Kechnini** of another Oujda-based weekly, *al-Hayat al-Maghribia*, were both sentenced to one year. The three were convicted for publishing a statement by an Islamist, **Zakkaria Boughrara**, himself tried alongside the journalists, praising the actions of the 'jihad movement in Morocco'. (RSF)

NEPAL

On 22 May, journalists **Murari Kumar Sharma** and **Uttam Hamal**, who had worked for state-owned Radio Nepal for eight years, were dismissed on the order of Information and Communications Minister Ramesh Nath Pandey for broadcasting reports about peaceful protest by five opposition parties. (RSF)

On 26 June, Nepal's National Union of Journalists, backed by the International Federation of Journalists, made presentations to Thakma KC, widow of journalist-poet **Krishna Sen** (*Index* 4/99, 3/01, 4/02, 3/03), editor of the weekly *Janadesh*, missing presumed killed while detained by the army, and Rita Sharma, widow of **Navraj Sharma**, editor of *Kadam Saptahik*, abducted and killed by Maoist rebels. The union gave both US$5,000 from a support fund, in part to shame the government into recognising their plight and the plight of others. (IPS)

It was reported on 19 August that auxiliary health worker **Bhanubhakta Sanjyal** had been transferred to a new posting in punishment for giving information to reporters covering an outbreak of the respiratory disease ARI earlier this year that claimed the lives of more than two dozen people. Sanjyal's employers in Kalikot district had attempted to claim that the disease had not affected the area. (Kathmandu Post)

Journalist and teacher **Gyanendra Khadka** was dragged from a village school, tied to a post and had his throat cut

DIE LAUGHING

ALI LMRABET

For almost a week I have been laid out in bed in the main ward on the sixth floor of the Avicenne de Rabat hospital, which serves as a place of seclusion for the sick inmates of Salé Prison. My legs no longer wish to support me. I have entered the seventh week of my hunger strike and I am aware that, inexorably and little by little, the other parts of my body will be invaded by this invisible illness which prevents you from doing just what you fancy with your limbs.

As the only activity permitted to me is reading, I happily take advantage by discreetly flicking through the occasional newspapers that light up my solitude. And often, I must admit, I really have to laugh, even if it seems out of place at this dramatic time.

I had to laugh when I read that our information minister, the ex-communist Nabil Benabdallah, during an official visit to Paris, declared publicly that I was not a 'journalist', rather a 'slanderer' who had scores to settle with the regime. I laughed because my journalist's permit for 2003 is signed by a certain information minister of the name of Nabil Benabdallah. I laughed at the memory: 6 June, outside the appeal court in Casablanca, the person being prosecuted by an ex-chief of police, for libel among other things, was none other than Nabil Benabdallah.

But the Right Honourable Minister was not altogether wrong when he said that I was not a journalist in the way this regime understands the term: an information tradesman accustomed to self-censorship, servility, the sacred 'yes, yes', and raised within the dogma of the verb 'compromise', the key word that will keep you out of trouble, safe from police surveillance, telephoned warnings, direct threats and, if that is not enough for you, a visit from the god called *the tax inspector*! And
if you do not learn your lesson, expect repeated legal action. But not trials for defamation or 'libel' as in the case of our minister, no . . . you will be accused of weightier crimes: 'disturbing public order', 'insulting the king', 'attacking the kingdom's territorial integrity' or 'attacking the monarchy'.

I laugh on the inside, well, inside the sheets – I am in a hospital bed after all – when I recall the reaction of one of our cartoonists when he read the official accusation: 'Is that really about us?' he enquired of me, worried. Incredible but true; 'that' was really about us. As if a few caricatures and humorous articles (printed in two satirical publications 'in business' thanks to the devotion of a skeleton crew) had the power to shake the regime that has reigned over the lives and souls of Moroccans for three and a half centuries.

I laugh when I remember the tone taken by the crown prosecutor in demanding the maximum penalty against me: 'The defendant Lmrabet deserves to feel the full force of the law upon him because he has committed a crime of extreme gravity.' It's true. What I did was very grave. I criminally poked fun at our good old regime. Irresponsibly, I mocked the hypocritical and opportunistic ways of our political class. Lastly, and perhaps most unforgivably, using caricatures I deformed the faces of our political leaders. I am guilty of having introduced satire and humorous journalism into a society that was in great need of it; a society sick of crying over its misfortunes and that found in my newspapers the chance to take revenge on the political class. Through laughter. Not by planting a bomb or by insulting anyone.

For those who lead us, these caricatures and photomontages are insults and slanders that deform their 'reality': the repressive system that they wish to impose on 30 million Moroccans. This regime does not accept humour as a peaceful form of expression; it has made the monumental mistake of believing that two amusing satirical publications were in fact a political party of the opposition. As if *Demain* and *Douman* magazines were one day going to give birth to a party of Laughter and Progress, a popular party which would steal their thunder.

That's it! I cannot go any further because my body calls me to order. My body does not joke. *He* points out that I do not have the strength to make a sustained physical effort and write with style, any style at all, without waking the invisible illness that prevents you from doing just what you fancy with your limbs.

In the end, I am left with a certainty, my certainty: that as long as I am conscious, I will not let the regime make an example of me in order to stifle the independent Moroccan press. As long as the invisible illness has not invaded my brain, I will continue to laugh at those who have sent me down because they believe I am a political party. ❑

Ali Lmrabet, *editor of the banned satirical weeklies* Demain *and* Douman

First published as 'Mourir de Rire' in Le Monde, *24 June 2003*
Translated by James Badcock

by Nepalese Maoist rebels on 7 September. Khadka, 36, who worked for the government news agency Rastriya Samachar Samiti (RSS) was well known for his articles in many national and local papers. (RSF)

NIGER

Around 50 Niamey University students arrived at the studios of Radio Télévision Ténéré following the broadcast of a report showing them selling stolen boxes of sardines. A number of people were assaulted and two vehicles vandalised in the ensuing violence. (RSF)

NIGERIA

State Security Service officials purchased the entire print run of 30 June edition of *Tell* magazine in a bid to block a story headlined 'Scandal in Aso Rock'. It alleged irregularities in the award of contracts for the supply of broadcast equipment for the All African Games and criticised the government of President Olusegun Obasanjo. The paper simply reprinted the article in the next two issues. (RSF, www.allafrica. com)

A draft code of 'General Conduct' for reporters covering the Nigerian National Assembly would require them to confirm 'sensitive information' with assembly officials, eschew use of leaked official documents and have their compliance with the code 'reviewed' before their annual accreditation is renewed. (IFJ, MRA)

Riot police stormed a workers rally in Abuja on 1 July, during the second day of a national strike over a government hike in fuel prices, beating journalists and union workers with whips and rifle butts. At least three journalists, including AP photographer **George Osodi**, were injured in the attack, AP reported. Osodi suffered cuts and bruises on his body, arms and face, and had his camera smashed. Police also assaulted two journalists from the daily *Vanguard*, **Rotimi Ajayi** and **Funmi Komolafe**, as they tried to leave the rally. (RSF)

The influential Islamic body Jama'atul Nasril Islam has reiterated the validity of a fatwa calling for the death of fashion journalist **Isioma Daniel** for an allegedly blasphemous article about the Miss World beauty pageant in 2002. (*Daily Independent*, IPC)

The Nigerian Union of Journalists is to contest the country's granting of asylum to Liberian President Charles Taylor in Nigeria's high court, urging that Taylor must answer charges of genocide and involvement in the killing of two Nigerian journalists, **Kenneth Ilodibe** and **Tayo Awotusin**. (www. allafrica.com)

Journalist **Ben Adaji** of *News* magazine was arrested and remanded in custody on 22 July after writing a report linking Taraba State Police Commissioner Nwachukwu Egbochukwu to corruption and abuse of prisoners' rights. Police also stormed the magazine's offices and demanded to see the editor. (MISA, RSF, www.allafrica.com)

Recent publication: *Obasanjo's new term*, West Africa, 9–15 June 2003

OMAN

Oman became the first member state of the Arab League to recognise the transitional Iraqi Council by notifying the Arab League on 7 August of its support of a proposal that the Iraqi Council assume Iraq's seat. (www.arabic news.com)

PAKISTAN

On 30 May, the government blocked local access to the Washington-based *South Asia Tribune News* website run by the exiled former editor of the *News*, **Shaheen Sehbai**. Sehbai is a major critic of rights abuses and corruption by the military government. (RSF)

Former *Frontier Post* subeditor **Munawar Mohsin** (*Index 2/01*) was jailed for life and fined 50,000 rupees (US$900) on 8 July for blaspheming the Prophet Mohammed by the publication of a letter titled 'Why Muslims Hate Jews' in January 2001. Former news editor **Aftab Ahmed** and computer operator **Wajeehul Hassan** were acquitted of the same charge. **Mahmood Shah Afridi**, the *Post*'s former editor, has been in hiding since the letter sparked violent protests. (RSF, CPJ, *Times*)

English lecturer Shahbaz Arif of Lahore's Punjab University called for the dropping of books he considered offensive to Islamists, according to a 10 July report. Among the books considered 'vulgar' by Arif for having too much sexual content were Alexander Pope's *The Rape of the Lock*, Ernest Hemingway's *The Sun Also Rises* and

Jonathan Swift's *Gulliver's Travels.* (*Guardian*)

The 28 July issue of *Newsweek* magazine was seized by Pakistani customs over an article headlined 'Challenging the Qur'an' that examines the theory of a German linguist that the Muslim holy book may have originally been written in Aramaic instead of Arabic. *Newsweek*'s local reporter in Peshawar fled the city in fear of reprisals after the magazine appeared. The magazine was also banned in Bangladesh. (RSF, *Newsweek*)

On 24 August, cable operators launched a week-long strike to protest against the refusal of state broadcast regulators to lift a ban on relaying Indian entertainment channels. Pakistani cable operators say 98 per cent of its viewers want to watch Indian-produced Urdu-language entertainment channels. (AFP, NDTV.com)

The media should project the issues being faced by the poor so that people with authority can make efforts to solve these problems, according to speakers at a workshop in the Pakistani city of Karachi in September. During the international workshop on 'Culture for Social Change', the participants said the commercial media should focus on the poor even if they were not the consumers and targets of its advertisers. (*Dawn*, EJC)

PALESTINE

On 5 August, 43 international solidarity movement activists from 11 countries – Canada, Denmark, France, Ireland, Israel, Italy, Japan, Palestine, Sweden, the UK and the US

– were detained while they attempted to block the Israeli Defence forces from demolishing a Palestinian family's home to make way for the separation wall cutting off the West Bank from Israel. (ISM)

Recent publications: *Israel and the Occupied Territories*, Amnesty International (4 July 2003); *Bush shrinks before Sharon*, Middle East International (8 August 2003)

PANAMA

On 7 August, journalists **Marcel Chéry** and **Gustavo Aparicio** of *El Panamá América* were jailed for a year for 'insulting' former interior and justice minister Winston Spadafora in a 2001 report. The independence of trial judge Secundino Mendieta was questioned, as Spadafora is now his superior in the judiciary.

PERU

On 25 June, journalist **Néstor Puicón** of Radio Señorial in Huancayo city, who has led an on-air campaign for an inquiry into municipal corruption, sought police protection after the kidnapping of his 23-year-old daughter and a series of telephone threats. (IPYS)

Channel 2 TV broadcast a recording on 18 August of a routine phone conversation between President Alejandro Toledo and an adviser. Journalist **Cesar Hildebrandt** said he aimed to highlight the security breach, but refused to reveal the source of the tape. Toledo now threatens legal action. (*Correo/El Comercio*)

PHILIPPINES

Reynaldo Cortes, a 'block-timer' (a broadcaster who rents airtime from a local station) at DYDD Bantay Radyo, was shot in the groin while on air in the studio. Cortes blames customs officers, the subject of a number of his critical comment pieces. (CMFR/IFEX)

Bonifacio Gregorio of the weekly *Dyaryo Banat* ('Attack Newspaper') was shot dead on 8 July in front of his home in the city of La Paz, Tarlac. He was a strong public critic of alleged corruption in the administration of La Paz mayor, Dionisio Manuel. (CMFR/IFEX)

Daily Tribune editor-in-chief **Ninez Cacho-Olivares** was arrested on 4 August on 19 charges of criminal defamation filed by President Arroyo's personal lawyer, Arthur 'Pancho' Villaraza. He and other presidential associates had been the subject of a *Tribune* investigation into a multimillion-dollar bribes scandal. It is the first time a newspaper editor has been arrested since democracy was restored in 1986. (RSF)

On 19 August, two gunmen shot dead radio journalist **Noel Villarante** in the city of Santa Cruz, south-east of Manila. His murder was linked to his on-air criticism of local corruption and gambling syndicates. (RSF/IFEX)

POLAND

In steps condemned as deliberate harassment, **Grzegorz Gauden**, president, and **Elzbieta Ponikio**, vice-president of the board of the

Presspublica media group, were interrogated by police on 16 June in an apparent bid to reopen an old and discredited charge of illegal payments to a former employee. (IPI)

PORTUGAL

The Portuguese government has pledged to step up its support for the mass media in Portuguese-speaking Africa – Mozambique, Angola, Guinea-Bissau, Cape Verde and São Tomé & Príncipe. Secretary of State Domingos Jeronimo said the focus of co-operation should shift from financial aid to staff training, the sharing of content and the development of co-productions. He said that simply providing funding had 'not always been effective'. (RN)

ROMANIA

President Ion Iliescu accused the Israeli daily Ha'aretz of 'ill will' by publishing an interview with him without submitting the text for his advance approval. It included references to the Holocaust that aroused Israeli anger; Iliescu said the paper's actions had damaged their countries' relations. (RFE, RN)

RUSSIA

On 18 June, the Russian parliament amended the law to allow the Media Ministry and federal and regional electoral commissions to close media deemed responsible for 'biased' reports during the forthcoming December 2003 parliamentary and February 2004 presidential elections. Election commission chief Aleksandr Veshnyakov said

the aim was to tackle the problem of candidates bribing journalists to write favourable articles. (CPJ)

On 21 June, the Media Ministry closed down TVS – the last major independent broadcaster in Russia and a strong critic of the Kremlin – replacing it with a state-run sports channel. Paralysed for months by a battle with pro-government shareholders, this is the third time that TVS editor-in-chief **Yevgenii Kiselyov** and his team of hard-hitting independent journalists have been pulled off the air by government officials and Kremlin allies. (CPJ)

Yurii Shchekochikhin, chief deputy editor of *Novaya Gazeta*, and member of the State Duma, died during the night of 2/3 July. According to the www.gazeta.ru website, the official cause of death was an 'acute allergic reaction'. But the deputy speaker of the Duma called for an inquiry into what he termed 'this death, this strange, sudden illness'. Shchekochikhin had a reputation for investigative journalism, particularly for unmasking corruption in the Moscow City Council and the Russian military forces in Chechnya. He had recently returned from Ryazan, where he had been investigating customs duties fraud.

On 9 July, officials denied a passport to journalist **Grigorii Pasko**, released from prison in January after serving more than two years of a five-year treason sentence for reporting on Russian navy nuclear dumping in the Sea of Japan. (CPJ/IFEX)

Alikhan Gulyev, a freelancer for TV Tsenter and *Kommersant* daily newspaper, was shot dead on 18 July outside his Moscow apartment. He was previously based in Ingushetia, where in the run-up to April 2002 polls, he successfully brought charges of electoral abuses against Ingushetian Interior Minister Khamsat Gutseryev, an ally of former Ingushetian President Ruslan Aushev. (RSF/IFEX)

On 15 August, **German Galkin**, publisher of *Rabochaya Gazeta*, was sentenced to a year in a labour camp for 'insulting' two vice-governors of the Chelyabinsk region in reports alleging corruption and abuse of authority. The hearings were closed to the press and the paper warned against analysing the case in its pages. (GDF)

Russian Union of Journalists General Secretary **Igor Yakovenko** reported on 21 August that 17 national newspapers and magazines in the Federation republic of Bashkortostan had been subject to direct censorship during May and July and the opposition radio station Retro-Ufa stripped of its licence. (*Nezavisimaya Gazeta*)

Russian media mogul **Boris Berezovskii** was granted political asylum in the UK on 10 September. Moscow seeks his extradition to face charges of fraud; Berezovskii says he is being victimised for his political beliefs. He still owns three newspapers and a television station. Berezovskii applied for asylum in the UK earlier this year, but was rejected. (BBC)

The Kremlin introduced a draconian election law to stem the slurs which marred past elections. The September decree places a blanket ban during campaigning on forecasting results and requires candidates to be given equal coverage – a practical impossibility between 44 parties. Media can be shut during the campaign after two warnings. One St Petersburg paper protested against the rulings by leaving its front page blank while filling its inside pages with articles about a fictional election in a distant land – in reality the St Petersburg vote, but with candidates' names changed. (*Guardian*)

SAUDI ARABIA

Editor **Jamal Khashoggi** of *al-Watan* was dismissed on 27 May on orders of the Saudi Information Ministry after prominent cleric Abdullah bin abd al-Jebrein issued a fatwa against the relatively liberal paper, urging Saudis to boycott it. (*Guardian*)

A Saudi TV channel broke new ground on 16 July with a debate entitled 'Saudi women speak out'. Eight women discussed prohibitions on driving, limitations on career options and the requirement that a family member accompany them while in public. (*Telegraph*)

The Saudi Information Ministry banned writer **Hussein Shobokshi** from writing a weekly column for the daily *Okaz*. No specific reason was given, but on 1 July Shobokshi's columm discussed issues including women's rights and democratisation. (Reuters)

SENEGAL

Abdou Latif Coulibaly, author and journalist with Sud FM, has begun receiving death threats since publishing a book critical of President Abdoulaye Wade, blaming his party supporters and instituting legal action against the party. (RSF)

SERBIA

The European Agency for Reconstruction has frozen a €300,000 grant to the country's new Broadcast Agency Council regulators, citing 'certain flaws' in the process of selecting board members. In April, some members resigned in protest at the choice of representative for Kosovo, among other issues. (B92)

Recent publications: *Memorandum on the draft Law on Free Access to Information of Public Importance*, Article 19, 14 July 2003

SOMALIA

Journalists **Abdurahman Mohamed Hudeyfi** and **Hussein Mohamed Gheedi** of local Banadir Radio were detained by Mogadishu police on 30 June. The seizures followed the station's reports on state corruption and illegal land purchases by private businessmen. (RSF)

SPAIN

A priest has claimed that he has been forced out of his position as a result of his opposition to the violent tactics of the Basque separatist group ETA, and his criticism of the Basque Nationalist Party. **Father Jaime Larri-naga**, the priest in the Basque village of Maruri, has accepted an armed bodyguard after accusing pro-nationalist political parties of a secret alliance with the ETA armed militias. He claims many Basques are too frightened of ETA to publicly criticise them. (*Guardian*)

Three Basque journalists had their detentions extended by six months and the ban on their Basque-language newspaper *Euskaldunon Egunkaria* renewed (*Index* 3/03). The state has claimed they and the paper were covertly supporting ETA activities. (WiPC, PEN)

Police in the southern Spanish city of Granada arrested al-Jazeera TV journalist **Tayseer Alouni**, a Syrian-born Spanish citizen, on suspicion of links to Islamic militants on 5 September, on orders of controversial Spanish prosecuting judge Baltasar Garzon. Alouni was well known for his work in Afghanistan during the US-led war there and one of the few reporters to interview Osama bin Laden. AP reported police sources as saying that Alouni was suspected of giving support to Edin Barakat Yarkas, also known as Abu Dahdah, arrested in Spain in November 2001 on suspicion of leading an Islamist fundamentalist cell in the country. (AP, BBC Online)

SRI LANKA

The offices of the *Lakmina* newspaper were set afire on 7 June by a gang armed with firebombs. Publisher **Ajith Gallage**, a front bench member of the opposition People's Alliance (PA), has broken links with the paper after death threats and a dispute with the company over a claimed debt of US$1,000,000. (*Sunday Times*)

Five people, including two policemen, were sentenced to death on 2 July for their role in the massacre of 27 suspected Tamil Tiger (LTTE) rebels at the Bindunuwewa detention centre in October 2000 (*Index* 1/01, 3/02). The court commuted the sentences to life imprisonment because of a moratorium on the death penalty. (Reuters)

The *Sunday Leader* reported on 27 July that Fisheries Minister Mahinda Wijesekera had threatened to kill **Lasantha Wickrematunga** (*Index* 2/95, 5/98, 2/00, 6/00), the paper's editor, in front of witnesses, including Water Management Minister Lakshman Seneviratne, who confirmed the incident to Reporters sans Frontières. Wijesekera allegedly boasted of his part in the killing of three journalists, including that of **Rohan Kumara** (*Index* 6/99, 2/00, 1/02) in 1999. (*Sunday Leader, RSF, AP*)

The Supreme Court ruled on 5 August that trying to convert another person to a different faith would violate freedom of conscience. The ruling focused on a draft law that senior Buddhists said would allow Christians to challenge the principal role given Buddhism in Sri Lankan society under the constitution. (*Sunday Times*)

A delivery truck run by *Thinamurasu*, a Tamil-language weekly (*Index* 4/02), was ambushed on 7 August by 50 Tamil Tiger rebels near the eastern city of Batticaloa. All 5,000 copies of the paper were taken from the truck and burned. (RSF)

On 7 August Amnesty International and Human Rights Watch jointly cited 'convincing evidence' that the LTTE was behind a series of 22 targeted assassinations of Tamil civilian political rivals since the ceasefire agreement between the Tigers and the government in February 2002.(AI, HRW)

Sugath Ranasinghe, the last remaining suspect in the January 2000 murder of Tamil political leader **Kumar Ponnambalam** (*Index* 2/00), was himself shot dead as he returned from court on 20 August. According to reports, Ranasinghe had recently tried to confess to a part in Ponnambalam's murder. Another suspect in the murder case, **Moratu Saman**, was shot dead on 18 May. (*Sunday Leader*)

Brigadier Rajitha De Silva, 23-3rd Brigade Commander in Batticaloa, barred filming inside Weber Stadium on 22 August. The stadium lies within an army-designated security zone. Five days before local journalist **T Vethanayagam** had been interrogated by soldiers after trying to photograph a football game at the stadium. (www.tamilnet.com)

Recent publications: *Sri Lanka: Political Killings During the Ceasefire*, HRW, 7 August 2003, 6 pp; *Open letter to Liberation Tigers of Tamil Eelam (LTTE)*, Sri Lanka Monitoring Mission (SLMM); *Sri Lankan Police concerning recent politically motivated killings and abductions in Sri Lanka*, AI, 12 August 2003, 4 pp; *Contempt of Court in Sri Lanka – Recommendations for Codification*, Article 19, 10 September 2003

SUDAN

Reporters sans Frontières Sudan correspondent **Faisal el-Bagir** was interrogated by security police on 8 June, on return from an Athens conference to discuss the future of the Iraqi media. The police quizzed him on his work for RSF, the Sudan Organisation Against Torture and the Khartoum Centre for Human Rights. (RSF)

The English-language *Khartoum Monitor* was closed by a 12 July court order citing a 2001 interview with **Santino Deng**, adviser to the regional government of Northern Bhar el-Ghazal state. Deng had said Muslim Arab clans were trading southern Sudanese women and children as slaves. Editor **Nhial Bol** and the interviewer were fined SP 400,000 (US$1,500) in May 2002 for the report. (CPJ, HRW)

Police seized all copies of the independent daily *al-Sahafa* on 29 July and detained reporter **Youssef al-Bashir Musa** over a 28 July article reporting the death of at least ten students in a bus crash on the way to an army camp. Some linked the order an article criticising a news blackout on talks between the government in Khartoum and rebels. (RSF, IFEX)

Recent publication: *Sudan: Empty promises?*, Amnesty International, July 2003

SWAZILAND

On 29 July, the government tightened the country's Secrecy Act, empowering it to ban any information the state declares 'secret' with sentences of up to five years in jail and fines of up to R25,000 (US$3,400) for transgressors. (MISA)

SWITZERLAND

The International Federation of Journalists criticised Swiss police tactics at the Group of Eight richest nations' summit in Evian in June. British photographer **Guy Smallman** was seriously injured by a stun grenade fired by riot police. (IFJ)

SYRIA

Fayiq el-Yusif's prize for winning a website design contest, a holiday in Turkmenistan, was withdrawn after organisers discovered he was the son of well-known Kurdish poet and journalist **Ibrahim El-Yusif**, a critic of discrimination against Syrian Kurds, it was reported on 29 June. (www.kurdishmedia.com)

There were new fears for the health of opposition MP **Mohamad Ma'mun' al-Homsi** (*Index* 1/02, 3/02), jailed since August 2001 on charges of seeking to illegally change the constitution and disrupt national unity. He was reported to have been hospitalised in July after a heart attack. (www.arabicnews.com)

TAJIKISTAN

The Committee to Protect Journalists has sent letters to Tajikistan deputy prosecutor-general Zizmat Tmomov and parliament chairman Mahmadsaid Ubaidulloyev with a list of 29 journalists murdered during and after Tajikistan's 1992–7 civil war and asked for more details about these cases. During a meeting on 21 July, Tmomov had agreed to receive the letter and respond within 30 days of its receipt. (CPJ)

The drive against the banned religious party Hezb-e-Tahrir in Soghd province, northern Tajikistan, continues. On 4 July, a large underground printing house was closed down. Computers and photocopying machines were impounded and more than 500 books and leaflets calling for civil disobedience and the establishment of a single Islamic state in Central Asia were seized. (Eurasianet)

OSCE officials have organised a series of human rights film showings in the cities of Kulyab and Nurek, the first time that cinemas have opened in southern Tajikistan in the ten years since the break-up of the Soviet Union. (RFE/RL)

TANZANIA

Ali Nabwa, veteran editor of the weekly independent newspaper *Dira*, has been ordered to reapply for citizenship and had his passport confiscated on 24 June. A Comoros citizen with dual Tanzanian nationality, Nabwa was granted a three-month permit and temporary passport. (MISA)

TOGO

Journalists **Dimas Dzikodo** and **Philip Evegnon** of *l'Evénement* and **Colombo Kpakpabia** of *Nouvel Echo* were arrested on 14 and 15 June and charged with 'attempting to publish false information and to disturb public order'. Evegnon and Kpakpabia were acquitted of all charges on 22 July. Dzikodo was found guilty but released two days later under a suspended 12-month sentence after his lawyers paid his US$864 fine. Media groups have condemned their treatment in custody. (MFWA, IRIN)

TONGA

Mateni Tapueluelu, editor of Tonga's controversial newspaper *Taimi 'o Tonga* was arrested by police who raided his office and home looking for an affidavit signed by former prison officer **Kivalu Halahingano**, who alleges that Police Minister Clive Edwards once ordered him to burgle Tapueluelu's office. Tapueluelu was released on bail pending trial. He claims the charge is just another attempt to close the paper. (*New Zealand Herald*)

TUNISIA

On 18 July, journalist **Abdallah Zouari** (*Index* 4/02), recently released from 12 years in prison, was sentenced to four more months in jail for defamation, in an incident in which Zouari complained about being barred from using a internet café. Zouari, formerly of *al-Fajr*, unofficial voice of the Islamist An Nahda movement, was then separately tried again on

29 August for breaking bail orders by not living in Tunis and given an additional eight months in prison. (RSF)

TURKEY

On 4 June, Istanbul Penal Court ordered the banning, seizure and destruction of all copies of a translation of *Philosophy in the Bedroom* by the Marquis de Sade, published as *Yatak Odasûnda Felsefe*. Translator **Kerim Sadi** and **Ömer Faruk**, administrator of the Ayrinti publishing house, were charged with 'insulting the moral feelings of the people'. Faruk was fined US$3,110. (*BIA-TIHV*)

Sixty-eight members of the women's wing of the pro-Kurdish Democratic People's Party (DEHAP) in Istanbul were detained for distributing red carnations during a protest calling for a general amnesty for political prisoners. On 15 June, 11 members of the women's wing of DEHAP in Cizre were detained during a press conference for the same reason. (*Milliyet, Özgür Gündem-TIHV*)

Abdülmecit Beyan and **Mehmet Demir**, distributors for the newspaper *Özgür Halk* in Urfa, were sentenced to three years and nine months in jail for 'aiding and abetting an illegal organisation' on 13 June. The Diyarbakir public prosecutor claimed that the journal was making propaganda for the Freedom and Democracy Congress of Kurdistan (KADEK) and the Kurdish PKK guerrillas. (*Özgür Gündem-TIHV*)

On 14 June, unidentified assailants carried out a bomb attack on the offices of the Turkish daily *Star* in Izmir. An anonymous caller, claiming responsibility, said it was retaliation for a news article that had been offensively headlined 'Ker-Kürt' ('Donkey Kurd'). (*Zaman-TIHV*)

Turkey's broadcast media regulators (RTÜK) imposed a one-month ban on Radyo Dünya on 10 July for broadcasting a programme called *Kurdish Language and Literature*. (*Evrensel-TIHV*)

A banner calling for a 'General Amnesty for Peace' was banned in Igdir by the Governor's Office on 26 June. The office claimed that banners were prohibited according to the Law on Administration of Provinces. (*Evrensel-TIHV*)

Kurdish musician **Ferhat Tunc** was arrested at the Ararat Festival in Beyazit after he allegedly made a speech in support of the Kurdish KADEK congress. Tunc, who sings in both Turkish and Kurdish, called for brotherhood, friendship and a general amnesty in Turkey. He was released pending trial. Ferhat Tunc's website: www.ferhattunc.net. (www. amude.com, www.kurdishmedia.com)

Orçun Mastçi, director of Van Trade Unions Theatre group, was detained and threatened by police in Hakkari, just before the opening of their play *Mikado'-nun Çöpleri* (*Mikado's Straws*) it was reported on 11 July. Mastçi was arrested for not standing when the Turkish national anthem was played in the yard outside. He was later released. (*Özgür Gündem-TIHV*)

A court in the eastern city of Dogubeyazit ordered the arrest of the singer **Rojin** and comedian **Murat Batgi** for activities during the city's Second Culture, Art and Tourism Festival, it was reported on 16 July. They were charged with 'aiding an illegal organisation'. Batgi had encouraged the crowd to sing a Kurdish folk song called 'Hernepes' and Rojin was charged for the inclusion of the word 'Kurdistan' in a song. (*Özgür Gündem-TIHV*)

The first issue of the newspaper *Devrimci Halkûn Birligi* was confiscated in Istanbul following allegations that some articles contained propaganda from the banned organisations – the Kurdish KADEK congress and the leftist Turkish Workers and Peasants Liberation Army (TIKKO) – according to a 17 July report. (*Özgür Gündem-TIHV*)

The author **Edip Polat** was beaten up on 17 July by members of the local village guard militia in the Bismil district of Diyarbakir, reportedly in retaliation for writing about one of the guard's fathers in his book *Sevgilim Sevgisiz Ölüm* (*My Dear Loveless Death*). (*Özgür Gündem-TIHV*)

Cartoonists **Askin Ayrancioglu** and **Seyit Saatçi** were charged on 17 July with 'insulting the armed forces' at a cartoon exhibition in the Black Sea coastal city of Sinop – which had been closed by the regional governor back in June 2001. (*TIHV*)

Muhbet Karaer and **Yusuf Süren**, distributors of the journal *Özgür Kadinin Sesi*

(*Voice of Free Women*) were jailed on 7 August for three years and nine months each by a security court in Izmir on charges of 'aiding an illegal organisation'. They had declined to take advantage of the Turkish 'repentance law' which offers qualified immunity from prosecution. (*Özgür Gündem*)

TURKMENISTAN

A *Deutsche Welle* report on the confiscation of homes belonging to holders of dual Russian–Turkmen citizenship led the country's foreign ministry on 1 July to accuse the network of a propaganda campaign against the country and to ask the German government to prevent the German media from reporting 'slanderous material' against Turkmenistan. (RFE/RL, www.turkmenistan.ru)

On 16 July, president Saparmurat Niyazov declared that Turkmen state TV was 'uninteresting' and ordered its reorganisation, appointing paediatrician **Gurbansoltan Handurdyeva** to head it. Niyazov said state TV failed to contribute to the 'upbringing of future generations in the spirit of love for their homeland and devotion to the tradition of their ancestors'. Niyazov also fined his press secretary **Akhmurad Hudaiberdyev** two months' salary for failing to prevent the problem in the first place. (RFE/RL)

UGANDA

On 22 June, Radio Kyoga Veritas FM was closed down after broadcasting interviews with people caught in fighting between government

forces and the rebel Lord's Resistance Army (LRA). On 17 June, Refugees and Disaster Preparedness Minister Christine Amongin had ordered media not to broadcast news of LRA attacks. (CPJ)

UKRAINE

Internet journalist **Edouard Malinivskii** of the online daily *Ostryv* was beaten up by unknown assailants in Donetsk on 12 August. The website has carried articles critical of powerful local leaders in Donetsk, but the police say there is no political connection. (RSF)

Victor Roncea, foreign editor of the Romanian daily *ZIUA*, was barred on 27 June from visiting Ukraine as part of a US/NATO mission to the Black Sea countries. The ban has been set for five years. It is believed that the Kyiv government was reacting to *ZIUA*'s reports on the murder of Ukrainian journalist **Ghiorghi Gongadze**. (IPI, IFEX)

On 9 July, the Ukrainian parliament passed a law allowing the detention of journalists suspected of revealing state secrets. The State Security forces will use the law to investigate reporters they say are illegally using information technology to break major stories. (IFJ, IFEX)

On 14 July, newspaper and television editor **Vladimir Efremov** was killed in a road accident when his car collided with a truck near Verkhnyodniprovsk town. Efremov was editor-in-chief of the *Sobor Dnipropetrovsk* newspaper. Friends recalled his fears,

voiced in October 2001 in the state newspaper *Golos Ukrainy*, that he would be killed because of his journalistic activities, probably in a 'staged road accident'. Efremov had agreed to testify at former prime minister Pavlo Lazarenko's upcoming 18 August trial in the USA on charges of 'embezzlement of public funds'. (RSF)

On 24 July, **Oleg Eltsov**, editor-in-chief and investigative journalist for the online bulletin *Ukraine Criminality*, was seriously injured by two unidentified assailants outside his Kyiv home. The attackers used an electric prod and a ten-kilo metal tube on him. Eltsov had written numerous articles criticising the higher echelons of Ukrainian political society. (IFJ/IFEX)

UNITED ARAB EMIRATES

Dubai-based broadcaster al-Arabiya TV was criticised by the US State Department for a 26 August broadcast that featured a group of masked Iraqis who threatened attacks against Iraqis who cooperated with the US-appointed Iraqi governing council, and members of the council themselves. The US has also brought pressure to bear on shareholders in the private channel. (BBC Online)

UNITED KINGDOM

The editor of the *Guardian* newspaper has failed in an attempt to force the abolition of a nineteenth-century treason law that makes advocating a republican government a criminal offence punishable by life imprisonment. The Attorney-General rejected

ON HIS MAJESTY'S SECRET SERVICE

UNNAMED BRITISH INTELLIGENCE OFFICIAL

The Hutton Inquiry into the death of weapons expert Dr David Kelly put thousands of private emails and memos into the public domain, giving us a revealing glimpse of the workings of government procedures that would normally be kept secret for 30 years under state secrecy rules – and an indication of what might be possible under an effective UK Freedom of Information Act.

The saga began with the claim that Prime Minister Tony Blair's government got the British intelligence services to 'sex up' their dossier on Iraq's weapons of mass destruction, to reinforce the government's public case for war. On 11 September 2002, a fortnight before it was published, Blair's office issued a 'last call' to the intelligence agencies for additional information that would make the dossier 'as strong as possible'. This email was the spies' private response. ❏

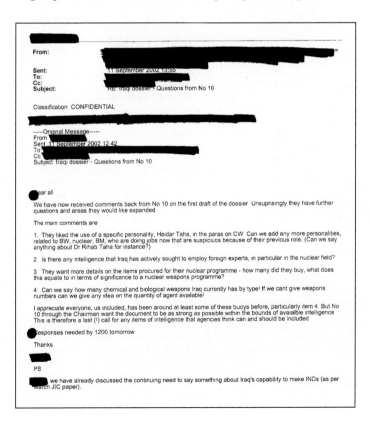

From:

Sent: 11 September 2002 13:55
To:
Cc:
Subject: RE: Iraqi dossier - Questions from No 10

Classification CONFIDENTIAL

-----Original Message-----
From
Sent 11 September 2002 12 42
To
Cc
Subject Iraqi dossier - Questions from No 10

Dear all

We have now received comments back from No 10 on the first draft of the dossier Unsurprisingly they have further questions and areas they would like expanded

The main comments are

1. They liked the use of a specific personality, Haidar Taha, in the paras on CW Can we add any more personalities, related to BW, nuclear, BM, who are doing jobs now that are suspicious because of their previous role. (Can we say anything about Dr Rihab Taha for instance?)

2 Is there any intelligence that Iraq has actively sought to employ foreign experts, in particular in the nuclear field?

3 They want more details on the items procured for their nuclear programme - how many did they buy, what does this equate to in terms of significance to a nuclear weapons programme?

4 Can we say how many chemical and biological weapons Iraq currently has by type! If we cant give weapons numbers can we give any idea on the quantity of agent available!

I appreciate everyone, us included, has been around at least some of these buoys before, particularly item 4 But No 10 through the Chairman want the document to be as strong as possible within the bounds of available intelligence This is therefore a last (!) call for any items of intelligence that agencies think can and should be included

Responses needed by 1200 tomorrow

Thanks

PS

we have already discussed the continuing need to say something about Iraq's capability to make INDs (as per March JIC paper).

the paper's claim that the law was a threat to freedom of expression, noting that there had been many words written arguing for the abolition of the royal family but 'these articles and letters have not led to prosecution or any threat of it'. (*The Times*)

The Broadcasting Standards Commission criticised 'shock-jock' radio presenter **Nick Ferrari** of London's LBC radio for encouraging racist attitudes towards immigrants and asylum seekers. (*Guardian*)

A family in South Wales received £50,000 from Gwent police in an out-of-court settlement after the Police Complaints Authority ruled that the installation of a secret camera in their home following a series of disputes with their next-door neighbour, a retired police officer, was illegal. (*Daily Telegraph*)

The UK government has rejected calls from MPs to introduce a privacy law that would guard against 'unwarranted' intrusions into the private lives of individuals by the press. (*The Times*)

Lord Hutton, the judge heading the inquiry into the events surrounding the suicide of disarmament expert **David Kelly**, barred TV cameras from hearings, arguing that it would put unnecessary strain on witnesses. He added that it did not violate free expression rights under Article 10 of the European Convention on Human Rights, as it did not cover the 'right of access to material not yet available to persons concerned'. The chief executive of ITN, Mark Wood, dis-

puted this claim, stating, 'We believe there is a strong public interest case for the public to see for themselves key witnesses giving evidence.' (*Guardian*)

Anti-abortion campaigners **Fiona Pinto**, 23, and **Joseph Biddulph**, 52, accused of insulting passers-by by displaying a large poster image of an aborted foetus, were cleared of all charges on 3 September. Welsh magistrates said they thought the poster was in 'poor taste' and its display in a public shopping area during the school holidays 'could be seen as unwise'. But they said that 'taken in light of modern-day images used daily in the media, and with regard to the laws of freedom of expression', they would clear the two. (BBC Online)

Almost 50 per cent of Scots polled in early July supported a ban on religious parades, traditionally organised by Protestants in Scotland and Northern Ireland, but the anti-sectarian campaign group Nil by Mouth said they opposed the idea of banning marches while arguing that they should be rigorously policed. The grand master of the Grand Orange Lodge of Scotland, Ian Wilson, said the banning of parades represented a 'slippery slope to a police state'. (*Sunday Herald*)

Former MI5 officer **David Shayler** lost an appeal on 29 July against his conviction under the Official Secrets Act for passing classified documents to the press. During his trial the judge restricted his questioning of MI5 officers and questions to witnesses had to be disclosed in advance.

Shayler claimed his rights to a fair hearing under common law and a fair trial under the European Convention on Human Rights had been breached. (*Guardian*)

BBC chairman **Gavyn Davies** accused the government on 27 July of trying to pressure the broadcaster into changing its coverage of the Iraqi crisis. He said the BBC had been under constant attack from politicians over coverage they perceived as 'anti-war' and that unidentified government figures had been quoted in media reports as threatening to cut its funding, rewrite its charter, and remove its director-general, Greg Dyke. (*Guardian*)

Convicted murderer **Harry Roberts** is challenging a decision barring him from seeing documents he hopes will win him parole after 37 years in jail for the killing of three policemen in 1966. The parole board has decided that a special advocate appointed by them, not Roberts' lawyer, should deal with the 'sensitive' evidence. The advocate would have no contact with Roberts or his lawyers once the evidence has been seen. (*Guardian*)

UNITED STATES

US military commanders have confessed their pleasure at important public relations victories during the fighting in Iraq. 'We've turned the media into a mechanism for communicating information from the action to the consumer including the enemy,' said Brigadier-General Vincent Brooks of the Joint Chiefs of Staff, speaking at a three-day US military conference on the media's role in Operation Iraqi Freedom. 'What we don't engage in is deception or manipulation.' But Major General James Thurman, who was chief operations officer for the land war command, noted: 'As a war fighter, I am going to leverage information. I'd be foolish not to. The power of information – it is phenomenal.' (Reuters)

The media monitoring organisation Fairness and Accuracy in Reporting (FAIR) has claimed that in the weeks after the invasion of Iraq US TV networks gave more airtime to political commentators who supported the war than those who opposed it. Almost two-thirds of the sources for stories (64 per cent) were pro-war, while only 10 per cent were anti-war. (FAIR)

The Federal Communications Commission (FCC) has introduced plans to relax the regulations that prevent companies from owning television stations and newspapers within the same market. Under current rules, a single broadcaster is allowed to reach 35 per cent of the population, but under the FCC proposal's this would increase to 45 per cent. Democrat senator Bryon Dorgan said: 'The airwaves belong to the people. The FCC ignores that requirement and advances corporate interests at the expense of the public's interest.' (Miami Herald, AP)

Attempts by al-Jazeera to sublease 17,000 square feet of studio space in Washington has been thwarted by the landlord, on the grounds that the Arab TV channel would potentially be 'a target for people who do not understand or do not agree with its business principles and philosophies of those of its ownership'. (Washington Post)

A radio presenter claimed that she was fired because she was opposed the war against Iraq. **Roxanne Cordonier**, who has filed a lawsuit against her former employees, alleges that she was subjected to jibes from her colleagues, both on and off the air, and that she was forced to attend a pro-war rally. (Greenville News)

US soldiers who criticised their government on ABC news may face disciplinary action after publicly voicing their frustrations with their mission in Iraq. One demanded the resignation of US Defense Secretary Donald Rumsfeld. Official response was rapid. One officer in Iraq said: 'It went all the way up to President Bush and back down again on top of us. At least six of us here will lose our careers.' (San Francisco Chronicle)

Wal-Mart Stores Inc. has demanded that five radio stations in the St Louis area stop running an advertisement that criticises the company's treatment of its staff. The advert is paid for by a local union. (STL Today)

Fox News sued the comedian **Al Franken** over his forthcoming book Lies and the Lying Liars who Tell Them: A Fair and Balanced Look at the Right, claiming that it has trademarked the term 'fair and balanced', and the title of the book would confuse its viewers. After Fox was refused an injunction it dropped the case on 25 August. (Los Angeles Times)

Pornographic film producer **Robert D Zicari** ('Rob Black') and his wife **Janet Romano** ('Lizzie Borden') appeared in court on 27 August in Pittsburgh, accused of violating federal obscenity laws with films specialising in dramatised hardcore recreations of rape and sex murders. US Attorney-General John Ashcroft said the Justice Department would 'continue to focus our efforts on targeted obscenity prosecutions that will deter others from producing and distributing obscene materials'. (Baltimore Sun)

Jayson Blair, the former New York Times reporter who resigned amid accusations of fraud and plagiarism, has won a book deal with New Millennium Press, a Los Angeles-based publisher. The book, Burning Down My Master's House, is scheduled to come out in March 2004, with a first printing of more than 200,000. New Millennium co-president Michael Viner said he was not concerned about the reliability of Blair's memoir. (CBS)

US Federal authorities are considering criminal charges against **ABC News reporters** who smuggled 15 lb of depleted uranium into Los Angeles from Jakarta, Indonesia – past Homeland Security anti-terrorism screeners for a second straight year – for an investigative piece on lax border security. ABC News said it believed its actions constituted legitimate investigative journalism. (AP)

UZBEKISTAN

On 19 June, two foreign internet sites covering religious issues in Uzbekistan were blocked by the authorities. Muslimuzbekistan.com relays reports on persecution of Central Asian Muslims. Centrasia.ru carries reports on religious issues in Central Asia and other news. Security officials have warned state employees not to visit 'undesirable' websites, and that access and use of the web should be limited and strictly monitored. (RFE/RL)

On 17 July, the entire staff of the Uzbek newspaper *Mokhiyat* resigned in protest at new director Sa'dulla Hakim's order barring articles critical of the government. Hakim formerly served as the head of the presidential information office. (RFE/RL)

On 14 August, the journalist and human rights activist **Ruslan Sharipov** was jailed for five and a half years on charges of homosexuality and child molestation, which he denied and which he said were politically motivated. Apparently under coercion Sharipov then changed his plea to guilty on 8 August, offered to plead forgiveness from President Islam Karimov and retract all critical web articles written between 2001 and 2003. On 5 September, he issued a statement from prison confirming that he had been 'tortured and pressured in ways I cannot describe with the aim of forcing me to confess and plead guilty at the trial for a crime I hadn't committed'. (PEN, CJES, RSF, IRIN, HRW)

VENEZUELA

On 27 June, Journalists' Day in Venezuela, an unknown assailant threw a Molotov cocktail into the car of journalist **Marta Colomina** of Televén TV, Unión Radio and the daily *El Universal*. It did not explode. On 21 July, a small bomb filled with leaflets attacking Colomina and others exploded near the Unión Radio office in Chacao, east of Caracas. (IPYS, RSF)

Community radio station Perijanera 95.1 FM in the city of Machiques was knocked off air on 4 July by armed men who stole the station's transmitter and other equipment. (IPYS)

On 10 July, community Catia TV serving Caracas's Lídice hospital was closed by police, allegedly on orders from the city's mayor and the municipal health secretary. No court order for the closure was presented and no court officials were present during the operation. (IPYS)

In a ruling issued on 15 July, the Venezuelan Supreme Court upheld the state's right to apply prior censorship. The court also found that laws protecting public authorities and institutions from criticism deemed 'insulting', were constitutional. (HRW)

On 20 August, Globovisión cameraman **Efrían Henríquez** was attacked with pepper spray by a government supporter as he covered a march organised by the opposition Democratic Coordinating Committee. (IPYS)

VIETNAM

On 18 June, writer **Pham Hong Son** was jailed for 13 years, later cut to five, with three years of house arrest to follow, on charges of espionage. He had circulated a series of articles online promoting democracy and human rights and was accused of spreading documents by e-mail that were 'anti-Communist Party and anti-Vietnam'. Foreign observers and family were barred from the court. (CPJ)

On 15 July, the Ho Chi Minh Young Communist Association's magazine *Sinh Vien Vietnam* was banned for three months. Its covers, which featured naked human statuettes and, last year, a photomontage of banknotes and an image of late President Ho Chi Minh floating in a toilet bowl, were judged 'offensive' by the Culture Ministry. Staff were ordered to engage in public 'self-criticism'. (RSF)

Jailed writer and publisher **Nguyen Dan Que** was told on 13 July that he would only be released if he agreed to leave Vietnam permanently and live in exile. A 61-year-old endocrinologist and prominent writer, he was arrested for the third time on 17 March in Ho Chi Minh City after issuing a statement criticising state restrictions on the media and calling for political reform (CPJ/IFEX).

YEMEN

The house of journalist **Hassan al-Zaidi** has been surrounded by security forces preventing him from leaving since the beginning of August. Al-Zaidi's two brothers were arrested on 7 August in what security forces describe as part of a campaign against the al-Zaidi tribe which is currently in dispute with the government, and not in response to any articles the journalist has written. (RSF)

ZAMBIA

Masautso Phiri, editor of the weekly *Today*, was quizzed by police on 24 June about an article criticising President Levy Mwambasa's policies and suggesting that it could trigger a coup. Phiri and article author **Wilfred Zulu** may face contempt of law charges. (MISA)

ZIMBABWE

Zimbabwe's Supreme Court has ruled that the *Daily News*, Zimbabwe's biggest selling daily and President Robert Mugabe's government most visible critic, is operating illegally because it has not registered under tough media

laws. The *Daily News*, the country's highest-circulating paper, had challenged the section of the law that requires news organisations to register with the state. The ruling means the publishers of the *Daily News* and its Sunday edition will have to register under the country's hardline Access to Information and Protection of Privacy Act (AIPPA) first before challenging the law. Lawyers for the *Daily News* had argued the rule was unconstitutional. (ABC)

On 30 June, chief executive officer **Sam Nkomo**, commercial director **Moreblessing Mpofu** and legal adviser **Gugulethu Moyo** of the *Daily News*, were convicted under clause 16 of the Public Order and Security Act (POSA) for publishing advertisements considered defamatory of President Robert Mugabe. The paper's editor, **Nqobile Nyathi**, was also charged for a similar offence. (MISA)

Compiled by: James Badcock (North Africa); Ben Carrdus (East Asia); Gulliver Cragg (Western Europe, North America); Ioli Delivani (Southern and Eastern Africa); Veronique Dupont (South America); Patrick Holland and Hanna Gezelius (Britain and Ireland); Monica Gonzalez Correa (Central Asia and Caucusus); Javier Gonzalez-Rubio (Russia, Poland, Ukraine, Baltic States, South-East Asia); Andrew Kendle (India and subcontinent); Gill Newsham (Turkey and Kurdish areas); Jason Pollard (Gulf States and Middle East); Jugo Stojanov (Eastern Europe); Mike Yeoman (Central America and Caribbean)

Edited by Rohan Jayasekera and coordinated by Natasha Schmidt

TALES FROM BAGHDAD

ROHAN JAYASEKERA LOOKS AT THE CHANGING
FACE OF THE MEDIA IN BAGHDAD AND THE
CHALLENGES FACING JOURNALISTS AFTER
30 YEARS OF RIGID CENSORSHIP

Baghdad 2003: poster of Saddam Hussein defaced by local people. Credit: Tuen Voeten / Panos

SCHOOL'S OUT

ROHAN JAYASEKERA

JOURNALISM TRAINING IS A KEY PART
OF THE PROGRAMMES OF RESEARCH,
PUBLICATION AND ADVOCACY THAT
INDEX ON CENSORSHIP IS CURRENTLY
RUNNING IN IRAQ

Working on media support programmes for *Index on Censorship* is a learning process for all concerned. That much should be obvious, considering how much we all thought we knew about the problems before the post-war newspapers and radio stations started up in Baghdad and Kabul, and how little those preconceptions turned out to be worth a few weeks later once the presses were finally running and the transmitters humming.

Index on Censorship runs a three-cornered programme in Iraq. We research; we publish; we are advocates for change. There is no defined quarter for training for its own sake, yet it is central to the process of how *Index* works with local partners, newspapers, magazines and media rights NGOs. Their interest in correctly analysing the situation, in accurately reporting it, in effectively making the case for change, is the same as ours.

It requires a professional, responsible, committed approach. But this skill set is not easily taught, at least not by conventional academic means. It requires basic human qualities that cannot be created, only enhanced by technique.

Still, the donor agencies that invest money in these programmes reasonably expect to quantify their return: to see a measurable number of trainees, a discernible agenda instilled, 'objectivity', 'balance', 'story structure'. This can be done to everyone's satisfaction. All these things have their virtues. It's just that they also have their place. Journalism, as I dully repeat to our 'participants' – I am reluctant to call them students – is a craft not an art, and is taught that way. I was indentured like a trade apprentice to my first newspaper: my father signed me away for four years on a sheet of vellum.

Basic skills are just that. Basic. Balance, don't judge until the facts are in, or until deadline, whichever comes first (add wry laugh), and Check, Check, Check. Even the Quran tells us so: 'O ye who believe! If an evil-liver bring you tidings, verify it, lest ye smite some folk in ignorance and

Baghdad, June 2003: Iraqi journalists at an Index *seminar. Credit: Yousef Ahmed*

afterward repent of what ye did,' from my favourite Sura, number 49, *al-Hujaarat*, which, as Egyptian editors say, is full of useful guidance for young reporters.

But practical skills alone don't take us very far. There are plenty of Western journalists who should take Sura 49, verse 6, to heart. Likewise, there are plenty of skilfully produced papers by Iraqis in Iraq, glorious full-colour broadsheets, part-produced in foreign cities by men who were rich and influential under Saddam Hussein and remain that way under L Paul Bremer III, the senior US administrator in Iraq. You can measure their success by booming circulation. You can also qualify it by noting how that success is built on paid agency photos of J-Lo, satellite TV listings and the cynical investment of millions of dollars in a tool for future political influence in a rapidly evolving Iraq.

Then there are the cultural differences and the need for a regional perspective. *Index on Censorship*'s programmes are run by Arabs in Arabic in Baghdad, with Kurdish programmes to come. Language in the hands of journalists is a dangerous weapon, so it helps to be trained in their use by someone who knows where the safety clip is.

But the experience of working at a senior level in Jordan, with its qualified free-speech rights, or in Palestine, cheek by jowl with an occupier, or in London's Arabic Press, where there is a solution for almost any technical problem, also neatly equips people for the kind of adaptable personal mentoring *Index on Censorship* prefers to see in Iraq. Half the problems of the Western media are due to our habit of taking basic rights for granted. There's nothing like working in an environment where no human right can be taken as read – even if you can read it in the constitution – to attune you to the realities and responsibilities of free expression.

Iraqi journalists still work reactively, not proactively. When you consider the fate that awaited the journalist who asked the wrong question under the old regime, it's hardly surprising that they got out of the habit of asking any questions at all. (The difference between post-war Iraq and post-war Afghanistan is startling. The Afghans had no media to speak of under the Taliban and nothing left when they went. But the Afghans bartered information like bags of grain and when they began taking up the alien art of journalism, they immediately grasped the point that the more accurate information was, the more value it had. Iraqis kept their information to themselves under Saddam. You never knew who around you had the power. The fact that Iraqis are so free with their criticism of today's US–British occupying forces, incidentally, is also a measure of just how little the average Baghdadi thinks of the Westerners' ability to do them either good or ill.)

But the gap's not so wide when it comes to communicating practical techniques of journalism. You can thank a globalised media for that. The brigade of privileged gentlemen who control the Iraqi print media today were all privately aware of al-Jazeera and the evolving standards being set by international Arab dailies such as *al-Hayat*, *as-Safir* and *an-Nahar*, even if the ordinary folk suffering under Saddam were not. Anyway, standardisation of media may not be welcome, but it sets standards by definition, and even if they are set so low they can only go up, it's a start.

Not everyone agrees. One editor told us that he believed that Iraqi journalists had nothing to learn from other Arab reporters. There's that kneejerk reaction against free expression as a Western self-indulgence, as if it was a tub of Häagen-Daz ice cream enjoyed in a brothel rather than a fundamental human right, recognised as such precisely because it transcends culture, race and nationality.

Yet that same Iraqi editor was looking at the prospect, for the first time, of having to defend his paper's work in a quasi-judicial forum, the press complaints council that the occupation authorities are proposing for the Iraqi media. He was talking to *Index* trainer Yahia Shukkier, who has made a national name in Jordan as a champion of free-expression rights in the courts on behalf of a score of its newspapers.

There's something the editor could learn from him, we thought. But not the 'who-what-when-where-how', the basic components of a news story that trainee journalists are taught make for an accurate account of a bus crash or a football match.

The fact is that the human qualities that make a good reporter – the professionalism, the sense of responsibility, the commitment – are not taught in seminars but instilled in men and women as they ply their trade in a professional environment that fosters responsibility and encourages commitment.

That's why media support programmes in Iraq – perhaps anywhere – have to pay more attention to the newsroom than the classroom, must support independent professional bodies, must encourage self-regulation and self-criticism and must defend journalists against legislation that seeks to control bad journalists first before supporting good ones, as has emerged in Iraq under the present occupation forces.

In the end it comes down to communicating the fundamentals – the basic principles of free expression. One editor told us that she had been approached by a businessman who had been the subject of a story in her paper. The story wasn't wrong, he just wanted to know who the source was. Before attending the *Index* seminars she would have probably told him, she confessed. Now, after the course, she knew she had to protect her sources. Well, she knew before, but now she understood why it was a principle. So she kept the name to herself. ❑

RJ

ADDING INSULT TO INJURY
MAJID JARRAR & SALAAM AL-JUBOURI

WHEN US TROOPS GUARDING ONE
BAGHDAD PETROL STATION CUT UP
ROUGH WITH STREET PETROL SELLERS,
IT LEFT IRAQI VICTIMS AND WITNESSES
EMBITTERED BY THE EXPERIENCE

Hamed Mehson Alaiwi was only trying to earn a little money to feed his family. His efforts cost him a beating from the US Army. And now he's angry. Alaiwi is one of the scores of Iraqis who used to fill cans with petrol and siphon it in to the tanks of drivers who did not want to join the long queues outside the city's filling stations. But the US troops who guard the petrol pumps changed the rules on him. When he tried to fill up at the Abu Qlam station the soldiers chased him and others away. They caught Alaiwi, he says, then pistol-whipped him and threatened him with a knife. He was left with two painful welts on his head.

'I never attacked them, they attacked me,' he says. 'They beat me with their guns and threatened me with a knife.' The soldiers used their blades to puncture the street sellers' cans, putting them out of a job. 'When they [the US forces] came, they were supposed to give us our freedom, not assault us,' Alaiwi adds.

Under the new order, only car drivers can fill up from the US military-supervised stations. The order, say the US forces, is to stop crowding round the pumps. Abu Qlam petrol station, in Baghdad's Karrada district, is a typical sight. Run-down cars filled with hot, sweating people line the streets outside the station from opening at 9am to closing time at 3pm. The US military believes that orderly queues for essential services are a fair way of dealing with the distribution of limited supplies.

But the soldiers are reacting violently to infractions of the rules, and are provoking angry responses from the Iraqis in return. Worse, the US troops are literally adding insult to injury by their casual replies. 'Hoo-yah! What guys?' responded one of the US troops said by witnesses to be involved in the beatings.

What the Iraqis did was to fail to obey – or fail to understand – an order in English to stay away from the pumps. But in the US military's eyes, the main crime the street sellers appeared to have committed was to have tried running away when challenged by a US soldier.

'People who run from us are bad people,' says another US soldier at the petrol station, name-tagged 'Smith'. The soldiers object to the street sellers crowding the pumps and holding up car drivers who sometimes can queue for hours waiting to fill their tanks. 'We told them not to do that,' Smith says. 'They ignored us and when we ordered him to stop, they ran away.'

It seems Alaiwi ran, became a 'bad person', got beaten. 'He insulted me,' says the angry and confused Alaiwi. 'If he was an Iraqi I would kill him. But he is an American and I can't do anything.' An eyewitness to the attack, who gave his name as Ahmed, said this kind of incident was becoming routine. 'The fight today was nothing,' he claimed. 'A few days ago an old man quarrelled with the Americans and they kicked him in the head.'

Compounding the problem is the knowledge that the whole scene – the petrol shortages, the queues and the violence – is taking place above land that holds the world's second largest proven reserves of oil. Before the war petrol was literally cheaper than water in Iraq. Today, with oil flowing freely over the border to Jordan and the first post-war tenders for fresh crude ready to be signed, many Iraqis believe that the petrol shortages are unnecessary and are deliberately engineered by the US to teach them a lesson about the value of their natural resources. The sheer irrationality and unfairness of the situation, combined with the casual insults and injury dealt out by the troops who man the filling stations, provokes bitter fury.

'The Americans came for the freedom?' says filling-station employee and high school student Ghassan al-Zubaidi. 'That's all lies. They robbed and they looted and they burned all the ministries, except for the Ministry of Oil, which wasn't touched because they wanted the oil. George Bush is a son of a bitch!' ❑

Majid Jarrar & Salaam al-Jubouri write for al-Muajaha *and are recent participants in* Index's *publication and training programmes in Iraq*

READING BETWEEN THE ENEMY LINES

ROHAN JAYASEKERA

HOW CAN IRAQI REPORTERS BALANCE
THEIR ARTICLES WHEN THE WAY TO
'THE OTHER SIDE OF THE STORY' IS
BLOCKED BY A TANK?

You're a tyro reporter on the streets and you pick up a juicy tale of alleged police brutality at a petrol station on the other side of town. You head down there and catch the alleged victim. He has lots to say through a mouthful of broken teeth.

Eyewitnesses point out the policemen allegedly responsible, still on the scene. The sergeant tells you the victim tried to run away and was forcibly stopped: 'People who run away are bad guys.' There's clearly something wrong here, but in the interests of fair and balanced reporting, before you write it up, you call the chief of police and ask him just what does he think his men are doing out there?

It didn't happen in Britain or the US. It happened in Baghdad. And it wasn't cops but US soldiers who pistol-whipped the man caught trying to jump the queue with a petrol can. What was missing from the story – not from this analogy, but from the real one written by two Iraqi reporters for the Baghdad monthly *al-Muajaha* (see p164) – was the quote from their commander.

Scores of such incidents of violence by patrolling US troops are reported weekly across Iraq, and you would assume that US Army public relations officers would be bombarded with requests for statements from the 100 or so newspapers that have set up in Baghdad alone since Saddam's fall. Not so: the PAOs – the so-called Public Affairs Officers – are virtually beyond reach to all of them. The path to 'the other side of the story' is blocked by the US 1st Armoured Division. The PAOs operate behind a ring of US steel in Saddam's old riverside complex of palaces, where they can only rarely be reached, and then only by unreliable and prohibitively expensive satellite phones.

The foreign media have the experience to manage the system, but the Iraqi press tackles a news agenda diametrically different from that of the internationals. While the Western media tackle the issues of economic (read

This cartoon was drawn by Dennis Draughon of the Scranton Times & Tribune in Pennsylvania, but the newspaper's readers never got to see it. Draughon was told by his associate editor that his drawing was 'not going to fly'. He accepted the decision. 'Editors and publishers run what kind of cartoons they want,' he told The Progressive magazine. 'I've learned to live with it.' Credit: The Progressive

oil) development and the assassinations of US soldiers, the Iraqi media is trying to deal with agonising stories of more direct consequence to its readers.

What to do, for example, about the chaotic courts system which, as Amnesty researchers note, can keep a traffic offender in a detention pen with murderers for days before his US and British guards can locate him and deliver him before a judge? Or the failure of the authorities to stop the unchecked sale of looted medicines in street markets, sold by the poor to the desperate – a trade that poisons, maims and claims lives every day?

None of this is on the PAOs' agenda, whose mission is to spread the good news about the US–British presence in Iraq. But the duty of the authorities to answer questions about these issues, and many more besides, goes far beyond the facilitation of 'balanced reporting' – these are questions that demand answers. And they are not being given.

In frustration, one editor has taken to printing accounts of violence by US troops as 'Letters to the Americans', simply reporting incidents as accurately as possible and ending each one with a public request for the US Army to respond.

The editor, Israa Shakir of *al-Iraq al-Youm*, deals in the same way with the flow of 'irrelevant' press releases from the PAOs – news of public-spirited efforts by US forces, including many genuinely sincere folk working off duty, covering such things as the laying of soccer pitches and the international collection of Beanie Babies for street children.

Unable to contextualise, balance or background any of this, Shakir simply marks it 'News from the Americans' and separates it from her own news, as if it were a paid advertisement.

Lack of access to information from the US forces – not any information, but information that the press wants – has not slowed the Iraqi media boom. Scores of titles are on offer, private radio stations are reappearing and, for those who can afford it, satellite dishes offering access to foreign Arab TV networks are on sale.

This unchecked growth provoked an immediate crisis for the occupation forces' media strategy. In June, L Paul Bremer III, the senior US diplomat in Baghdad, released strict rules on the operation of the media. His Order 14 comes with a list of prohibited activities, which include incitement to political, religious or ethnic violence; advocating support for the banned Baath Party of Saddam Hussein, and publishing material that is 'patently false and is calculated to provoke opposition to the CPA [Coalition Provisional Authority, the occupation powers] or undermine legitimate processes toward self-government'. Order 14 has been enforced as well, with a string of raids on newspapers, arrests and the closure of half a dozen papers in Baghdad and Najaf.

The tough line, though hardly surprising given the rising death toll among US forces in Iraq, is in part over-compensation for the Pentagon's abject failure to manage its own corner of the Iraqi media – the state broadcasting network it captured after Saddam's fall. Both the US and British ran so-called 'psy-ops' (psychological operations) broadcasts in the run-up to the war, beaming coalition-approved TV and radio to Iraq, by long-range shortwave transmitters and from orbiting US Air Force planes. The reconstruction of the post-war media was contracted out by the Pentagon to the

US defence technology giant Science Applications International Corp (SAIC). But SAIC was chosen for its record in managing psy-ops technology; it had no obvious record in conventional media management. It was supposedly overseen by former Voice of America (VoA) chief Bob Reilly, perhaps appointed because of, not in spite of, his past differences with VoA over 'taking sides' in the 'war on terror'. The so-called Iraqi Media Network (IMN), essentially a reconstructed Iraqi state broadcaster, was an abject failure under SAIC management. Plagued by management conflicts, missed deadlines and overspending, operated by overworked, under-resourced, undertrained and sometimes unpaid staff, it delivered a network that could barely cover Baghdad, let alone Iraq, and was derided by its target audience. Iraqis turn instead to the print media and the satellite dish for their news.

The determination of the CPA to regain the PR advantage, fired by its failure to win hearts and minds through the IMN, appears to have blinded it to another, not necessarily exclusive strategy. The failure of the US authority to tackle crime, economic collapse and the repair of public utilities fuels ever more fiery criticism and dubious opinion in the press.

Both sides are split on the difference between 'spreading incitement' and what counts as 'coverage of the people who incite' – key players in the new Iraq, like it or not. News-gathering on the ground remains a precarious activity. The CPA is making some efforts to poke holes in the information wall. Tenuous attempts are being made, through Arabic-only CPA press conferences, to try to engage with the Iraqi media. And, eventually, Iraqi journalists will pick up the news-gathering skills they need to extract news from a complex system, imported wholesale from the media free-fire zone inside the Washington Beltway.

But the general inaccessibility of the US authorities in Iraq gives the excuse for precisely the kind of specious speculation and adoption of rumour as fact that Bremer wants stamped out among the Iraqi media – with jail sentences if necessary.

It's no answer to say that the present system is better than anything Iraqi journalists experienced under Saddam. Today the present system treats the Iraqi journalist with no more respect than it does any other Iraqi citizen. ❏

RJ

- While working on this comment in Baghdad, Rohan Jayasekera made five separate attempts over a week by email formally requesting an interview with a US official to discuss media policy in Iraq; he received no reply.

SHOOTING THE MESSENGER

RAMI G KHOURI

TAKING THE 'HATE SPEECH' AGENDA
BEYOND OCCUPIED IRAQ, THE
US ACCUSES ARAB MEDIA OF
BROADCASTING 'INCITEMENT'

Deputy US Defense Secretary Paul Wolfowitz and other senior American officials have accused the pan-Arab media of broadcasting material they consider to be 'incitement' that could lead to further attacks on US troops in Iraq. The American administration in Baghdad temporarily shut down another Iraqi newspaper for the same reason recently.

It is not surprising that Wolfowitz and friends are seeking culprits to blame for the daily, often deadly, attacks. But from my vantage point inside the Arab media in a region plagued by occupations and ideological battle-grounds, Washington's 'incitement' charges are childishly unconvincing.

The accusations show just how different are the US and Arab perceptions of the difficult situation in Iraq. But they probably reveal even more about the tortured mindset of Wolfowitz and vintage American neo-cons who successfully inititated America's war against Iraq but now find themselves flailing at enemy ghosts that torment and elude them. There is something pitiful about a person of Wolfowitz's stature, experience and power responding to the regular killings of young Americans in Iraq by lashing out against Arab satellite television channels such as al-Jazeera and al-Arabiya.

Are the charges accurate and fair? On the strength of having watched US television and these two Arab stations daily for the last year, I think not. The specific complaints against the Arab media include:

- Calling the US presence in Iraq an occupation and labelling those who commit acts of violence in protest against it as the local armed resistance. *Almost all the non-Anglo-American world uses this same language because it is deemed factually accurate.*
- Airing strong anti-American sentiments on talk shows and interviews. *The Arab channels also routinely give the uncensored American official version every day and night.*

- Showing how American troops' and administrators' behaviour in Iraq often humiliates and angers ordinary Iraqis. *This happens and is rarely shown on US television.*
- Providing political narratives and testimonies that contradict the American portrayal of daily events in Iraq. *The Arab channels offer far more extensive and comprehensive coverage of the region and thus include a wider and more accurate range of views than do most US media.*
- Allowing many hosts and anchors to express anti-American biases. *These are regularly countered by the views of American and other guests.*

At the technical level, the Arab media does exactly what the mainstream American media has done since March: they mirror and pander to the dominant emotional and political sentiments of their own public opinion, because they seek to maximise their market share of audience and advertising. In choosing, framing and scripting their stories, Arab and American television stations alike unabashedly and unapologetically cater to their respective audiences' sentiments: the flag-adorned US media emotionally support the US troops, and the Arab media are equally fervent in opposing America's occupation of Iraq.

Mosul, Iraq, July 2003: Iraqis chant support for Saddam. Credit: Farah Nosh / Panos

Like it or not, the media have become part of the arsenal of the political conflicts that define many aspects of US–Arab relations. This is not incitement: this is digitised combat.

But although the Arab channels clearly offer an alternative point of view, and although they, like millions throughout the world, have made it clear that they believe the US occupation of Iraq is wrong and is creating a powerful, spontaneous resistance movement, they do not and have not supported the violence against Americans. The correspondents and anchors of al-Jazeera and al-Arabiya have not praised the attacks or called for them.

They are not the enemy: they are simply the messengers.

Wolfowitz's incitement accusation takes us back to the strange time of Richard Nixon, Spiro Agnew and John Mitchell. These intellectually ignoble Americans in their criminalised White House found it easier to attack messengers bearing bad news than to try to grasp the important anti-war message being transmitted.

In today's Iraq, the Arab media are only the latest to be blamed by an increasingly desperate Washington for attacks against US forces (having already named former Baathists, Saddam Hussein loyalists, local criminals, Iranian agents, residents of the 'Sunni Triangle' north of Baghdad, anti-American groups from other Arab countries and Islamist terrorists from around the world).

Politically, all these and more are probably involved in fighting the American occupation army in Iraq. But as Associated Press correspondent Niko Price more soberly reported from Baghdad in September, Iraqis who shoot American soldiers are often motivated not by love of Saddam Hussein or Islamist fervour but by their anger at the humiliating and degrading way US troops have treated their families and communities.

The very simple reality of Iraq, as old as time, is the message sent by most of the Arab media: occupation begets resistance. Calling it incitement because your occupation troops are the target of both a spontaneous and an organised resistance movement is faulty media analysis, amateur politics and Agnew- and Nixon-style sour grapes taken to those frightening edges of logic and truth where these days only nervous neo-cons dare tread. ❑

Rami G Khouri *is executive editor of the* Beirut Daily Star

Credit: Martin Adler / Panos

Credits: Tuen Voeten / Panos

TAKING LIVES AND LOSING WARS

Reuters cameraman Mazen Dana was shot dead on 17 August by a US soldier while filming near the US-run Abu Ghraib Prison in Baghdad. Eyewitness Stephan Breitner of France 2 TV spoke frankly. 'They knew we were journalists. After they shot Mazen, they aimed their guns at us. I don't think it was accident. They are very tense. They are crazy.'

To most journalists the root of the threat appears to be combat stress – not the kind of total breakdown triggered by intense fighting, but the cumulative effect of loss of morale, exhaustion and the tension brought on by constant fear of a hit-and-run attacker.

It's what the US Department of the Army's own field manuals call 'Misconduct combat stress behaviour' – combat stress leading to breaches of the laws of war. Field Manual No. 22–51 notes the risk, 'especially in guerrilla warfare, when some seemingly non-combatants, such as women and children, are in fact un-uniformed combatants', and 'likely when the sympathies of the civilian non-combatants have become suspect'.

But the manual also makes a clear point: 'Note. Commission of murder and other atrocities against non-combatants must be reported as a war crime and punished if responsibility is established. This must be done even though we may pity the overstressed soldier as well as the victims.'

The US military may even be playing into the enemy's hands. Many observers suspect that Iraqi opposition forces intend to provoke increasingly violent responses from the US occupation forces in the hope of further turning the populace against them, just as the 1972 'Bloody Sunday' massacre turned Northern Irish Catholics decisively against the British Army.

Field Manual No. 22–51 is blunt in this respect: 'The fact is that overstressed human beings with loaded weapons are inherently dangerous.' It also makes the point that the key to tackling misconduct stress behaviour is to maintain and enforce a unit self-image that regards misconduct behaviours as unacceptable.

Essential to this is the full, fair and transparent investigation of such incidents. *Index on Censorship* in London, the Committee to Protect Journalists in New York and the Reporters sans Frontières media rights group in Paris have called for a full investigation into Dana's shooting, and a public accounting. It is the very least the US Army itself requires. ❏

RJ

DO AS YOU WOULD BE DONE BY

RAMZI KYSIA

IF WE WOULD TRULY HELP THE IRAQI PEOPLE,
THEN THAT INTENTION DEMANDS THAT WE
SEE AND TREAT THEM AS OUR EQUALS, AND
THEREFORE TAKE RISKS WITHIN OUR OWN
LIVES COMMENSURATE WITH THE RISKS THAT
HAVE BEEN REGULARLY IMPOSED ON IRAQIS,
OVER LONG YEARS, BY THE REST OF THE WORLD

Institutionally, Iraqis face enormous challenges in constructing a modern, democratic state. Some of these challenges stem from internal conflicts and competing interests among Iraq's varying religious and ethnic groups. Some of them stem from decades of a tyranny that infiltrated and corrupted all aspects of civil society.

Some stem from decades of war, internal repression and embargo. And some of these challenges stem from the military occupation by the United States and United Kingdom – nations that promoted an increasingly violent and unproductive strategy against Iraq for decades, ranging from support of Saddam Hussein to massive bombing of civilian infrastructure to the most comprehensive embargo in modern history, policies that resulted in the deaths of hundreds of thousands of Iraqis.

In the face of these post-war challenges, international humanitarian and peace workers have descended on Iraq in numbers that recall the 'carpet-bagger' invasion of the Southern Confederacy in 1865 following the US Civil War. Less than a dozen international, non-governmental organisations (NGOs) operated in Iraq prior to the fall of Saddam Hussein. By mid-July 2003, the United Nations had registered 173 NGOs operating in the country, many with no previous experience working in Arab or Muslim countries.

While the similarities with post-Civil War America should not be over-stated, they are striking. In both examples, corporate interests dominated US government policy, helping to provide essential services but also exploiting local populations in order to maximise profits. In both examples, US policy was torn between competing desires to provide 'stability' for American political and economic interests by co-opting and re-empowering existing elites, and eliminating those elites in order to prevent the resurgence of the defeated regimes they represented.

In both examples, occupying US military forces were viewed alternatively as 'liberators' and 'oppressors' by the local population in a post-war environment of great devastation and the breakdown of local governance and law and order. And in both, Iraq and the Confederacy, 'foreign' humanitarian workers and occupying government policymakers, attempting to provide assistance to long-brutalised local populations, often met with failure stemming from internal and unrecognised prejudices towards the very people they were hoping to help.

This failure was demonstrated, for me, in Iraq, by a well-meaning soldier guarding the Hotel Palestine, then home base for the international media in the days after the fall of the city. Catching two crying eight-year-old boys who had staked out a begging patch outside the lobby, he found nearly US$300 in their pockets – more than a year's salary for most Iraqis.

When I tried to speak to one of the soldiers about the situation, he brushed me off, saying, 'It's OK. I've seen those kids around before. They work here.' It was at that moment that I knew that there was no possible chance that the US occupation of Iraq could ever succeed.

The inability of that one soldier to see Iraqi children as anything other than 'natural' beggars, or Iraq as anything other than a society where such begging must be 'normal', is partially reflected in the extreme security measures adopted by internationals living in Iraq today.

US policymakers are tucked away inside Saddam's former palaces, with 24-hour-a-day electricity, water, food and sanitation services. UN workers are under an 8pm curfew and are not supposed to travel anywhere except between their workplaces and the hotels they live in.

NGOs have adopted varying security measures, with many requiring body armour to be worn outside, and forbidding independent interactions with Iraqis. For recreation, these internationals tend to hold parties inside locked compounds, interacting only with each other. For most of these people, this is their first and only vision of Iraq.

Post-war Iraq is dangerous. Iraq is suffering from military occupation, violent resistance from some sectors of society, the breakdown of governing structures and an unprecedented wave of violent crime. However, the security measures adopted by internationals in Iraq isolate them from Iraqi society, and provoke bitterness among ordinary Iraqis who do not have the ability to 'protect' themselves quite so thoroughly, or in anywhere near so much comfort.

The international community in its works worldwide has tried to promote cultural understanding and prevent the exploitation of local populations receiving aid. Unfortunately, it is unlikely that this can be done when internationals isolate themselves, and with comforts that few Iraqis can afford. Nor can existing, and perhaps unrecognised, prejudices be confronted and overcome in such isolation.

This self-imposed isolation is not simply limited to our work in Iraq – its mirror is our institutional failure to see the reflection of international policies and of our own lifestyles at home on the problems of Iraq. Western-based humanitarian organisations and solidarity movements have often constrained themselves to what happens 'over there'. While this is an essential element of our work, by itself it becomes arrogance. If we are truly to help people in Iraq, then it will be as much through the work we do at home as the work we do there.

Kerbala, Iraq, April 2003: seven-year-old Mirtatha Abbass joins a Shia Iraqi religious pilgrimage, banned for over a quarter of a century under Saddam Hussein's regime.
Credit: Farah Nosh / Panos

If our end goal is promoting, nurturing and protecting human rights – economic, social and political freedoms that are the birthright of all human beings – then we cannot ignore violations of those rights by our own governments. Nor can we ignore how our own lifestyles in our own countries contribute to human rights violations around the world.

Un Ponte Pe . . . (A Bridge To . . .) is an Italian NGO that has been operating in Iraq for the last ten years. In Iraq, they help rehabilitate water-treatment plants and schools, and directly operate a health clinic for children in Basra. In Italy, they do grass-roots organising and education, governmental lobbying and direct action aimed at changing international policies that contribute to the humanitarian crisis in Iraq.

Fabio Alberti, president of Un Ponte Pe . . ., told me: 'It's not enough to help people without targeting the causes of their suffering, and it's not enough to do political work without having a concrete element to help people . . . We are the most powerful people in the world – white, Western people. We are trying to manage the world as our property. We are consuming 80 per cent of the resources of the world and that, finally, brings us here – to this situation in Iraq. Our security depends on finding a new way to manage our lives.'

The one constant in international policies towards Iraq, particularly US and UK policies over the last 13 years, has been an absolute indifference to the suffering those policies have inflicted on the Iraqi people. Given US hyperpower and dominance in our world, directly challenging those policies can be extremely difficult – difficult politically, socially and economically. Are Iraqis facing any lesser challenges in reconstructing their society today?

If we would truly help the Iraqi people, then that intention demands that we see and treat them as our equals, and therefore take risks within our own lives commensurate with the risks that have been regularly imposed on them, over long years, by the rest of the world. ❑

Ramzi Kysia is an Arab-American peace activist and writer who has worked in Iraq with Voices in the Wilderness (www.vitw.org) for over a year and has been helping young Iraqis establish the independent newspaper al-Muajaha (The Witness).

Al-Muajaha is available online ➪ www.almuajaha.com

EVERYDAY LIFE IN IRAQ

DESPITE THE TANKS, THE GUNS AND
THE CHAOS, LIFE GOES ON IN THE
TOWNS AND VILLAGES OF IRAQ

Baghdad, 6 June 2003: Riyad and Maya celebrate their wedding.
Credit: Marco di Lauro / Getty Images

Above: north-east of Baquba, 7 May 2003: tanks, sheep and shepherd tangle on the highway. Credit: AFP Photo / Roberto Schmidt

Opposite, top: Baghdad, 11 April 2003: braving smoke-filled streets for a little loot. Credit: Scott Nelson / Getty Images

Opposite: 26 March 2003: blind and bewildered in the face of attack. Credit: AFP Photo / Eric Feferberg

Opposite: Mosul, 4 February 2003: Saddam's finest, the women's militia, line up to face the impending US/UK invasion. Credit: AFP Photo / Awad Awad

Top: Baghdad, 13 April 2003: bank robbers divested of their loot. Credit: AFP Photo / Awad Awad

Above: Karbala, 22 April 2003: after years of exclusion, Shias approach the shrine of Imam Hussein to express their devotion. Credit: AFP Photo / Romeo Gacad

*Baghdad, 24 April 2003: a former prisoner revisits her
place of torment under Saddam. Credit: Spencer Platt*

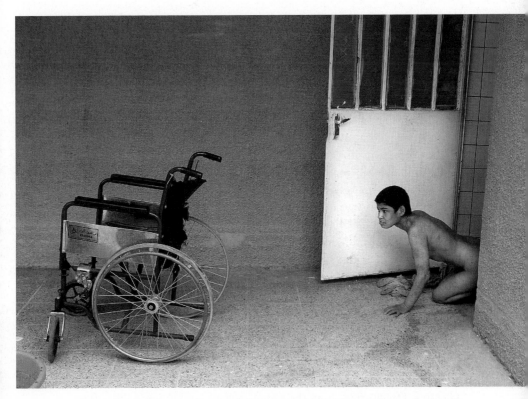

*Baghdad, 4 June 2003: inside an orphanage for mentally
disabled children. Credit: Mario Tarna / Getty Images*

BAGHDAD DIALOGUES:
30 JUNE–7 JULY 2003
TURI MUNTHE

Andrew Erdmann is the US civil affairs officer attached to the Ministry of Higher Education. He must be 35 years old. He's the man ultimately responsible for the entire Iraqi university system. As we walk through Saddam's gigantic presidential palace in Baghdad, where he lives and works, he tells me the first few weeks there, without electricity for air conditioning, were 'brutal'.

On 16 May, L Paul Bremer III, Iraq's civil administrator, issued a statement excluding any high-ranking members of the Baath Party from public office. Erdmann has sacked about 2,000 professors. He admits he might not have ordered the same himself, but he's following orders – energetically, as energetically as he is trying to supply books, funds and building materials to the rubble that is Iraq's higher education system. Erdmann is liked by most university administrators.

In the 1970s and 80s, Iraq's universities were the pride of the Arab world. The children of the rich flocked there from across the region. 'Baghdad University' on a name tag was a common sight at top-level academic conferences worldwide. Quality was achieved only because the professors, Baathists or not, were so adept at resisting the politicisation of their subjects. That was until sanctions began in 1990. 'Every aspect of higher education has been debilitated,' Erdmann tells me, 'by the previous regime.'

Erdmann is a man of rigorous principle. 'Analytical' is his favourite adjective. He worried about the timing of the war, but joined the effort because he felt he had to. 'For better or worse, international affairs are now guided and defined by US concerns. Analytically, if this goes wrong, the fallout in world politics will be way worse than it was after Vietnam.' He wants to ensure it doesn't go wrong. 'When my kids are ten, and the world is a bad place, I don't want to tell them I did nothing to improve it, however unimportant whatever I did was.' Erdmann is scrupulously reasonable – it's the way he parcels up his life. He is also scrupulously sincere. In a microcosm, he represents the very best reasons the US went to war. He's idealistic and he runs on well meaning. He is also grossly naive.

Most of those excluded by the Bremer directive claim they had to join the system in order to work. 'I don't pity them,' he tells me. Erdmann, whose standard short back and sides and mail-ordered clothes make him look like a caricature of the normal American, is asking these men and women to have bucked a system that was as violent as it was all-pervasive. Analytically, Baathism was a bad thing. Analytically, these men and women should not have played a part in it. The very nature of Baathism has meant that for 25 years no Iraqi has ever had the luxury of making analytical decisions.

Erdmann believes they should have fought the good fight. He believes 'education and politics should not mix'. Erdmann works for the State Department. His number two, Steve Curda, is an army colonel. Erdmann joined the war to watch the political application of intellectual models. He was 'fascinated by the practice of my PhD subject'. Erdmann's Harvard doctorate was entitled 'Conceptions of Victory in Twentieth-Century American Foreign Policy'. Colonel Curda's doctorate from the University of Oklahoma was, ominously, in Distance Learning.

I met Hussam al-Rawi al-Rifa'i beneath his portrait in the architecture school of Baghdad University, the second to last in a long line of serious-eyed, diffidence-inspiring sepia headshots of the successive heads of department. They represent the intellectual history of the school from its founding in 1948. Hussam himself is beautiful: he has German glasses and warm skin. He has poise. He is delicate and confident. He looks like he's been careful with his life. Hussam is a Section-Level Baathist, the third-highest rank in the party. He can no longer teach.

Hussam joined the Baath Party aged 15, just after the 1958 coup that toppled the monarchy. Conservative, from an old Baghdad family, he, like many, felt the Baath were his only hope against the rising power of the communists. He believed in them and he still has an ideological commitment to their ideas. The Baath slogan is Unity, Freedom, Socialism. Hussam wants a union of Arab states modelled on the EU, and he believes (like many) that light socialism (à la British Labour Party) is the only economic model that will work for Iraq. He went to RIBA – the Royal Institute of British Architects in London – and then began work there. Between 1975 and 1978, he was president of the General Union of Arab Students in Britain.

Most Iraqis think of Baathism as a system, not an ideology. To most, a Baathist is a brute, a bully-boy, a paid hand, a torturer, a mafioso. Hussam is the counter-example. Between 1982 and 1985, he was Dean of the College of Engineering. Then, last year, Lu'ay Khairallah, Saddam Hussein's nephew, who was studying at the college, hospitalised a professor for failing him in his end-of-year exams. Hussam expelled him, and was sacked himself. 'I would challenge any independent person to have done that,' he says. 'I paid a price I could live with. Others would not have – literally.'

Jihane was his departmental coordinator at the time. She is half-American. She has always been politically independent. She says she would never have got the job had it not been for him. Because he was such a high-ranking Baathist, Hussam could protect her. 'He helped ensure I stayed independent. In fact, over 80 per cent of the architecture faculty are non-Baathists because Hussam was able to stall pressure on us joining.'

Hussam has lived in a fracture. He has had to hack his integrity out of tarnished stone. 'We loved Michel Aflak [Baathism's progenitor]: he was romantic, he was a believer, he was almost a Sufi.' I asked him why, when he knew what Baathism was doing to his country, he stayed in the party. 'We kept hoping that something would change. We didn't want to leave because we loved the party, we loved its ideas. I thought we might just be able to fight from within.

'It looks as if I've been living in an old dream-world of ideals. I believed in an ideology that no longer existed, whose leader contravened all its principles. My conflict was between my hatreds: Western imperialism and the bastard who stood against it – Saddam, the man I hated, and the US, the power I hated. The US has never shown us Arabs any kind of moral justice.' Hussam says the Baath Party has never ruled Iraq.

Hussam is complicit in Baathism's cruelties, if only complicit in silence. He understands this all too well. What he doesn't understand is why men like Erdmann and Bremer are entitled to establish the parameters of morality by which he is judged.

I had dinner with Isam and Sadeq, two recently returned exiles. They're sharing a flat. One is a political theorist, one a poet. We met in their apartment building: plastic-cheap, dust and broken lifts. The apartment walls are grey-brown and bare, the kitchen is unused and there's a two-thirds empty bottle of the cheap Dimple Scotch you find here perched

Kathimiya Mosque, Baghdad 2003: a tribute to the martyr Muhammad Baqer al-Sadr replaces the image of Saddam. Credit: Turi Munthe

on the sill of the little I can see of Sadeq's room. Isam has stopped drinking. Two weeks ago, he fell apart over a bottle of arak and it terrified him.

We had thick tea in the main room. Threadbare, rubber-velvet furniture, an imitation-wood coffee table, and al-Jazeera playing fuzzily on a 1970s TV in the corner. Isam grins: 'A life of militancy has given me low requirements.' I feel as if I'm on a film set, talking hard, idealistic politics in a room that looks like a crack den. The place has dissidence and danger written all over it. They had no food, so we went out.

Sadeq is acutely depressed. His eyes are not so much dead as burrows of sadness. He has spent two decades at poetry gatherings apologising for his exile, trying to excuse the failure of his generation, taking the blame for Saddam. Isam spent 24 years outside the country. If the war had taken place six months earlier, he would have been with his mother when she died. Neither can believe they have returned. Isam is tormented by snapshot nostalgia. I'm smoking. 'My father used to keep Craven A cigarettes in the guest bedroom.' Sadeq returned to the house where he was born and kissed its bricks. 'It's magical. It sounds ridiculous, but it's *magical*.'

There's no true romance to exile. 'Exile makes you free and lost. You have no context; you have no reason for morality; you have nothing concrete left to fight for.' Isam tells me he is a womaniser, as he thinks I am. He is trying to show off. I don't believe him. On the contrary, he has had little else but his morality, his fight to ground him. I think that enforced integrity embarrasses him.

Both Isam and Sadeq work for the Coalition Provisional Authority (CPA). Both say accepting that work was the hardest decisions of their lives 'in a life of hard decisions'. Both are on the edge of resignation. They hated General Jay Garner, the first civilian viceroy of Iraq: 'A brute, a fool. His people hated Iraqis and disrespected them in what amounted to straightforward racism,' says Sadeq. But Bremer, his successor, is little better. 'His Iraqi advisers – us – are decoration. No one will listen to us. The CPA *still* has the most simplistic view of Iraq. They still divide us up into Shiites and Sunnis, they still obsess about our imagined tribalism. They don't *want* to disabuse themselves,' says Isam.

'And they're going to blow this country apart if they try to turn it into a satellite. Sweeping economic liberalisation will bring this country down and hurl it into civil war. It will create massive wealth disparity and bring on enormous political unrest.' Since those who profit now can only be those close to the US, internal civil unrest will yoke itself to already-virulent anti-occupation sentiment. 'We'll fall apart.' Isam's work on the liberalisation of developing economies is world class and ground-breaking. 'The only thing to save us will be a light welfare state. And for that, there is absolutely no political will.'

Sadeq is convinced his battle – the battle for secularism, for his kind of culture (a stitching of Sorbonne thought and Beirut colour) – is lost. Lost to religion. 'The problem with the secular is it can offer nothing absolute. As a result, a secular democracy has no absolute authority. Men are prepared to die for absolutes, not for relative principles. The Iranian Revolution of 1979, a combined putsch of clerics and leftists, became the Islamic Revolution for just that reason.' Sadeq, who is breaking inside, can say this; Isam could not. He asks: 'I wonder if we are still Iraqis. I know I am. I have always known I am. But will they believe we are? Won't they see us as foreign? Will we be allowed to be?'

We left the restaurant too close to the 11pm curfew to find a taxi. I, a Westerner, hailed an open-backed van to take us home. They sat in the front, I in the back, and I watched battered Baghdad roll up to us in the space between their two heads. Framed like that, I watched a tragedy, a requiem for a dream.

Al-Kathimiya is a district in the north of Baghdad named after the Kathimiya Mosque, a gigantic golden-domed Shiite complex crawling with people. Outside it, the colossal portrait of Saddam has been pulled down and replaced with one of Muhammad Baqer al-Sadr, luminary of the religious aristocracy, martyred in 1999. It looks as if it has always been there. The limbless gather outside the Kathimiya gates, so many of them they look like a separate species: an army of early human prototypes with design flaws.

Two hundred metres away, down a back street washed by raw sewage that smells of pig, lives Sayyed Ali al-Wa'adh, imam of the mosque and deputy of Ali Sistani of Najaf, perhaps the highest religious authority in Iraq. In the antechamber to his study, a fat mullah with rotten teeth and exquisite Arabic is hurtling through Quranic exegesis with four middle-aged men. An older man sits near me. 'Under Saddam, say a word against God and they'd promote you. Say a word against Saddam, and they'd cut out your tongue.' This isn't rhetoric.

Sayyed Ali is an old man, with a beard that fans out like a grouse tail, a speech impediment and a black turban, which tells you he's descended from the Prophet. His position is somehow both acquired and hereditary. I go to shake his hand, but he withdraws it. It is kissed by his attendants. I can't touch him. Sayyed Ali's family has lived in this house – 'the house of learning' – for 120 years. He himself has spent the last 23 years under continuous house arrest.

'The Americans have freed us, they have ended the tyranny. This is truly a beautiful thing. But if they want to stay and govern us, we will say no. We have already lived occupation under the British. Do you remember the 1920 rebellion? We do not want to live that again.' He feels powerful enough to threaten: 'We hope the US will leave peacefully. We hope there will not have to be any deaths.'

Sayyed Ali is looking forward to a new Iraq. He wants a multi-party, Islamic, democratic government free of foreign interference. He wants a Muslim-Arab president, Shia or Sunni. 'The Just' is one of the 99 names of God. He wants a president whose true quality is justice. Ali believes democracy – the rule of the people – is Islamic. He does not believe in the Wilayat al-Faqih doctrine of Ayatollah Khomeini. He believes in a state *inspired* by Islam.

'The US are responsible for daily rapes and daily deaths. They have freed the thieves and stripped the hospital and prison guards of their weapons. They understand nothing. They desecrate our mosques, and harass our women. They are surrounded by quislings, exiles, men who are no longer Iraqi but want to use Iraq for themselves. There will be demonstrations, and then there will be bullets.'

There are two large photographs by the bed on which he sits. Both show him leading prayers at the Kathimiya. The first, black and white, gold-framed, was taken in 1971. He stands alone at the head of his congregation, arms raised to his head, facing Mecca. The second was taken in April this year. It's the same scene: he can hardly hold himself upright, but there are three times as many people standing behind him. ❏

Turi Munthe is a writer and editor. He is the author of The Saddam Hussein Reader (Thunder's Mouth Press, New York, 2002)

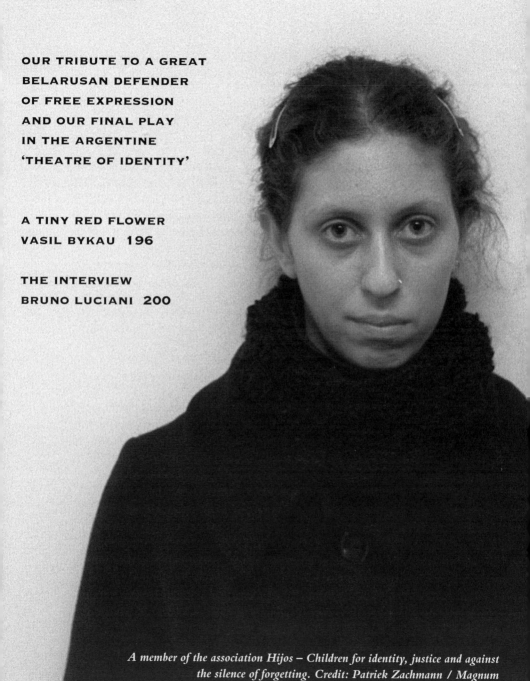

CULTURE

OUR TRIBUTE TO A GREAT
BELARUSAN DEFENDER
OF FREE EXPRESSION
AND OUR FINAL PLAY
IN THE ARGENTINE
'THEATRE OF IDENTITY'

A member of the association Hijos – Children for identity, justice and against the silence of forgetting. Credit: Patriek Zachmann / Magnum

A TINY RED FLOWER . . .

VASIL BYKAU

VASIL BYKAU, the most eminent Belarusan writer of the past half-century, died of cancer on 22 June 2003, three days after his 79th birthday.

Bykau came to prominence on the Soviet literary scene with the publication of his novel The Third Flare *(1962) set during World War II. This, and the novels that followed,* The Dead Feel No Pain *(1965),* Alpine Ballad *(1966),* The Accursed Hill *(1968),* The Kruhlanski Bridge *(1969),* Sotnikau *(1970),* Obelisk *(1971) and* Pack of Wolves *(1981), revolutionised the war-reportage/novel genre throughout the Soviet Union, replacing the hitherto standard stereotypes of 'good' Soviet partisans, wicked Nazis and treacherous collaborators with more complex individual characterisation and the grim realism of war. His books became bestsellers throughout the USSR, translated into Russian and other Soviet languages, and he won a number of leading Soviet literary prizes.*

Fame, however, did not protect Bykau from the attentions of the censors, who disliked critics of the Stalinist regime.

With the arrival of Mikhail Gorbachev, perestroika and the collapse of the Soviet Union, Bykau was at the forefront of the campaign for Belarusan independence and the revival of the Belarusan language and culture which, under Soviet rule, had been downplayed. He became a leading member of the pro-democracy pro-independence Belarusan Popular Front and of Martiraloh – the organisation set up to honour the victims of Stalin's purges in Belarus – and was elected first president of the new Belarusan PEN Centre.

The arrival of Alaksandr Lukashenka as president of Belarus in 1994 changed all that: control over all aspects of life increased; Belarusan language and culture were discouraged; freedom of speech and of the press was under constant threat.

Under Bykau's leadership, Belarusan PEN resisted these trends. The regime retaliated with various forms of bureaucratic harrassment. At the end of 1998, Bykau left Belarus under the auspices of the 'Cities of Refuge' initiative. He finally settled in Prague at the personal invitation of Czech President Vaclav Havel. Back in Belarus, literary magazines were forbidden to publish any of Bykau's works.

Bykau repeatedly stressed that his stay abroad was purely temporary, but his health was deteriorating; in March this year he underwent surgery for cancer and, as soon as he was able to travel, returned to Belarus where his death on 22 June coincided with the anniversary of Hitler's invasion of the Soviet Union, an event that had been so central to his work.

Vera Rich

He had a great love for the people, and the people had a great love for him.

Especially since the Uprising, which he had nursed, prepared and commanded and in which he had won the first victory. The Uprising was no easy matter: victories alternated with defeats, but the people believed in him and followed him. Indeed, he did not grudge time or strength or the work of his deep understanding for the holy cause – the victory of the People's Uprising.

At first these were few and the forces of long years of oppression were ten times greater, but his will gave the insurgents the strength not to go under completely. They endured everything – defeats under the walls of the fortress, persecution, torture in prison, death sentences, captivity, exile. He never gave up, he always said: 'Liberty will come, victory will come: the sun will shine in at our little window too!' And he called on them to struggle, sparing nothing, neither people nor lives nor wives nor themselves. Nor did he spare himself, nor his wife and children, who were tortured to death in captivity.

When the great victory was won, and the impenetrable fortress taken, the people's love for him knew no bounds. In the fortress, which he had stormed for 20 days, they raised him high on crossed lances, draped with the twin colours of the patriots. There, in the bailey of the fortress, a newly formed guard – a company of hand-picked young insurgents – swore allegiance to him. The city fathers brought him platters full of gold coins. Ten of the fairest women in the city pulled off his boots and bathed his tired feet. They vowed to serve him throughout their lives, in war and in peace. In the eyes of the people, he became the most handsome and noble-minded man alive. And utterly generous – he owned nothing and was satisfied with what they gave him. When he spoke from the steps of the cathedral a crowd of thousands listened with bated breath. Always he spoke like God, giving not the least reason to doubt a single one of his words.

He rose to the peak of universal glory and recognition which, it seemed, none could take from him, neither god nor devil. In the eyes of the people, he was no less to be honoured than either of them.

Unfortunately, the struggle did not end with the fortress. The oppressors did not lie down. Those who survived the attack fled abroad, where they found support. The brief breathing space lasted only months. He did not waste this time: he strengthened his household and defence. Day and night people toiled to repair the fortress, to rebuild the shattered towers and gates and walls. He perfected his army, appointed commanders, gave posts to the ablest and bravest. But those abroad were not asleep; they established alliances, recruited mercenaries whom they armed and fed with hate for the insurgents. Their money was plentiful; the army they assembled was great. And one sunny day, this army appeared under the fortress walls.

He called the people to defend it and the people rose as one. A siege began, and continued into the late autumn. At first the defenders held their own, but gradually things became harder. Reserves began to run low. There was a shortage of water. People could bear the short commons, but without water things were impossible. They started to murmur together saying that some people were taking too much water, that spies had poisoned the wells, that there were spies all over the place and he was failing to expose them. And then the attacks began again, every day. The besieged fought heroically from turrets and walls, their siege engines hurled shot, rained boiling water and hot oil and Greek fire on the heads of the enemy. But the enemy did not give up – and they were innumerable. In the fourth month of the siege, they delivered an ultimatum: unconditional surrender.

He called a great assembly which unanimously resolved to fight on to victory. He promised the people victory, and the people, as ever, believed him.

The struggle went on, but the forces were ill-matched, and the advantage swung more and more towards the enemy. In the fortress, food ran out, and then powder. Half the defenders had been wounded. On the walls of the fortress, women, old men and even half-grown children fought on. Everyone believed they would be victorious. No one wanted to surrender.

But their strength proved unequal to the task and finally the enemy broke into the fortress. He himself led the counter-attack and the breach was held. He was gravely wounded during that battle, shot in both legs, but he continued to command the resistance. And he still assured everyone that victory would come. And the people shouted 'Hurrah!' But they were less than before . . .

And when the fourth breach came they had no forces left. The enemy took over the bastion and there, beside the twin colours of the insurgents, they killed him. Some faithful women managed to get his body away in the night and buried it by the cathedral. One of them tried to kill herself on his grave, but they stopped her.

The people suffered the full horror of defeat. Most of the insurgents were killed, the rest taken captive. The captives were put into fetters and sent to the quarries. Soon the enemy occupied the whole fortress. Those women who had washed his feet were sold into oriental harems. The simple people died of hunger and disease. In the spring, the Black Death broke out.

The victors told the people this was punishment for the crimes of their idol; that he was an adventurer and anti-Christ. Otherwise he would not have sent so many to their deaths for something unattainable. Victory over the victors – impossible! Now the people must pay for his adventures and the price would be enormous. The people feared and believed their words; how can one not believe the victors? As time went on, people grew to hate their late leader and wondered how they could ever have listened to him.

It was said that some of those who once swore allegiance to him came by night and dug up his grave and threw out the body. And ravening dogs tore it apart and dragged it over the cobbles.

But many years later, one spring, when the grass had grown green on the place that had been his grave, someone laid a tiny red flower. It lay there a long time, unwithering . . . ❑

Translated by Vera Rich

THE INTERVIEW ('LA ENTREVISTA')

BRUNO LUCIANI

*In June 2000, under the title 'Theatre for Identity' ('Teatro x la Identidad'),
a series of short plays was launched by the Grandmothers of Plaza de Mayo in
Buenos Aires. Their purpose was to remind Argentines of those – including their
own loved ones, children and grandchildren – who had disappeared during
Argentina's dictatorship from 1976 to 1983.*

On 23 June 2003, the third of the trilogy, The Interview *by Bruno Luciani,
a young playwright from Argentina, had its first staging in English at the Arcola
Theatre in London along with the first two plays* A Propos of Doubt *by Patricia
Zangaro (Index 1/01) and* In Labour *by Marta Betoldi (Index 1/03). Index
is happy to follow its publication of these with the final part.*

*The performances stress that memory and identity are matters of international
importance in a world dominated by civil and global wars. The loss of identity forced
on large sections of some societies is a pain that will remain when the wounds of the
flesh have healed. Governments toy with these at their peril.*

*Since Bruno Luciani's play was written, events in Argentina have changed.
President Néstor Kirchner took office on Argentina's National Day, 25 May 2003.
His government passed a bill through the lower House of Congress reversing 1987
legislation that granted immunity to members of the armed forces who served the
dictatorship. If the bill, passed on 12 August 2003, becomes law, the men and
women who stole lives and newborn babies, who murdered and tortured people
with impunity, will finally have to face trial, almost 20 years after the event.
The psychological effect of this has been to throw an entire society into a state of
anxiety; Argentines in general do not want to rake through the torments of the
past at every trial.*

Andrew Graham-Yooll

The stage is in darkness. There is a sound of computer keyboards, telephones ringing, voices of sales staff in a telemarketing company. It is deafening. Above the noise a deep male voice calls, 'Next . . . name?' The words that follow are unclear and the interviewers and their interviewees overlap. The impression is of many interviews, many offices, many people. A spotlight comes on slowly and shines on a woman's legs. She is seated. Waits anxiously, nervous and fidgety. Her feet move often, but stop at a ten-to-two position. On hearing the male voice, the feet come together sharply. She takes off one shoe and shakes out a stone. 'Next.' But she is too busy with her shoe. 'Hey, you!' The voices rise. Light shines fully on a young woman, shoe in hand, smelling her sock.

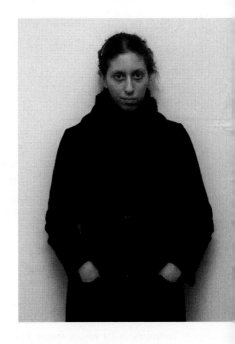

YOUNG WOMAN What d'you mean, what's my name? My name's in my CV. With the letter of introduction . . . from Mrs María Antonieta. I was her secretary until recently. I can operate a PC, I speak English, type . . . no, not very fast, but I have elegant handwriting. It is a family trait. Mrs María Antonieta has a very round hand, perfect. Mine's OK, she forced me to learn when I was little, it took time, but I learned. When I was smaller I used to draw very well. On walls. But not at my home. I was very small, before . . . before I was small with . . . Small from when I can't remember . . . much before . . . before.

I sold subscriptions for private medicine. That lasted three months. The business closed because of a little problem with the books at an old people's home which was not registered. Or something. You know. The usual fiddle. Well, then I went on holiday to the seaside with some friends. I was responsible for a stall where people tasted those new American potato crisps which are all the same size, delicious. What else did I do . . . ? Oh, yes.

Music comes up and, followed by a spot, she does a couple of cabaret steps.

One, one, four. Twenty million pesos. National Lottery, the one that pays and pays. The old bastard who won didn't even throw me a hundred.

She goes back to the interview chair.

I wanted to stay there but the director-general of Lotteries and Casinos of Buenos Aires said: 'The girl has a nice voice, but she can't tell the difference between a flute and a kettle boiling.' That was it, boiling water, that was used to remove the drawings from the walls. I was quite good at painting. I said so, didn't I? Can't remember much, but I know it was when I was small. From before . . . I have memories that are cloudy, but I have some . . . I painted with crayons and a little boy took them from me, all the time. The crayons . . . the walls . . . that I remember. Well, really only the crayons because the walls he told me about because he was older. And now he is incredibly big, enormous. Wherever you look at him. Those feet, that nose . . . he is very tall, like Dad . . . he showed me some photos from when he was small, when his dad held him in his arms. He was a giant. Not me, I have tiny feet, like Mum, small. Short. No feet, no stability. You know those inflatable dolls one punches and punches and punches and they always come upright? That was the old man. He doesn't look like it in the photo but he was. Shall I go on? If you would rather I can speak slower. Right, slower, more elegant.

She walks downstage as if to tell the audience a secret.

D'you know what the girls at school called him? 'Lovely Hunk'. I also called him that. He was so lovely . . . he still is . . . has huge eyes . . . and a hard flat stomach . . . but at school, when we met, he was like that and he drove the girls in my class mad. He was in fifth and we were in third. Fat chance we had. Whenever there was a tournament we went to cheer, wherever it was held.

She moves about slowly, mouthing as if chanting with the fans in a stadium.

Bunch of droolers we were, watching every move of his hand, each breath, every move! Never seen anything more boring than chess. But we didn't miss a match. And when the event was over, after five or six hours of sheer boredom, we just sat there . . . waiting for him to acknowledge us . . . that he should see we were the fans from third B . . . the ones who did not miss a single game . . . his girls.

Sounds off, footsteps which she follows with her eyes as they seem to walk across centre stage.

And he went right past the stands, the quickest look and walked right on. A whole morning doing our hair, making up, lashes, heels, miniskirt, cleavage, uplift. None of us admitted it, but each time he walked past us it was a relief. We were so nervous when he came close. Just imagine how we'd feel if he talked to us . . . help! We would have probably looked like 'The Stutterers Choir', trying to find the best way, the best tone, the most relaxed posture, to tell him how much we had liked his game. I had not the slightest idea about chess! Lucky he walked past us. Nowadays I do understand everything. The bishop moves across, the pawn doesn't . . .

Do you play chess? None of my business, is it? Look, if you don't stop me I'll talk, talk, talk. I secrete saliva very well. I've never been hoarse. That's good for the job, isn't it?

As I was saying I now have my own private chess tutor. The 'Lovely Hunk'. I wouldn't touch him with a barge pole now, but in those days, phhhoaaarrhh . . . And the girls from school that I still see die for him. The 'Lovely Hunk'. At first when he started to come closer . . . my God. The first time he stopped me in one of the passages I began to shiver from the nerves. Spring at its best, the heat beat the shit out of you! And all I did was shiver, nod my head and utter: aha, aha, aha . . . as he was leaving, at the end, I was able to find a thread of a voice to say: OK, I'll go . . . see yah there . . . jeans or frock? For a gig. I'd never been to one. I was scared shitless. The 'Lovely Hunk' really liked ME. The trouble was afterwards, when I saw him in the hall at school I avoided him. I felt terribly ashamed . . . but he came over again. Sure, the lad had to question me, and he is so pig-headed. The thing is, I went to no meetings, no demos and no students' union, so there was no place we had in common. One day, though, yes. I was dragged back to the chess, by my friends. After an endless tournament, where I fell asleep halfway through, as he was passing the stands he stopped, instead of going straight on. He told La Turca, my friend, to call me. I was fast asleep. She shook me and, only half asleep, I saw him, standing there, serious. I felt the eyes of all the girls, they drilled holes right through my neck. Never gave it a thought. Rather than stay with them like a bunch of hens, I stood up, grabbed his hand, and walked away. He didn't know what had hit him either, I think.

Sounds off: two pairs of feet running quickly along an empty hallway. One of the pairs trips . . .

I dragged him along a passage which ran the length of the school, from the gym to the patio.

She drags the chair from stage left to centre stage.

We got there, up against a wall, I had not looked at him the whole way. There was nobody because it was Saturday, start of the month, when the chess tournament begins, I turned, and we stood looking at each other.

She faces the chair.

We were panting as if we had run the marathon. I was terrible at games. But anyway, have a look at my report, the next page, where my name is, you will see that my average was always among the ten best at school.

She acts a conversation changing from Her to Him, using a teenager's body language and imitating a boy's deep voice.

'Thanks, I was really embarrassed with your friends watching me.'
   Me, speechless.
   'You get quite bored at the chess games, don't you?'
   Me, speechless, and with a need to run away.
   'I get bored.'
   This bloke's mad, I thought.
   'I play because my granny taught me when I was very small. And I play well . . . against her. At the matches I don't concentrate, I get nervous because of the pressure of a guy opposite. That's why I never say hi to you. I've never won a match.'
   I never noticed.
   Suddenly somebody yelled at him, 'Go on, kiss the cow!' I had my heels on, but just in case I rose a little, willing. I lost my balance and went down on my arse. I looked up at him, fixed, if he laughed I'd kill him. But

I giggled. I had tried so hard to be serious I couldn't stop laughing, and he laughed too.

She imitates his deep laugh.

We walked out to find a bar.

A second time, in a bar. She sits on the chair as if at a table, and again acts her own and his part. Offstage, sounds of a coffee bar.

'What's your name? Where d'you live? How old are you?'
    'You look older. What's your zodiac sign? D'you like barbecues?'
    No. I'm a vegetarian.
    'Funny, so am I.'
    Runs in the family . . .
    Any brothers and sisters?
    'Yeah, a younger sister, but I don't know her. Do you?'
    No. I don't know her either.
    'Who?'
    Your sister.
    'I meant do you have any?'
    Oh, me? No. Only child.
    'Your parents?'
    My mother has a brother, my uncle Alfredo.
    'Nah . . . D'you live with your parents?'
    With my mum.
    'What happened t'yer dad?'
    Killed in battle. And you?
    'I live with my gran.'
    And your parents?
    'Disappeared.'
    In the war against subversion?
    'No, the dictatorship.'
    Same thing, the war.
    'There was no war.'
    Ah.
    He said nothing.
    I said nothing.

And I was so nervous I blurted.

Nice eyes.

'Thanks, same as yours.'

D'you think so?

'Yes. And your nose also looks the same. Look.'

Bar sounds stop.

And he looked at his image in the bar window.

I looked at mine, and looked at his, and looked at him. The fans were off. I was sweating like a pig.

Yes . . . funny, isn't it? So? I said for something to say.

'Nothing. Just that. It's nice to find somebody that looks like one.'

I was short of air.

D'you know the time?

'No.'

Oh, well. Then it's getting late. I want to go. I must go.

A stranger in front of me makes me very nervous.

'OK. D'you want my phone?'

As you like, I answered.

He wrote the number on a paper napkin.

Sound of vigorous hand with pen on paper.

He put it on the table, I grabbed it, stood and reached the door.

Bye, I said to him.

Sound of thunder and heavy rain.

I ran off like a fool.

She runs in short quick steps around the chair.

I felt more of a fool when my heel broke. I looked like the Hunchback of Villa Crespo. I ran three blocks, to the little square. I went to the swings.

She stands behind the chair and moves slowly back and forth.

I swung, very hard. Very high. I flew.

She is illuminated by one small spot.

Sounds off: pleasant noises. Drops of water, frogs. The squeal of the chains of a swing. A telephone rings. A light shines on a telephone at stage right, close to the proscenium.

Shall I answer? I have always been told that my telephone voice is very agreeable. As if people were talking to me right here.

Telephone continues to ring until she lunges and sits on it. Light only on the telephone area.

After that day, every time the telephone rang at home I always answered. What an idiot! He didn't have my number. The first time it rang I lunged at it. I'd never let her answer, she wasn't too well those days . . . now . . .

Hello . . . fine, Turca, fine.

My friend asked me if things were OK with the 'Lovely Hunk'. What the hell was I going to answer?

Yes, Turca, we have many things in common. Many . . . No, Turca, he hasn't kissed me, but he said his nose is as awful as mine. What did he mean? I'll tell you some other time.

Some other time? There was fuck all to tell. I became ill. That week was endless. An endless shit. I didn't go to school, I didn't see the girls. I saw nobody. I even had to listen to herself ask if I was pregnant. Yes . . . by the Holy Spirit. I was thinking, 'How the fuck will you understand what is happening, if I hardly know myself.'

But she understood, she didn't miss a beat, and as I saw him again after that week, she started to restrain me. I couldn't go out, I had to be home right after school, I wasn't to answer the phone. She was super-paranoid. And I never said a word to her, I never asked her. I didn't dare, I was too afraid. Too afraid. The widowed mother, the dead hero father killed in battle and the only, perfect daughter, 'can't say, won't say'. What a family portrait. Fine to put up over the mantelpiece, and smash it against the wall and throw it in the fire. Let it burn, let it burn. To Hell.

Then she told me I'd have to go if I carried on with those ideas. If I continued to dishonour the memory of 'my' father. 'Your husband,' I said.

She nearly died.

She picks up the phone, then throws it on the floor.

But that first week, while I was at home, ill, all I ever wanted was for him to explain what the hell all that about the eyes and the nose was about. I couldn't get out of bed.

   Eyes . . . nose? *(pause)* Too many coincidences. I called him.

She nervously starts to sharpen a pencil.

Hello . . . yes, it's me, with the eyes and the nose. Look, I don't think it is the least bit of a joke. Tonight? Who? . . . never heard of him. Yes, I'll go. Plaza de Mayo? OK . . . but I don't know anything about those things . . . only a gig . . . yes, but won't it be dangerous? Well, if you say so, let's. I'll see you there.

   I rang off.

She snaps the pencil and flings the pieces over her shoulder.

A gig in the street. Plaza de Mayo, the Town Hall, Casa Rosada, the cathedral. Obvious: there's no getting laid there. I arrived.

She stands on the chair and searches the distance.

Bunch of heads. I went to where he told me, 'Under the banner that says HIJOS (children of the "disappeared").' Some detail. All I needed was a badge and him to say, 'Welcome to the club.' I waved from some distance and he signalled to get closer to the stage.

Off: sounds of a band at a gig. She starts to jump, partly dancing, as she speaks she looks as if she were on a pogo stick.

There was I in the middle of a gig listening to a baldie in pyjamas who was singing, people threw bottles at him, and he talked about identity. Yes. Lots of identity, lots. But in the crush I got my crotch grabbed several times and I never knew who did it.

Sudden stop in sound. She picks up the chair and drives away imaginary attackers. Puts the chair back in its first position.

Well, what d'you think. I always found it easy to speak and I have a good voice. You noticed? Tact. If there is something men don't have it's tact. Sorry, I don't mean you, of course.

And I don't mean just when they want a grope, but also when they have to say things.

My brother, tact . . . less than anybody. It is not that I realised in the bar and suddenly knew the whole story. The truth is I noticed nothing at the time. But something did happen. My stomach turned, I didn't know why. But it was more obvious at the gig. Couldn't he have gone a little slower? OK, so he didn't show me the photo of the two of us, very small, playing in the sandbox, that he told me about.

She goes to look for it in a bag. Sits.

That photo, the one with the flowered pants, where we are together . . . he didn't show it to me because there isn't one. If there had been, he wouldn't have hesitated.

So, now, Mrs María Antonieta, what is she to me? I asked one day. She brought me up . . .

A door slams.

Hey, careful. You trying to make it revolve?!

It wasn't easy.

You could have been a bit more pedagogical at first, I told him recently, remembering that day. I am studying psycho-pedagogy, so I know something.

'Pedagogy, fuck . . .' he answered. 'I didn't force you into anything. True, I went looking for you. But after that you started to doubt on your own, and you're no fool. You were sixteen and had a right to know.'

Yeah, the right to know. He knew he couldn't get a leg over right from the start. But he didn't give a damn. Now we meet regularly. Every Wednesday. We get on all right. Sometimes we see a film, when we agree on what to see. Other days we look at photos, or he tells me things he remembers when we were kids. It's OK. He's a brute, really. But he's right, really, he's right.

Light goes down over her.

Shall I go on? What d'you think of my voice.

What's my name. It says there on the CV. Yes, I use both names, but my surname is my dad's, not the captain's. The captain, who died in battle, the woman's husband. Dad and Mum are Dad and Mum. Those are the captain and his wife. What a ffff . . . mess. It's what there is.

She looks at her feet, positioned at ten to two . . .

Yeah, I've got flat feet. My brother does too. My father did. Some gift. But sitting you hardly notice, look.

She straightens her feet.

You want me to read you this? I went to a seminar on public speaking. Did I tell you? 'Welcome to our customer attention centre. Thank you for choosing us, my name is blank, to be completed by the employee. How can I help you?'

There. How did that sound? I told you I had a good voice. My mother's was also good. She sang at the family meals. The Beatles.

That I didn't get from her. But the voice is the same. My grandmother told me.

The phone rings. She answers and recites the short welcome speech. Her voice merges with other voices saying the same, they are unclear, the sound eventually is fused into the opening audio. The light goes down until only her feet are seen.

Blackout. ❑

First staged in 2001 at the General San Martin Cultural Centre in Buenos Aires; also staged at El Ateneo on 8 October 2002, directed by the author and performed by Paula Barrientos

WHEN THINGS FALL APART

CYNTHIA SCHARF

Beni, north-eastern Congo (DRC)

Dawn on a Sunday, and the sticky, white heat of the tropics already hangs heavy over the slumbering town of Beni, gateway to some of the richest and most violently contested territory in the Democratic Republic of Congo (DRC). Beni is just one of many hot spots in a war that has claimed some 3–4 million lives since 1998, a shocking statistic that makes Congo the world's deadliest conflict of the last half-century. Most of these deaths are from disease and hunger, a direct consequence of the war's violent displacement of millions of families, including some 80 per cent of the population in the north-eastern areas.

I am roused from sleep by the sound of loud chanting and quickened footsteps on the dirt road outside my hotel. Either this is a group of gospel-belting Congolese Christians en route to church, or a contingent of child soldiers marching through town in a display of preening adolescent militarism. I decide to cast my vote for the forces of faith over fear – deliberate wishful thinking on my part – and roll over back to sleep.

The street-side chanting continues, however, and I get up to investigate. My colleague, a British aid worker with the medical charity Merlin, one of the leading international humanitarian groups in DRC, cautiously informs me that several dozen Kalashnikov-toting, half-naked boy soldiers have just marched by. The hotel workers look supremely bored when we ask about the soldiers. Kalashnikovs, rebel soldiers, warrior chants: to them, it is just another Sunday morning in one of the world's worst neighbourhoods.

Eastern Congo is home to one of the world's worst, and least publicised, humanitarian crises. But unlike Iraq or Afghanistan, the war in Congo goes virtually unnoticed by the media, international parliaments or the public. Despite the huge death toll, Congo's tragedy is greeted with a shameful silence.

Several factors collude to shroud this war in obscurity. For starters, Congo is difficult to access. Imagine a nation bigger than Germany, France, Poland, Ukraine, Belarus and Hungary combined, one with virtually no roads, phones or infrastructure, no functioning local government, police, postal, education or health systems. Add to this Congo's unpredictable violence, and it becomes clear why few journalists venture here.

Second, and more fundamentally, Congo is not in the strategic sights of the USA, and in this unipolar world has fallen off the map of international attention. Third, news of calamity, be it famine, Aids or warfare, dominates (and distorts) our perceptions of Africa, and anaesthetises our sense of moral outrage over a war in which millions of civilians have died.

'The international community is prepared to fly out a handful of children from Iraq for expensive medical treatment because it suits their political purposes,' said Geoff Prescott, CEO of Merlin. 'Millions are left to die in DRC, however, because there is no PR benefit to be gained from helping them. This may be realpolitik, but it is a reality for which there is no morality.'

The war in DRC is at once both a civil war and an international conflict located within the borders of one of the continent's largest countries. But what is the war really about? Like so much about this incredibly huge, verdant, violent and complex country, no one really knows (*Index* 1/01).

It is much easier to state what it is not: it is not a conflict about ideology, nor is it about territory. Unlike Cold War era conflicts in Africa, the war in Congo is not about one group proclaiming its ideological superiority over the other. No army – Congolese, foreign or rebel – swears allegiance to any ideology other than that of pure self-interest. Nor are any of these armed groups seeking to redraw Congo's borders.

In part, the war has its roots in the Rwandan genocide of 1994. That year, 1 million Hutu refugees, including tens of thousands of *interahamwe*, Hutu extremists responsible for the genocide, flooded across the border into eastern Congo. Rwanda's current president, Paul Kagame, has vowed to hunt down every last *interahamwe*, and cloaks Rwanda's repeated military incursions into Congo in the robes of international justice.

Money is also a motive. Congo's vast natural resources – cobalt, copper, gold, rubber and coltan, a little-known mineral now found in every mobile phone and laptop – have proved an irresistible lure to outsiders since Congo was first brutally colonised. What the Belgians started under King Leopold II (the only European leader to claim an entire African country as his own personal property), Africa's own leaders have continued apace, shamelessly looting and plundering Congo's mineral wealth with impunity.

In 1965, soon after independence, Washington's client dictator, Mobutu Sese Seke, established a 30-year kleptocracy, which further drained the nation's wealth. His rule also left the state apparatus in shambles. Today, Uganda, Rwanda, Zimbabwe and Angola, in addition to assorted rebel factions, all vie for a piece of the action, trafficking in natural resources that help prop up their own systems. Significantly, the only ones who don't share in Congo's wealth are its own citizens – the millions of Congolese living on the very margins of survival.

In a crowded bar in Beni, I watch as the local fixtures in Congo's illegal, highly lucrative export economy assemble for the evening: Congolese prostitutes saunter up to drunken European businessmen and 'vodka pilots' from Russia. A soldier in camouflage taps his fingers on his ever-present Kalashnikov, beating out the rhythm of a Madonna song (ironically, the song is called 'Holiday') that blasts from a tinny stereo powered by one of the town's few generators. For the other 100,000–plus residents of Beni, this evening, like every other evening, passes in utter darkness. No electricity, no running water, no Madonna-inspired 'Holiday' – just the familiar din of child soldiers parading through dirt streets.

Since 1998, eastern Congo, particularly the mineral-rich Ituri region, has become the centre of savage violence between rival ethnic groups and proxy militias backed by Rwanda and Uganda, both recipients of vast amounts of British aid. In April of this year, Hendu and Lendu tribes openly slaughtered hundreds of civilians in the town of Bunia, prompting long-overdue international action to stem the bloodletting that has displaced up to 80 per cent of the population in Ituri and claimed an estimated 50,000 lives.

A French-led multinational force deployed to Bunia in June seemed to offer some hope for ending the orgy of violence. However, with an extremely limited mandate, the mission came under strong criticism from local Congolese and some NGOs for providing only the pretence of protection while thousands of civilians were left stranded without sufficient aid. The French departed on 1 September, and were replaced by a beefed-up contingent of UN troops (known by their French acronym, MONUC) authorised by the UN Security Council to keep the peace not only in Bunia, but throughout Ituri, a region roughly the size of Ireland.

It remains to be seen whether 5,000 MONUC troops can quell the pervasive violence in Ituri, or whether they will use their Chapter VII UN mandate actively to protect the thousands of Congolese civilians threatened by marauding militias. To date, the UN's track record in Congo does not provide much hope on this key point. Troop strength is also an issue: at most, MONUC has roughly the same number of troops authorised for its work in DRC as it did in Sierra Leone, a country about 3 per cent the size of Congo. A peace deal signed in April between rival Congolese factions could mark a turning point. The agreement called for the establishment of an interim government and the first free elections in Congo's history. While the agreement has lifted hopes for a viable political settlement, few hold their breath given the degree of savagery and corruption that has devastated this country.

In the meantime, the war slogs on for a fifth year, barring sustained pressure from UN Security Council members to enforce the stronger UN Mission mandate, provide sufficient resources for peacekeeping, and apply pressure on Congo's neighbours to stop funnelling men and arms into DRC in an effort to exploit the country's chaos.

According to Véronique Aubert, an Amnesty International researcher recently in the area, 'MONUC have failed to protect civilians, and failed to be present in Ituri where they are most needed and where the most egregious human rights violations are occurring.' To be fair, the 5,500 UN troops presently in Congo (another 3,200 are expected to join them) can do little to pacify a country as massive and chaotic as Congo. The UN mission in Sierra Leone, for example, had 17,500 troops.

What is most needed is, unfortunately, what is least likely to happen: namely, a commitment by the US, first and foremost, to invest the political capital and financial resources needed to push for a settlement between all warring parties. But Congo does not figure in the US-led 'war on terrorism'. Aid workers joke darkly that the best thing that could happen to Congo is the allegation that Osama bin Laden had formed a terrorist cell inside the country. There are few places in the world today where the gap between humanitarian needs and available resources is as cavernous as in the Congo. Perhaps only south Sudan and Somalia can contend for this infamous honour.

We justify our callousness with a world-weary sigh – 'but after all, this is Africa' – as if millions of lives could be written off because geography alone robbed them of their dignity and value. One might look at our collective callousness and conclude – not unjustly – that we seem to value human life most when it most closely resembles our own.

This form of ethical exceptionalism is deeply imbedded in the

Democratic Republic of Congo 2002: living on the margins
of endless war and devastation. Credit: © Cynthia Scharf

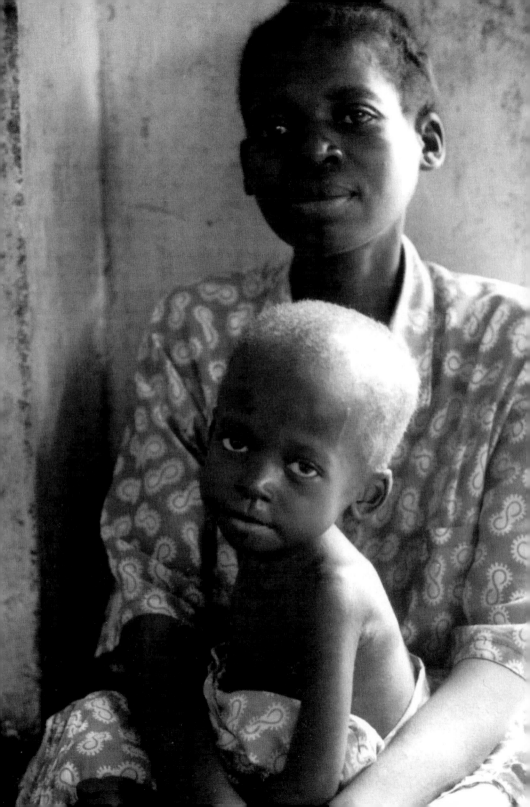

Western mindset, and derives in part from the power of narrative to frame perceptions of the world around us. For better or worse, Congo inevitably evokes for the Western imagination images from Joseph Conrad's *Heart of Darkness*. A recent visit to this enormously complex and chaotic country, however, brought to mind another literary masterpiece, this one indigenous to the African continent. The title: *Things Fall Apart*. And how.

The title of Chinua Achebe's novel serves as an all-too-apt moniker for the Congo, an enormous country virtually bereft of infrastructure or any of the normal trappings of state governance. No one knows the rate of HIV/Aids infection here, though health experts assume it is high – and climbing rapidly. Another human tragedy among many in Africa.

Another symptom of the country's breakdown is growing malnutrition. There is a tragic irony to the presence of hunger in Congo, a country so teemingly fertile it is said one can throw a stick in the ground and watch it grow. But there is little food available in key provincial towns. Not because it cannot grow, but because the fields cannot be harvested due to the ongoing violence.

In Kindu, a city of 150,000 now surrounded by Mayi Mayi soldiers, the central market place is nearly bare. One day I enter a feeding centre set up by Merlin, and watch as a six-year-old boy with prematurely whitened hair and pencil-thin limbs is checked by a nurse. Severely malnourished, the boy will soon die without immediate medical care. He emits a barely audible call for his mother. But neither she, nor his father, is anywhere to be found. The father was likely dragged off to war; the mother is presumed dead after being kidnapped in the fields by the Mayi Mayi.

Humanitarian assistance is vitally necessary to prevent further loss of life in the Congo. In itself, however, aid is an insufficient response to the crisis. Congo's swift and steady decline cannot be halted by international aid workers, as heroic and life-saving as their efforts are. As we have seen in Bosnia, Kosovo, Sierra Leone and elsewhere, humanitarianism is not – and should not be – a figleaf for political inaction and cowardice.

Ending the war in Congo is not simply a matter of humanitarian concern. Given the country's size and significance in regional politics, forging peace in the Congo is vital to ensuring stability throughout the whole of Central Africa.

The UN clearly has a role to play in bringing an end to the conflict, but with its effectiveness severely compromised during the Iraq debacle, analysts hold out little hope for immediate progress. In the meantime, what is to be done? Despite all they have been through, the Congolese people still evince a palpable yearning for national unity. In eastern Congo, the dream for reunification with Kinshasa, the capital city, remains.

We leave Beni the next day to return to Goma, a town covered in hardened black lava flows following last year's volcanic eruption. Somehow the chanting of boy soldiers still rings in my ears, their defiant tones haunting me. The echoes of their singing, the swagger of their naked limbs sheathed only in weaponry: these images stay with me as our plane lands in London some days later.

Back in the West, the news is still of Iraq, and now possibly Iran, as the US's obsessive search for a worthy enemy continues. Meanwhile, the carnage in Congo continues unabated, and the calamity that is DRC continues to fall on all-but-deaf ears among the media and most politicians. The West's collective indifference to the world's most lethal conflict is a shocking, but not surprising, stain on our conscience. ❏

Cynthia Scharf is a writer and journalist living in London

POINT OF ARRIVAL

*Within the present decade, and thanks largely to an influx of Asians from Africa in the late 1960s and early 1970s, Leicester, a modest and somewhat unprepossessing town in the Midlands — what has become known to the tourist trade as 'The Heart of England' — will be home to the UK's first majority non-white population (*Index, *3/02). Not that Leicester is any stranger to migration: since at least the nineteenth century, the city's prosperity has been built on the labour of incomers from less fortunate parts of the UK as well as from the former empire.*

For some years, the East Midlands Oral History Archive at Leicester University has been recording the personal histories of many of the migrants. Below, we present a range of their voices.

MR ABDUL HAQ came to Leicester from India in 1938

I came to Leicester in March 1938 and I've lived in the city ever since. My father lived here, and that's why I came, but soon the war started and my father went back, one month after the war started. I stayed here. It was my intention to go back to India in 1947, but along came the partition of India and I couldn't go because my people lost their home and everything, and they left their place. They went to live in Pakistan, 200 miles away.

When I first came here I couldn't speak English very well, but as soon as I mastered the language I was all right. The people, when they get to know you, are quite friendly, see; but it's getting to know you. From the time I've come to this city I've got on very well with English people all round. I've got nothing to grumble about: nice and friendly. Of course it was up to me as well. I respect everybody, and I find the people are the same to me, very much the same, and I've enjoyed a lot of their hospitality.

MRS N NAAN moved from Ireland during World War II to work at The Towers psychiatric hospital in Leicester

I can't remember what my fare was, but there were no night sailings during the war. So I had to come from the west of Ireland up to Dublin, stay a night in Dublin, get the boat in the morning and travel in the day . . . It was two days coming on the boat, *The Princess Maude*. It was terrible; there

*Point of arrival: Leicester's
Clock Tower and town centre –
'rather better than most'.*
Credit: Leicester Mercury

were cattle down underneath it . . . People had never heard of Leicester
. . . When you went home and said you were in Leicester, they'd say,
'Where's Leicester?' Even now, 'Where's Leicester?'

It was still the blackout when I came, and it was the trams then, they all
finished at nine o'clock at night. Well, everything finished at half past ten –
dances, everything . . . I was so homesick when I came here I cried myself
to sleep every night for about a fortnight. And another girl from Castlebar
came the same day to The Towers, and we used to say, 'What brought us
here? We'll go home tomorrow.' And here I am, 52 years on! I used to say
that I wanted to go back, but now all my family are here, and my
husband's buried here. So here I'll be.

MRS E MORTON came to Britain from Nevis in 1959 to work
as a nurse and moved to Leicester from Birmingham after she
got married

In the Caribbean there was no such thing as racism. We knew nothing
about racism. So we weren't trained to handle the situation when we came
here. I mean, when I came here first, even though I came to the hospital,
I still had to go to the Labour Exchange to show my passport . . . and to fill
a form out. And when I fill this form out, because she didn't see me fill it
out and put my signature, she asked me to fill one out in front of her,
because she didn't think I could write *that* good! You see, that was the sort
of racism we met, and we didn't experience those things in the Caribbean,
and we weren't ready for those things. I mean, even on those days you
come here, you see another Black person, and it doesn't matter how far
away that Black person is, you're moving closer and closer to get to know,
and just to be near that person, because you feel a little bit safer.

I mean, you go into the market, and you stand in the queue and you
wait, and they will pass over you, and serve everybody at the back, and
then they will tell you, 'What do you want, me duck?' Well, I got so
annoyed one day, I call for two pounds of everything on this stall, and then
walk away, you know, because I was really annoyed that these things could
happen, when you've been taught everything about England, and England
knew nothing about you. We had the Union Jack, we flew the Flag,
we had Empire Day, 24 May. We had Prince Charles's birthday. We had
everything that's going . . . We knew everything about England . . . And
yet they know nothing about us.

To be told, 'Why don't you go back where you come from,' was really
hard. We had the extended family. We had to save for our family, send
something back home. It was ten years before I got back home to see my
mum and dad. The Caribbean women, the Black women from the
Caribbean, we were the ones who paved the way . . . We were the ones
that put the first stone down, and from that stone, we are quite satisfied
with our lot, because we know we have brought our children up not to
hate. We have had that hate, we have asked them not to hate . . . The
amount of things we have been through is worth telling. We need to say
what really happened to us here when we came to this country.

MR D PATEL came to Leicester from Kenya in 1974

Now, I was in East Africa before I came to Leicester, and before that I was in India. I was born in India, and at the age of 16 I went to Africa. First I landed at Mombasa where my parents were, and there I had my education, further education and lived there for a total of 22 years in Nairobi and Mombasa . . . When I first came here I was 40 years old. Then I came with my family, my wife, four children and myself, and we settled here . . .

The reason why I came to Leicester and stayed was that before I came here to settle permanently in 1974, I came here for a holiday from Nairobi. I came here for an eight-week holiday. That time I travelled all over the UK, especially from up around Blackpool and other places. That was in 1971. So, from Nairobi I came here for a holiday, I travelled here, and that time I met all my friends and relatives, and after that I saw the country, and at that time I was so impressed that, well, if I had to come in this country, for me, well, persons like myself, I didn't have any problems deciding where to settle.

So I made up my mind that if I could choose anywhere I could come, that I would come and settle in Leicester . . . I particularly liked Leicester because, I don't know, but when I went to the city centre with my friends I was much attracted by the flatness of the city, you see. It's very much geographically visible, with an easy approach. It's nicely built, and it's not a confusing city, you see – that's what my view is, you see – and therefore I liked it.

Secondly, the roads leading out of the city centre are very straightforward. So I thought that would be very good as well for communications in the future. And also the business system I had seen at that time was spread all over the city in different areas. So I am a businessman, and I thought that if I had to come and choose a business, I would have a much wider choice here in Leicester, rather than going into one particular city and then not finding much environment or obvious availability of that sort of thing.

Thirdly, I was attracted because the Asian community was a good number in 1970–1 and I knew that. So that is also one of the reasons that I came to Leicester . . .

Racism: it was there, and even today it is still there. Now racism is something like a disease. You can cure and you cannot cure; in my opinion you know it won't be cured. It will be a relief, and that relief only you can achieve by good neighbourhood relations, good understanding within the community, and mainly by teaching. More than anything, it is the sound and voice of politicians. If the sound and voice of politicians is positive for the betterment of the entire population of this country, that message works faster than anything else . . . You see, the support of the bigger cities, whatever will happen is in the large cities like London, Birmingham, Leicester, Bradford, Preston. These are the cities that count, not the small places. Race relations in Leicester are much better than other cities. I go around the cities, and we are lucky that we have very good race relations.

ANONYMOUS WOMAN who came to Britain in 1965 and went back to India for the first time after 32 years

Almost everything seemed to be changed. It was a different world altogether. When I landed in Delhi, because I was already missing my children on the way, on the plane, I was saying what am I doing here, why am I doing this . . . I suppose I had forgotten the way people live, this culture, different. I'd got used to so much of British culture or the British way of life. I expected people to behave in a sort of British way . . . It wasn't a good experience, and I wanted to come home straight away, I wanted to catch the plane back home . . .

The village had changed. I didn't recognise it at all. We have a farmhouse, we have a guest house, we have a living house. When I went to the farmhouse, I didn't recognise it. The car stopped and I said, 'Why have we stopped here?' They said, 'We're here, this is our farmhouse.' I could not recognise anything at all. It seemed small; I don't know why it seemed so small. It used to be a vast open space but this time it was so small. It looked so tiny and very messy. The sugar cane, the maize, all that was all over the place, because there's nobody who's looking after the place very well. I was astounded, really, to see that it's changed, that it's so different. And certainly, because my parents and my grandparents are not there, nobody I knew. It was a very emotional feeling. ❑

Excerpts compiled by **Cynthia Brown** *from recordings in the East Midlands Oral History Archive*

The complete archive is available at the Centre for Urban History, University of Leicester ⇨ emoha@le.ac.uk

WWW.INDEXONCENSORSHIP.ORG
CONTACT@INDEXONCENSORSHIP.ORG
TEL: 020 7278 2313 • FAX: 020 7278 1878

SUBSCRIPTIONS (4 ISSUES PER ANNUM)
INDIVIDUALS: BRITAIN £32, US $48, REST OF WORLD £42
INSTITUTIONS: BRITAIN £48, US $80, REST OF WORLD £52
**PLEASE PHONE 020 8249 4443
OR EMAIL TONY@INDEXONCENSORSHIP.ORG**

Index on Censorship (ISSN 0306-4220) is published four times a year by a non-profit-making company: Writers & Scholars International Ltd, Lancaster House, 33 Islington High Street, London N1 9LH. *Index on Censorship* is associated with Writers & Scholars Educational Trust, registered charity number 325003 **Periodicals postage:** (US subscribers only) paid at Newark, New Jersey. Postmaster: send US address changes to *Index on Censorship* c/o Mercury Airfreight International Ltd Inc., 365 Blair Road, Avenel, NJ 07001, USA